Plane Geometry Problems
with Solutions

*the text of this book is printed
on 100% recycled paper*

The Authors

The late Marcus Horblit was principal of the Fairfax Hall School. His original work on plane geometry problems was thoroughly reorganized and revised by Professor Nielsen in 1947.

Kaj L. Nielsen received the degrees of B.S. from the University of Michigan, M.A. from Syracuse University, and Ph.D. from the University of Illinois. He has held teaching positions at Syracuse, Illinois, Brown, Louisiana State, Purdue, and Butler. He has been associated with a number of industries and the U.S. Navy Department as a research engineer and scientist. He is at present Director of the Systems Analysis Group at Battelle Memorial Institute, Columbus, Ohio. Dr. Nielsen has written numerous articles based upon original research in mathematics and published in leading mathematical and engineering journals. He is the author or coauthor of *Differential Equations, College Mathematics, Plane and Spherical Trigonometry,* and *Logarithmic and Trigonometric Tables,* in the College Outline Series, and of four other mathematical books.

COLLEGE OUTLINE SERIES

PLANE GEOMETRY
PROBLEMS WITH SOLUTIONS

MARCUS HORBLIT
KAJ L. NIELSEN

BARNES & NOBLE BOOKS
A DIVISION OF HARPER & ROW, PUBLISHERS
New York, Evanston, San Francisco, London

Library of Congress catalogue card number: 47–19284

SBN 389 00059 0

78 79 80   12 11 10 9 8 7 6

PREFACE

This is a problem book in Plane Geometry; it contains more than 300 problems and their solutions. The purpose of this book is manifold. Originally designed to aid students in their preparation for college board, Annapolis, and West Point entrance examinations, the manuscript was expanded and revised so that it may be used profitably by anyone who finds a need to review, test, or expand his knowledge of this fundamental subject of mathematics. It is well known that a true test of your knowledge of any mathematical subject is the manner in which you handle original problems, but equally important is the additional knowledge which comes with the solution of any problem. It may be said that the solution of problems gives added experience and in any endeavor there is no substitute for experience.

If you are contemplating taking any kind of examination which requires knowledge of Plane Geometry, this book will prove invaluable in your preparation; but, as has been said, it has other purposes. It may be used by students and teachers alike as a reference book for source material to supplement the work in any class in Plane Geometry. Draftsmen and designers will find it useful as a "brush-up" on their two-dimensional geometric concepts. College students will find that it serves as a good review of their high school mathematics.

The book is divided into two parts. The initial chapters of Part I deal with the technique of solving geometrical problems. Special comments are made on the solutions of construction and loci problems and examples are given throughout the discussion. The subject matter has been divided into five parts: circles, constructions, loci, polygons, and triangles. A chapter has been given to each of these parts. The beginning of each of these chapters contains some illustrative examples before the problems are listed. The problems are arranged more or less in order of their difficulty and therefore it is advantageous to take the problems in order. Part II contains the solutions of the problems stated in Part I. The solutions list each step of the problem and sufficient reasons are given so that the reader should have no difficulty in following the logic of the steps.   A figure accompanies each problem so that the solution can be followed visually.

The authors gratefully acknowledge their indebtedness to Mrs. Carlene Nielsen for her aid in the preparation of the manuscript, to Mrs. Gladys Walterhouse for her careful reading and checking of the manuscript, and to the staff of Barnes and Noble, Inc., for their pleasant co-operation in the publication of this book with the minimum of typographical errors.

January, 1947.   K. L. N.

TABLE OF CONTENTS

PART ONE

TECHNIQUE OF PROBLEM SOLVING AND THE PROBLEMS

PART TWO

SOLUTIONS OF THE PROBLEMS

Part One

TECHNIQUE OF PROBLEM SOLVING
AND
THE PROBLEMS

ABBREVIATIONS AND SYMBOLS

A', A prime.

Adj., adjacent.

Alt., alternate; altitude.

Bis., bisector.

Comp., complementary.

Cons., construction.

Cor., corollary.

Corr., corresponding.

Def., definition.

Ex., exercise.

Ext., exterior.

Fig., figure.

Ft., feet.

Hyp., hypotenuse.

In., inch(es).

Int., interior.

Opp., opposite.

P_i, P sub i.

Prop., proposition.

Quad., quadrilateral.

Rect., rectangle.

Rt., right.

St., straight.

Supp., supplementary.

$=$, is equal to; equals.

$\neq$, is not equal to.

$\sim$, is similar to.

$\cong$, is congruent to; congruent.

$>$, is greater than.

$<$, is less than.

$\parallel$, is parallel to; parallel.

$\therefore$, therefore.

$\perp$, is perpendicular to; perpendicular.

$\ldots$, and so on.

$\angle$, angle.

$\not\angle$, angles.

$\frown$, arc.

$\odot$, circle.

$\circledS$, circles.

$\square$, parallelogram.

$\boxed{S}$, parallelograms.

$\square$, rectangle.

$\boxed{s}$, rectangles.

$\sqrt{n}$, square root of n.

$\triangle$, triangle.

$\triangle$, triangles.

$'$, feet; minutes.

$''$, inch(es); seconds.

s.a.s. = s.a.s. Two triangles are congruent if two sides and the included angles of one are equal, respectively, to two sides and the included angle of the other.

a.s.a. = a.s.a. Two triangles are congruent if two angles and the included side of one are equal, respectively, to two angles and the included side of the other.

s.s.s. = s.s.s. Two triangles are congruent if the sides of one are equal, respectively, to the sides of the other.

CHAPTER I

TECHNIQUE OF SOLVING ORIGINAL PROBLEMS

Introduction.

There is no cut-and-dried method of doing original problems in Geometry. As its very name implies, an original problem calls for ingenuity, mental agility, and insight. However, it is not true that those who lack these qualities are precluded from successfully solving geometrical problems; for there are certain general rules and directions which, if carefully followed, will be found very helpful in the solutions of problems. These general rules may be divided into four classes, to which we shall give the following names: (a) *the forward movement;* (b) *forcing the issue;* (c) *reductio ad absurdum;* (d) *the backward movement.* Before proceeding to a detailed discussion of the rules it should be pointed out that a careful study of the examples will also greatly benefit the student and help to develop a technique. However, may he be cautioned not to read the examples carelessly but to study them in detail.

The Forward Movement.

This method of attack may be called the natural method. You start with the given and then move forward, drawing deductions from the given and deductions from your deductions, until you arrive at the final conclusion, the Q.E.D. The method will be illustrated by some examples.

Example 1. If a median of a triangle is drawn, prove that the perpendicular from the other vertices upon this median are equal.

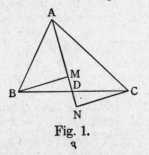

Fig. 1.

Solution. In Fig. 1, it is given that AD is a median to BC, and that BM and CN are perpendiculars from B and C respectively to AD or AD extended.

From the definition of the word "median," it is deduced that $BD = DC$; furthermore, since it is given that BM and CN are perpendiculars, we deduce that triangles BMD and CND are right triangles in which BD and DC are hypotenuses. Since BC and AN intersect at D, $\angle BDM = \angle NDC$; therefore, we conclude that, since the right triangles have the hypotenuse and an acute angle of one equal to the hypotenuse and an acute angle of the other, the triangles are congruent. Hence, we conclude that BM is equal to CN, since corresponding parts of congruent triangles are equal. This proves the statement of the problem.

Sometimes, the forward method involves the drawing of construction lines.

Example 2. If NO is the base of the isosceles triangle MNO and if the perpendicular from N to MO meets MO at A, prove that the angle ANO is equal to one-half the angle at M.

Solution. It is given that MNO is an isosceles triangle and that NA is perpendicular to MO. See Fig. 2.

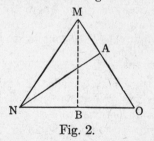

Fig. 2.

Since it is asked to prove that $\angle ANO = \frac{1}{2} \angle NMO$, it is natural to draw MB bisecting angle NMO. The problem now is to prove that $\angle ANO = \angle BMO$. Since MB is the bisector of the vertex angle of an isosceles triangle, it is perpendicular to the base, NO. In the two triangles MBO and NAO, angle AON is common, and angle NAO equals angle MBO since each is a right angle. Therefore we conclude that angle ANO must equal angle BMO, because, when two triangles have two angles of the one equal to two angles of the other, the third angles must be equal.

This natural method, which we have called the forward movement, cannot be easily applied to all problems, but it should be borne in mind by the student as a possible method of attack.

Forcing the Issue.

The second method, which we have called "forcing the issue," is really a variation of the first method. It is generally used when relationships between angles or lines are in question. To make this method clear let us again consider Example 2 above.

Solution. Since we are to prove $\angle ANO = \frac{1}{2} \angle NMO$, we ask ourselves what angle ANO does equal. From observation of the right triangle NAO, it is obvious that

$$\angle ANO = 90° - \angle NOA.$$

Our aim now should be to change the right side of this equation by the method of substituting equals for equals until it is ultimately changed into one-half of the angle NMO. Since the right side must contain only the angle NMO, the substitutions should be made with that in mind. First, $\angle NAO = 90°$, therefore the equation becomes

$$\angle ANO = \angle NAO - \angle NOA.$$

Since $\angle NAO$ is the exterior angle of triangle NMA, it therefore equals $\angle NMA + \angle MNA$. Thus

$$\angle ANO = \angle NMA + \angle MNA - \angle NOA.$$

Notice further that $\angle MNA = \angle MNO - \angle ANO$ and by substitution the original equation becomes

$$\angle ANO = \angle NMA + \angle MNO - \angle ANO - \angle NOA$$

and since $\angle MNO = \angle NOA$,

$$\angle ANO = \angle NMA - \angle ANO.$$

Solving this equation we get

$$2 \angle ANO = \angle NMA$$

or

$$\angle ANO = \frac{1}{2} \angle NMA. \quad \text{Q.E.D.}$$

In the above example we have thus "forced" the right side of the equation into the required form. Problem 40, Chapter VIII, is another example which lends itself to this type of solution. This method should usually be employed when it is a question about the relationship between one angle and another.

Reductio ad Absurdum.

The third method is called *reductio ad absurdum*, or, in plain English, it is a method of proving that, if the proposition in question is not true, an absurdity results.

Example 3. Consider the proposition that two straight lines can intersect only once.

Solution. Let the given straight lines, AB and CD, intersect at P.

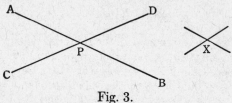

Fig. 3.

If we assume that the proposition is not true, in other words, that the two straight lines will intersect again, say at X, the result will be that between the two points, P and X, we shall have two straight lines, PDX and PBX. However, this is an absurdity, since between two points there can be only one straight line. Therefore, since the assumption that the proposition is not true leads to an absurdity, the proposition must be true.

Problem 45, Chapter VIII, is a good example of a problem to which this method is applicable. The method is of limited application, but it should be borne in mind.

The Backward Movement.

The last and most important method has been called the *backward movement* because we assume the conclusion and then draw deductions from the conclusion until we arrive at something known or something which can be easily proved. In other words this method is the opposite of the forward movement in which we begin with the given and proceed forward to the conclusion; in the backward movement we begin with the conclusion and move backward till we arrive at the given or the known. After we arrive at the given or the known, we then reverse the movement and proceed forward to the conclusion. Some examples will make this clear.

Example 4. Given that $ABCD$ is a rhombus and BD is a diagonal. Prove that $\angle m = \angle n$. See Fig. 4.

Solution. First assume that $\angle m = \angle n$. Now $AB \parallel DC$, since the figure is a rhombus, and consequently, $\angle m = \angle p$. Therefore, $\angle p = \angle n$ since we assumed that $\angle m = \angle n$; but if $\angle p = \angle n$,

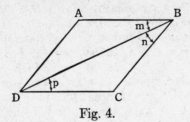

Fig. 4.

then DC must equal BC. We have now arrived at a known or a given, for we know that $DC = BC$ since the figure is a rhombus. The backward movement is now ended and we are ready to give the final proof by reversing our steps as follows:

$DC = BC$ since the figure is a rhombus; therefore $\triangle DCB$ is isosceles and $\angle p = \angle n$; but $\angle p = \angle m$ since $AB \parallel DC$; therefore $\angle m = \angle n$.

Example 5. Given: AOB is a diameter of the circle O; BM is tangent to the circle at B; CF is tangent to the circle at E and meets BM at C; the chord AE, when extended, meets BM at D. Prove that $BC = CD$. See Fig. 5.

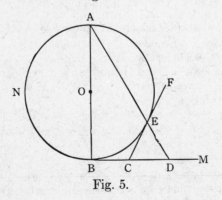

Fig. 5.

Solution. First assume that $BC = CD$. We note that $CE = BC$ since tangents from one point to a circle are equal. The first deduction, therefore, is that, since by assumption $BC = CD$, CE must equal CD. This deduction, however, does not lead to a known or a given, since we do not yet know that $CE = CD$.

Therefore, we proceed further with our deductions. The next deduction is that, since $CE = CD$, $\angle CED = \angle CDE$. This deduction cannot be directly confirmed since there is no theorem which gives us the measurement of $\angle CED$, although there is a theorem which pertains to $\angle CDE$, an angle between a tangent and a secant. We proceed further back with our deductions. Next note that $\angle CED = \angle AEF$; therefore, we deduce that $\angle AEF = \angle CDE$. Since $\angle AEF = \frac{1}{2}$ arc AE, and $\angle CDE = \frac{1}{2}$(arc ANB — arc BE), we deduce that arc AE = arc ANB — arc BE; but since arc ANB = arc AEB, we then have that arc AE = arc AEB — arc BE. At last we have arrived at a known, for arc AE + arc BE = arc AEB, or arc AE = arc AEB — arc BE. We have, therefore, reached the end of the backward movement and we are ready to reverse the steps for the regular proof. These steps are as follows:

Arc AE + arc BE = arc AEB; arc AE = arc AEB — arc BE; arc AE = arc ANB — arc BE; $\frac{1}{2}$ arc AE = $\frac{1}{2}$(arc ANB — arc BE); $\angle AEF = \angle CDE$; $\angle AEF = \angle CED$; therefore $\angle CED = \angle CDE$; therefore, $CE = CD$; but $CE = BC$; therefore, $BC = CD$.

This method is sometimes called the *analytic method*. It is very important and deserves the student's closest study.

Other Rules.

The four general rules which have been presented pertain to the method of attack and should be systematically applied to any problem under consideration. In addition to these rules, the student should bear in mind the following directions:

1. *Draw the figures carefully*. A good drawing will often reveal a clue to the solution.

2. *Remember to make use of the given*. It often happens that a student loses sight of the given and attempts to solve a problem without it.

3. *Ask yourself what propositions deal with the given*. A mere enumeration of pertinent propositions may reveal a clue to the solution. In this connection, the student is advised to know the book propositions thoroughly; this includes the corollaries.

4. *Note the significance of certain facts*. For example:

If one line is twice as long as another there may be a 90°, 60°, 30° triangle present; or the shorter line may connect the midpoints of two sides of a triangle.

If the $\sqrt{3}$ appears, there may be a 90°, 60°, 30° triangle present.

If the $\sqrt{2}$ appears, there may be a 90°, 45°, 45° triangle present.

If the three sides of a triangle are given, it may be of advantage to find out whether the square of the longest side is equal to the sum of the squares of the other two sides.

If an equality of two products is given ($\overline{AB} \times \overline{CD} = \overline{EF} \times \overline{GH}$), rewrite the equation in the form of a proportion ($AB : EF = GH : CD$), in order to discover possible similar triangles or polygons.

The systematic application of the four general methods of attack and the observance of the more specific directions given above should be very helpful to the student in his geometric endeavors.

Presentation of a Solution.

Thus far in the examples no attempt has been made to present the solutions in a systematic form. We have been more interested in the discussion of a method of attack than in the actual solutions of the examples. However, it cannot be too strongly emphasized that in the presentation of a solution, a systematic form should be followed. Such a form will develop clear, logical thinking as well as present an orderly, easy-to-read solution. Most textbooks on Plane Geometry present the proof of the propositions in a standard form listing the steps (conclusions or deductions) in one column and the reasons in a second column. It may not always be possible to follow this form, or any standard form, in the solutions of problems, but an attempt should be made to have a well-organized solution.

A good form should have the following characteristics:

1. Statement of the given or hypothesis.
2. Statement of the conclusion or question specified in the problem.
3. Organization of the steps which arrive at the Q.E.D.
4. Organization of the reasons for the steps.
5. Specific indication of any constructions.

Two examples will be given here to illustrate the possible form. Other examples throughout the book may also be studied for their form.

Example 6. If the angle C of a triangle ABC is equal to the sum of the other two angles, prove that the side AB is equal to twice the line joining C with the midpoint of AB.

Solution.

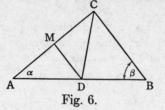

Fig. 6.

Given: $\angle ACB = \alpha + \beta$; D is the midpoint of AB.
Prove: $AB = 2\,CD$

1. $\alpha + \beta + \angle ACB = 180°$.	Sum of ∡ in △ = 180°.
2. $\angle ACB = \alpha + \beta$.	Given.
3. $2\angle ACB = 180°$.	Substitution of equals.
4. $\angle ACB = 90°$.	Solution of (3).
5. Draw $DM \perp AC$ from D.	Construction.
6. $\therefore DM \parallel BC$.	Both $\perp AC$.
7. DM bisects AC.	D is midpoint of AB and (6).
8. $\therefore AM = MC; MD = MD$; $\angle AMD = \angle DMC$.	(5) and (7).
9. $\therefore \triangle AMD \cong \triangle DMC$.	s.a.s. = s.a.s.
10. $CD = AD$.	Corr. parts of $\cong$ ▲.
11. $AB = AD + DB = 2\,AD = 2\,CD$.	Given and (10). Q.E.D.

Example 7. Given an acute angle and the sum of the legs. Construct the right triangle.

Solution.

Let x be the given angle and let BC be the sum of the legs.

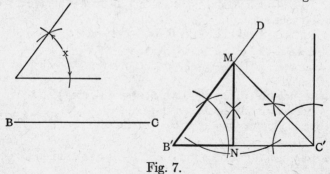

Fig. 7.

Constructions.

1. Draw $B'C' = BC$.
2. At B' construct $\angle DB'C' = x$.
3. At C' construct $\angle B'C'M = 45°$.
4. From M drop a perpendicular MN to $B'C'$.
5. $\triangle B'NM$ is the required right triangle.

Proof.

(1) $MN = NC'$ because $\triangle MNC'$ is a right $\triangle$ and $\angle NC'M = 45°$.
(2) $\therefore\ B'N + MN = B'N + NC' = B'C' = BC$.

CHAPTER II

SPECIAL NOTES ON LOCI AND CONSTRUCTIONS

The solutions of loci and construction problems call for more ingenuity and insight than other problems. Consequently, this chapter deals with a special note on each of these two types. A careful study of the examples and close adherence to the rules may overcome the usual difficulties encountered in these problems.

Loci Problems.

The difficulty in doing loci problems can be reduced if the following three rules are carefully observed.

1. *Draw the given points or lines in various positions.*

2. *From observation of these carefully drawn points or lines, deduce the probable shape of the locus which contains them.*

3. *Confirm this deduction by a deep consideration of the given.*

The application of these rules will be illustrated by two examples.

Example 1. Find the locus of the midpoints of all chords that can be drawn from a fixed point on the circumference of a circle.

Solution. In Fig. 8, we have followed the first rule by drawing the given chords and points in various positions.

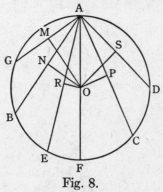

Fig. 8.

Among the chords drawn from the fixed point A is the diameter AOF. The midpoints of the chords are M, N, R, O, P, S. Rule 2 is now applied. Careful observation indicates that the probable shape is a circle. However, we must be more specific in the description of the locus. It is not enough to say that it is a circle; we must prove that it is a circle by locating its center and calculating its radius. It is here that Rule 3 is applied. Since M, N, R, O, P, and S are the given midpoints of their respective chords, we should think of theorems that pertain to such midpoints. There is a theorem which says that the line from the center of a circle to the midpoint of a chord is perpendicular to the chord. Therefore, draw the lines OR, ON, OM, OP, OS. The result is a series of right triangles, ORA, ONA, OMA, OPA, and OSA, all having the same hypotenuse, AO. This should remind us of another locus problem (see Problem 1, Chapter VI) which states that the locus of the right angle vertices of right triangles with a fixed hypotenuse is the circle having the hypotenuse as its diameter. Applying this problem to the one under discussion (this problem, however, should be proved, since a problem cannot be quoted in the proof of another problem) we may now say that the required locus is a circle having AO as its diameter. However, this statement needs a little refinement. The point A cannot be included in the locus since it is not the midpoint of any chord drawn from A. Moreover, it is better to relate the required locus to the given circle by stating that its diameter, AO, is one-half the diameter of the original circle. The final statement, therefore, is that *the required locus is a circle, omitting the fixed point, having a diameter equal to one-half the diameter of the given circle and having its center midway between the fixed point and the center of the given circle.* The student should note the generality of this statement.

Let us now consider a more difficult type of locus problem.

Example 2. From the vertex A of the isosceles triangle ABC a line is drawn cutting the base at D. On AD produced a point P is taken so that $\overline{AD} \times \overline{AP} = \overline{AB}^2$. What is the locus of P as D moves along the base?

Solution. In accordance with Rule 1, we draw several positions of points D and P. See Fig. 9.

Applying Rule 2, it may be conjectured that the locus is a curved line, probably the arc of a circle. We now try to define the locus more specifically by applying Rule 3 and making use of the given. It is given that $\overline{AD_1} \times \overline{AP_1} = \overline{AB}^2$. This can be written in the form of a proportion: $\overline{AD_1} : \overline{AB} = \overline{AB} : \overline{AP_1}$. This form of the statement hints at similar triangles. If B is connected with P_1, then triangle ABD_1 is similar to triangle ABP_1 because $\angle BAD_1$ is common and the including sides are given proportional. Hence $\angle AP_1B = \angle ABC$. Similarly, we can prove that $\angle AP_2B$ and

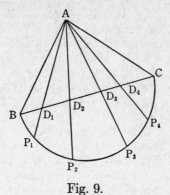

Fig. 9.

$\angle AP_3B$ are equal to $\angle ABC$. Therefore, the circle which we conjectured was wholly or partly the locus of P_1, P_2, and P_3 must be such that the arc subtended by $\angle ABC$ must equal the arc subtended by the angles at P_1, P_2, and P_3. A reasonable guess, from observation of the figure, is that the locus lies in the circumference of the circle circumscribed about triangle ABC. This guess may be confirmed by taking any point, say P_4, in the arc BC and proving that $\overline{AP_4} \times \overline{AD_4} = \overline{AB}^2$. In $\triangle ABD_4$ and ABP_4, $\angle BAD_4 = \angle BAP_4$. Moreover, $\angle ABC = \frac{1}{2}$ arc AC and $\angle AP_4B = \frac{1}{2}$ arc AB, but since chord AB = chord AC, then arc AB = arc AC; therefore, $\angle ABC = \angle AP_4B$ and the triangles are similar. Consequently, $\overline{AP_4} : \overline{AB} = \overline{AB} : \overline{AD_4}$ or $\overline{AP_4} \times \overline{AD_4} = \overline{AB}^2$. The locus, therefore, is the minor arc, omitting points B and C, intercepted by the chord BC in the circle circumscribed about $\triangle ABC$. With greater generality, *the required locus is the minor arc, omitting the extremities of the base of the triangle, intercepted by the base in the circle circumscribed about the triangle.*

These two examples illustrate the use of the rules given above which will be found sufficient for the solution of most loci problems. A form for the presentation of the solution to a loci problem will be illustrated in Example 3.

Example 3. Find the locus of the intersections of the diagonals of all rhombuses which have a fixed line-segment AB as one side.

Solution.

1. Figure 10 shows the conditions of the problem in two positions.

2. Since the figure is a rhombus, we recall the theorem: *The diagonals of a rhombus are perpendicular to each other.*

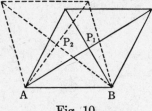

Fig. 10.

3. Therefore, the angles AP_iB ($i = 1$, 2, 3, etc.) are right angles.

4. The right triangles AP_iB ($i = 1$, 2, 3, etc.) have a fixed hypotenuse AB.

5. This problem then becomes Problem 1, Chapter VI, and by this problem the locus is a circle with AB as the diameter except for the points A and B.

Note. The complete solution to this problem should display the solution to Locus Problem 1. However, we shall simply refer the student to this problem.

Construction Problems.

Construction problems are generally done by means of the *backward movement*. They call for much ingenuity and insight. Additional aid may be derived from the following two rules.

1. *Draw a rough sketch of the completed figure, checking the given parts.*

2. *Then analyze the problem, combining any knowledge of theorems with the given, until the solution is found.*

It must be admitted that ingenuity plays so large a part in these problems that these rules, though helpful, must be supplemented by a certain amount of insight. Two examples will be given in order to see how the rules are applied and how the mind should function.

Example 4. Construct an isosceles triangle, the vertex angle and the sum of the equal sides being given.

Solution. Let angle A be the given vertex angle and let the line MN represent the sum of the equal sides.

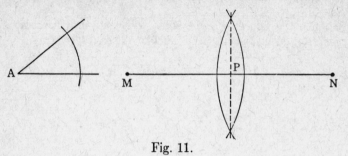

Fig. 11.

In accordance with the first rule, draw a triangle which more or less represents the completed figure and check the given parts (Fig. 12a). Now apply Rule 2 and analyze the problem. We know that $AB = AC$ and since $AB + AC = MN$, we arrive at the conclusion that $AB = \frac{1}{2} MN$ and $AC = \frac{1}{2} MN$. Since MN is given, we bisect MN at P and let $MP = PN = AB = AC$.

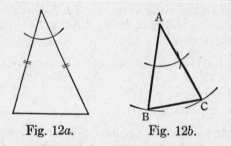

Fig. 12a.   Fig. 12b.

We can now draw AB by making it equal to MP. Then at point A draw an angle equal to the given angle and mark out a distance $AC = MP$. Finally, connect B with C.

Example 5. Through a given point within a circle, draw a chord of a given length.

Solution. First apply Rule 1 and draw a rough sketch of the completed figure (Fig. 13a). A is the given point and BC is the chord required.

Here a little more insight is required than in the previous example. It is clear that many chords equal to BC can be drawn in this circle. Let this picture persist for a few moments in our minds. By an association of ideas we think of the theorems that equal

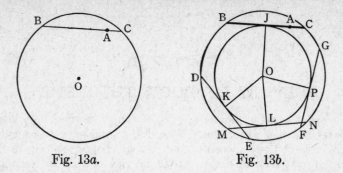

Fig. 13a.   Fig. 13b.

chords are equally distant from the center of the circle and all
perpendiculars from the center bisect the chords. This picture
may be represented by Fig. 13b. We can now see that, since
$OK = OL = OP = OJ$, a circle having O as its center and OK as
its radius will pass through the points K, L, P, and J, and that
BC will be tangent to that circle. This analysis leads to the
solution. Draw any chord, say DE, equal to the given length;
draw OK perpendicular to DE; with O as a center and OK as
radius, draw a circle; to this circle draw a tangent from A. This
tangent-chord is the required chord.

For a form which may be used to present the solution to construction problems see Example 7 of Chapter I.

It is suggested that the student learn the special rules for loci
and construction problems thoroughly and remember that prac-
tice makes perfect. This completes any advice that we can give
on the methods of attack and analysis of solutions of problems in
Plane Geometry.

CHAPTER III

REVIEW OF BOOK THEOREMS

In order to solve problems, it is, of course, necessary to know the regular book theorems. To aid the student in testing his knowledge of these theorems, the present chapter contains a list of questions which are designed to be a review of the book theorems of Plane Geometry. The questions will pertain to diagrams which will divide the review into groups. No attempt has been made to cover every theorem, but it is believed that a knowledge which permits the student to answer these questions will go a long way in doing the problems. If, on the other hand, the student has considerable trouble with these questions, it is suggested that he consult any standard textbook on Plane Geometry.

I. Questions Pertaining to Figure 14.

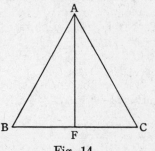

Fig. 14.

1. If $AC = AB$, what two angles are equal?
2. If $\angle ABC = \angle ACB$, what two sides are equal?
3. If $AB = AC = BC$, what angles are equal and how many degrees are there in each angle?
4. If $AB = AC$ and AF is the bisector of $\angle BAC$, how many degrees are there in $\angle AFC$? What is the ratio of BF to FC?
5. If the three angles of $\triangle ABC$ are equal to one another, what is the ratio of the sides to one another?
6. If AF is perpendicular to BC, can another perpendicular from A to BC be drawn?

18

7. What is the sum of the angles in triangle ABC?

8. If in triangles ABF and AFC, $\angle BAF = \angle FAC$, $\angle ABF = \angle ACF$, and $AF = AF$, are the triangles congruent?

9. If in triangles ABF and AFC, $AB = AC$, $AF = AF$, and $\angle BAF = \angle FAC$, are the triangles congruent?

10. If in triangles ABF and AFC, $AB = AC$, $\angle BAF = \angle FAC$, and $\angle ABF = \angle ACF$, are the triangles congruent?

11. If in triangles ABF and AFC, $AB = AC$, $AF = AF$, and $BF = FC$, are the triangles congruent?

12. If the triangles AFB and AFC are right triangles, with the right angles at F, and if $AB = AC$ and $\angle ABF = \angle ACF$, are the triangles congruent?

13. If the triangles AFB and AFC are right triangles, with the right angles at F, and if $BF = FC$, does $\angle ABF = \angle ACF$? Are the triangles congruent?

14. If AFB and AFC are right triangles, with the right angles at F, and if AB and BF are respectively equal to AC and FC, are the triangles congruent?

15. If AF is perpendicular to BC and if $BF = FC$, does $AB = AC$?

16. If AF is perpendicular to BC and if $BF = FC$, is every point on AF equally distant from B and C?

17. If, in triangle ABC, AC is greater than AB, compare angle ABC with angle ACB.

18. If, in triangle ABC, angle ABC is greater than angle BAC, compare the lengths of two sides of this triangle.

19. If AF is perpendicular to BC, is AF shorter than AC?

20. If AF is the shortest line from A to BC, is AF perpendicular to BC?

21. Would the bisectors of the three angles of $\triangle ABC$ meet at one point?

22. Would the perpendicular bisectors of the sides of $\triangle ABC$ meet at one point?

23. Would the medians of $\triangle ABC$ meet at one point?

24. If, in triangles ABF and AFC, $AB = AC$, $AF = AF$, and $\angle BAF > \angle FAC$, what is the relationship between BF and FC?

25. If, in triangles ABF and FAC, $AB = AC$, $AF = AF$, and $BF > FC$, what is the relationship between $\angle BAF$ and $\angle FAC$?

26. If, in triangle ABC, $AF \perp BC$ and $FC > BF$, compare AC with AB.

27. If, in triangle ABC, $AF \perp BC$ and $AC > AB$, compare FC with BF.

28. If, in triangle ABC, AF is the bisector of angle BAC, state the relationship of BF, FC, AB, and AC with one another.

29. If AF is perpendicular to BC, what is the area of triangle ABC?

30. If one-half the perimeter of $\triangle ABC$ is represented by s and if the three sides are represented by a, b, and c, express the area of $\triangle ABC$ in terms of s, a, b, and c.

31. In $\triangle ABC$, where would the center of the inscribed circle lie? Where would the center of the circumscribed circle lie?

32. In $\triangle ABC$, where, numerically, would the meeting point of the medians lie?

II. Questions Pertaining to Figure 15.

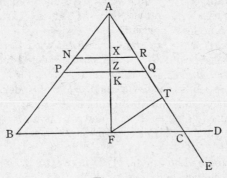

Fig. 15.

1. Angle ACD is equal to the sum of what angles of triangle ABC?
2. What angle does angle ACB equal?
3. If the two angles TFC and CAF have their sides respectively perpendicular, FT to AC and FC to AF, what is the relationship between the angles?
4. If, in triangles ANR and ABC, angle NAR is common and $\angle ANR = \angle ABC$, does angle ARN equal angle ACB?
5. What is meant by the phrase "distance of a point from a line"?
6. If K is equally distant from B and C, does it lie on the perpendicular bisector of BC?
7. If K and A are equally distant from B and C, what is the relationship of line AK to BC?
8. If P and Q are the midpoints, respectively, of AB and AC, what is the relationship of PQ to BC?

9. If, in $\triangle ABC$, NR is parallel to the base, complete the following proportions: $AN : NB = \quad ; AN : AB = \quad ; AN : AR = \quad ;$ $AB : AC = \quad .$

10. If PQ is parallel to BC and bisects AB, what is the relationship of Q to AC?

11. If, in $\triangle ABC$, NR and PQ are parallel to BC, complete the following proportions: $AN : NP = \quad ; NP : PB = \quad .$

12. If, in $\triangle ABC$, $AN : NB = AR : RC$, what is the relationship between NR and BC?

13. If, in $\triangle AFC$, $\angle AFC$ is a right angle and $FT \perp AC$, what triangles are similar (a) to AFC? (b) to AFT? (c) to FTC? (d) State the relationship between FT, TC, and TA; (e) between FC, AC, and TC; (f) between AF, AC, and AT; (g) between AF, FC, and AC.

14. If, in $\triangle ABC$, $NR \parallel BC$, is triangle ANR similar to triangle ABC?

15. If triangles ANR and ABC are similar, what does the ratio of their corresponding altitudes equal?

16. If triangles ANR and ABC are similar to each other, complete the following proportion: area of ANR : area of $ABC = \quad .$

17. If $PQCB$ is a trapezoid and ZF is its altitude, what is its area?

18. If $\angle NRC = \angle RCD$, what is the relationship between NR and BD?

19. If $\angle RCD =$ the supplement of $\angle NRA$, what is the relationship between NR and BD?

20. If $NR \parallel BD$, what is the relationship between angles NRC and RCD? between angles NRC and RCB?

III. Questions Pertaining to Figure 16.

1. If AG and LM are both parallel to NO, is AG parallel to LM?

2. If AN is parallel to GC and if NR is parallel to CD, what is the relationship between angles ANR and GCD? between angles ANR and GCF?

3. If BG is the bisector of $\angle ABC$, is every point on BG equally distant from AB and BC?

4. If AG, LM, and NO are parallel lines and if $AL = LN$, what is the relationship between GM and MO?

5. If G is equally distant from AB and BC (extended, if necessary), what is the relationship between BG and angle ABC?

6. In the quadrilateral $ABCG$:
   (a) If the diagonals AC and BG bisect each other, what kind of figure is $ABCG$?
   (b) If AG equals BC and is parallel to BC, what kind of figure is $ABCG$?
   (c) If $AG = BC$ and $AB = GC$, what kind of figure is $ABCG$?

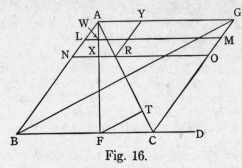

Fig. 16.

7. If $ABCG$ is a parallelogram, what is the relationship between the diagonals AC and BG? between AG and BC? between AB and GC? between angles GAB and BCG? between angles BAG and ABC? between angles BAG and AGC?
8. If $AG \parallel BC$, compare the distances of A and G from BC (extended, if necessary).
9. Name at least three conditions under which two triangles, say ANR and ACG, could be similar to each other.
10. If $ABCG$ is a parallelogram and $AF \perp BC$, what is the area of $ABCG$?
11. If $ALMG$ and $LNOM$ are parallelograms and AW and WX are their respective altitudes, complete the following proportion: area of $ALMG$: area of $LNOM$ =   .
12. If $ANOG$ and $ANRY$ are parallelograms and AX is their common altitude, complete the following proportion: area of $ANOG$: area of $ANRY$ =   .
13. If $ANRY$ and $ABCG$ are parallelograms and AX and AF are their respective altitudes, complete the following proportion: area of $ANRY$: area of $ABCG$ =   .
14. If $ABCG$ is a rhombus, express its area in terms of AC and BG.
15. If BG and FT are both perpendicular to AC, what is the relationship between BG and FT?
16. If BG and FT are parallel and $AC \perp BG$, what is the relationship between AC and FT?

IV. Questions Pertaining to Figure 17.

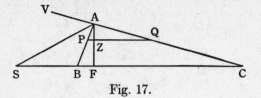

Fig. 17.

1. If AS is the bisector of the angle VAB, state the relationship of SB, SC, AB, and AC with one another.
2. If triangles APQ and ASB have equal bases and if AZ and AF are their respective altitudes, complete the following proportion: area of APQ : area of ASB = .
3. If triangles ABC and ASB have the same altitude, AF, complete the following proportion: area of ABC : area of ASB = .
4. If AZ and AF are respectively the altitudes of triangles APQ and ASB, complete the following proportion: area of APQ : area of ASB = .

V. Questions Pertaining to Figure 18.

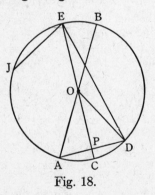

Fig. 18.

1. What is the longest chord in circle O?
2. If $\angle AOC = \angle COD$, what is the relationship between arcs AC and CD?
3. If arcs AC and CD are equal, what is the relationship between angles AOC and COD? between the chords AC and CD?
4. If $\angle AOC > \angle COD$, what is the relationship between arcs AC and CD?

5. If chord AC equals chord CD, what is the relationship between arcs AC and CD? If chord AC is greater than chord CD, what is the relationship between arcs AC and CD?

6. If arc AC is greater than arc CD, what is the relationship between chords AC and CD?

7. If $EC \perp AD$, what is the relationship between AP and PD? between arcs AC and CD? between arcs AE and ED?

8. If P is the midpoint of AD, what is the relationship between CE and AD?

9. The perpendicular bisector of chord JE would pass through what point?

10. If chords AD and JE are equal, what is the relationship of their distances from the center of the circle? If chord AD is greater than chord JE, what is the relationship of their distances from the center?

11. If chords AD and JE are equally distant from the center, what is the relationship between AD and JE? If AD is farther from the center than JE, what is the relationship between AD and JE?

12. Express in the form of a proportion the relationship between angles AOC and DOB and their respective arcs, AC and DB.

13. The number of degrees in angle AOC is equal to the number of degrees in what arc?

14. What is the measure of $\angle JEC$? What is the measure of $\angle EPD$?

15. If CE is a diameter of the circle, how many degrees are there in angle CDE?

16. Through points D, O, and B, how many circles can be passed?

17. What does the product of AP and PD equal?

18. If PD is perpendicular to the diameter CE, what is the relationship between PD, CP, and PE? between CD, CE, and CP? between DE, CE, and PE?

19. If AD is the side of a regular inscribed hexagon, what is the relationship between AD and OD?

20. State the formula which expresses the relationship between the circumference of a circle and its radius.

21. Express the length of arc AC in terms of its intercepted central angle and the radius.

22. State a formula which expresses the area of a circle.

23. Express the area of sector AOD by means of a formula.

24. If the circumference of a circle were divided into equal arcs, would the chords of those arcs form a regular inscribed poly-

gon? Would the tangents erected at the extremities of those chords form a regular circumscribed polygon?

VI. Questions Pertaining to Figure 19.

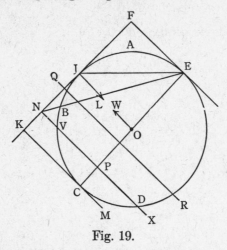

Fig. 19.

1. If *FE* is tangent at *E* to the circle whose center is *O* and *OE* is a radius, what is the relationship between *FE* and *OE*?
2. If *OE* is a radius and *FE* is perpendicular to *OE*, what is the relationship between *FE* and the circle?
3. If *JL* is perpendicular to the tangent at *J*, what is the relationship between *JL* and the center *O*?
4. If *OW*, when extended, is perpendicular to the tangent *FJ*, what is the relationship between *OW* and *J*?
5. If *FJ* and *FE* are tangents to the circle at *J* and *E*, respectively, what is the relationship between *FJ* and *FE*? What is the relationship between angles *JFO* and *OFE*?
6. If *KM* is a tangent and is parallel to the secant *QR*, what is true about their intercepted arcs? If *NX* and *QR* are parallel secants, what is true of their intercepted arcs? If *FE* and *KM* are parallel tangents, what is true of their intercepted arcs?
7. If *CE* joins the points of tangency of two parallel tangents, what is the relationship between *CE* and the center *O*?
8. What is the measure of angle *JFE*, formed by tangents *FJ* and *FE*? What is the measure of angle *END*, formed by two secants *NX* and *NE*? What is the measure of angle *FEJ*,

formed by the tangent *FE* and the chord *JE*? What is the measure of angle *JND*, formed by the tangent *NJ* and the secant *ND*?

9. If *NJ* is a tangent and *ND* a secant, what is the relationship between *NJ*, *NV*, and *ND*?

VII. Questions Pertaining to Figure 20.

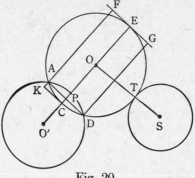

Fig. 20.

1. If the two circles having *O* and *O'* as their centers intersect at *A* and *D*, what is the relationship between *OO'* and *AD*?

2. If the two circles having *O* and *S* as their centers are tangent at *T*, what is the relationship between *OS* and *T*?

3. Express, in the form of a proportion, the relationship between the circumferences and the radii of the circles having *O* and *O'* as their centers.

4. Express, in terms of a proportion, the relationship between the areas and the radii of the circles having *O* and *O'* as their centers; the relationship between their areas and their diameters.

5. If *KAPC* and *APEF* are rectangles, having the common altitude *FE*, complete the following proportion: area of *KAPC* : area of *APEF* =   .

6. If *KAPC* and *PDGE* are rectangles, complete the following proportion: area of *KAPC* : area of *PDGE* =   .

7. If *KAPC* is a rectangle, what is its area?

VIII. Questions Pertaining to Figure 21.

1. Express by a formula the sum of the interior angles of polygon *ABCDE*.

2. Express by a formula the sum of the exterior angles of polygon *ABCDE*.

3. If the interior angles of *ABCDE* are equal to one another, express by a formula the number of degrees in each.

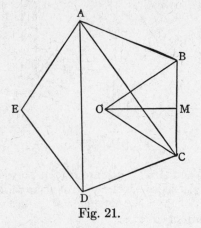

Fig. 21.

4. If *ABCDE* is a regular polygon, can a circle be circumscribed around it? Can a circle be inscribed in it?

5. If *ABCDE* is a regular polygon and *O* is its center, express by a formula the number of degrees in angle *BOC*.

6. If *ABCDE* is a regular polygon, having *O* as its center and *OM* as its apothem, and if *p* represents its perimeter, what is its area?

IX. Questions Pertaining to Figure 22.

1. If polygons *ABCDE* and *A'B'C'D'E'* are similar to each other, what is the relationship between △*ABC* and *A'B'C'*? between △*ACD* and *A'C'D'*? between △*ADE* and *A'D'E'*?

2. If in polygons *ABCDE* and *A'B'C'D'E'* triangles *ABC*, *ACD*, and *ADE* are similar, respectively, to triangles *A'B'C'*, *A'C'D'*, and *A'D'E'*, what is the relationship between the two polygons?

3. If *ABCDE* and *A'B'C'D'E'* are regular polygons of the same number of sides, are they similar?

4. If *ABCDE* and *A'B'C'D'E'* are similar polygons, what does the ratio of their areas equal?

5. If polygons *ABCDE* and *A'B'C'D'E'* are similar to each other, what does the ratio of their perimeters equal?

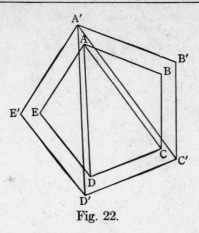

Fig. 22.

6. If *ABCDE* and *A'B'C'D'E'* are regular polygons of the same number of sides, express the ratio of their perimeters in terms of the radii of their inscribed circles; in terms of the radii of their circumscribed circles.

CHAPTER IV

PROBLEMS ON CIRCLES

Before proceeding to the list of problems a few examples will be considered. It is hoped that a careful study of these examples will not only serve as a guide but will also prepare the student for the problems that follow. The problems are arranged, more or less, in the order of their difficulty.

Example 1. Find the number of degrees in the angle subtended at the center of a circle by an arc 5 ft. 10 in. in length if the radius of the circle is 9 ft. 4 in.

Solution.

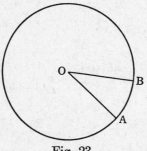

Fig. 23.

Given: Circle O whose radius is 9 ft. 4 in.; arc AB of length 5 ft. 10 in.

To Find: The number of degrees in $\angle AOB$.

1. $OA = r = 9$ ft. 4 in. $= 112$ in.	Given.
2. $AB = 5$ ft. 10 in. $= 70$ in.	Given.
3. Circumference of $\odot = C = 2\pi r = 360°$.	Corollary.*
4. $2\pi r = 2\pi(112) = 224\pi$ in.	Substitution.
5. $AB : 2\pi r = \angle AOB : 360°$.	Corollary.*
6. $\therefore 70 : 224\pi = \angle AOB : 360°$.	Substitution.

7. $\therefore \angle AOB = \dfrac{(70)(360°)}{224\pi} = \dfrac{225°}{2\pi} = 35° \ 48' \ 36''$ approximately.

* The reader should supply the statement of the corollary.

Example 2. From an external point P two secants, PAB and PCD, are drawn. If $PB = 27$ in., $AB = 21$ in., and $PC = CD$, what is the length of PD?

Solution.

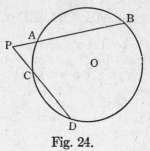

Fig. 24.

Given: PAB and PCD secants from external point P; $AB = 21$ in.; $PB = 27$ in.; $PC = CD$.

To Find: The length of PD.

1. $PA = PB - AB = 27 - 21 = 6$ in.	Substitution in given.
2. $\overline{PA} \times \overline{PB} = \overline{PC} \times \overline{PD}$.	The product of each secant by its external segment is a constant.
3. $PC = \frac{1}{2} PD$.	$PC = CD$.
4. $\therefore 6 \times 27 = \frac{1}{2} \overline{PD} \times \overline{PD}$.	Substitution in (2).
5. $\therefore 324 = \overline{PD}^2$ or $PD = 18$ in.	Solution of (4).

Example 3. A triangle ABC is formed by the intersection of three tangents to a circle. Two of the tangents, AM and AN, are

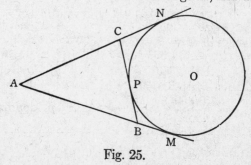

Fig. 25.

fixed in position, while BC touches the circumference at a variable point, P. Show that the perimeter of the triangle ABC is a constant and is equal to $2\,AN$.

Solution.

Given: AM, AN, and BC tangents to the circle O at M, N, and P, respectively, and intersecting to form the $\triangle ABC$; M and N are fixed but P is a variable point.

To Show: The perimeter of $\triangle ABC = 2\,AN$, a constant.

1. $BM = BP$ and $CP = CN$. Also $AN = AM$.	Tangents to a circle from an external point are equal.
2. $AB + BP = AB + BM = AM$.	Substitution of equals.
3. $AC + CP = AC + CN = AN$.	Substitution of equals.
4. $\therefore AB+BP+PC+AC = AM+AN$ $\qquad\qquad\qquad\qquad\quad = 2\,AN$	Substitution of equals.

Example 4. Prove that the center of a circle inscribed in a triangle does not coincide with the center of the circumscribed circle, except when the triangle is equilateral.

Solution.

Given: $\triangle ABC$, the inscribed circle with center at O, and the circumscribed circle with center at O'.

To Prove: O coincides with O' if $\triangle ABC$ is equilateral. O does not coincide with O' if $\triangle ABC$ is not equilateral.

I. Consider the equilateral $\triangle ABC$. (Fig. 26a.)

1. Let M be the midpoint of BC.	
2. $AB=AC$; $AM=AM$; $BM=MC$.	Given and (1).
3. $\therefore \triangle ABM \cong \triangle AMC$.	s.s.s. = s.s.s.
4. $\therefore \angle BMA = \angle AMC = 90°$.	(3) and $\angle BMC = 180°$.
5. $\therefore AM \perp$ bis. of BC.	(4).
6. AM is bisector of $\angle BAC$.	$\angle BAM = \angle MAC$ by (3).
7. Similarly for BR and CN.	Steps similar to (1)–(6).
8. O is the point of intersection of the bisectors of the angles of $\triangle ABC$.	Construction.
9. O' is the point of intersection of the $\perp$ bisectors of sides of $\triangle ABC$.	Construction.
10. $\therefore O$ coincides with O'.	(5), (6), and (7).

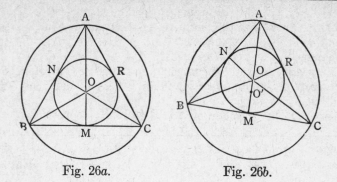

Fig. 26a.   Fig. 26b.

II. Consider any △ABC which is not equilateral. (Fig. 26b.)

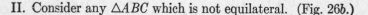

1. Assume O and O' coincide.	
2. $ON = ON$ and $OA = OB$.	By (1) $OA =$ radius of circle O'.
3. ∴ rt. $\triangle ONA \cong$ rt. $\triangle ONB$.	Leg and hypotenuse equal.
4. ∴ $AN = BN$.	Corr. parts of $\cong$ ▲.
5. $BN = BM$.	Tangents from external point.
6. Similarly, $\triangle BOM \cong \triangle MOC$.	Steps similar to (1) and (2).
7. ∴ $BM = MC$ and $MC = CR$.	(6) and (5).
8. Similarly, $CR = RA$ and $RA = AN$.	Steps similar to the above.
9. $AN + NB = BN + BM$ $= BM + MC$.	(4), (5), and (7).
10. ∴ $AB = BC$.	Postulate.
11. Similarly, $AB = AC = BC$.	(4), (5), (7), and (8).
12. ∴ $\triangle ABC$ is equilateral.	Definition.
13. This contradicts the given.	$\triangle ABC$ is not equilateral.
14. ∴ O and O' do not coincide.	Q.E.D.

Example 5. The circumferences of three unequal circles, whose centers are A, B, and C, pass through a common point, O, from which lines are drawn through A, B, and C meeting the circumferences in A', B', and C'. Show that the sides of the triangle $A'B'C'$ pass through the other points of intersection of the circles and are respectively parallel to the sides of the triangle ABC.

Solution.

Given: Three circles whose centers are A, B, and C, passing through O and also intersecting at P, Q, and R. The lines OC, OB, and OA intersect the circles at C', B', and A', respectively.

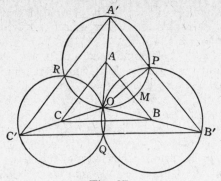

Fig. 27.

To Prove: $A'B' \parallel AB$, $B'C' \parallel BC$, $A'C' \parallel AC$, and $A'B'$, $B'C'$, $A'C'$ pass through P, Q, and R, respectively.

1. Connect A' with P and B' with P and draw the line of centers AB.	
2. Draw the common chord OP.	
3. $AB \perp$ bis. of OP.	Theorem.
4. AB is bisector of arc OP.	Theorem.
5. $\angle PA'O = \frac{1}{2}$ arc $PO =$ arc MO.	Theorem.
6. $\angle MAO =$ arc MO.	Theorem.
7. $\therefore \angle PA'O = \angle MAO$.	(5) and (6).
8. $\therefore PA' \parallel AB$.	Theorem.
9. Similarly, $PB' \parallel AB$.	Steps similar to (1)–(7).
10. $\therefore A'P$ and PB' form a st. line.	Through P only one line can be drawn parallel to another line.

11. Similarly, we may prove that $B'C'$ passes through Q and $A'C'$ through R, and that they are respectively parallel to BC and AC.

PROBLEMS

1. Two chords intersect within a circle. The segments of one chord are 1 in. and 6 in. Find the segments of the other chord if its length is 5 in.
2. Prove that a trapezoid inscribed in a circle is isosceles.
3. Find the angle formed at the intersection of two secants if the intercepted arcs are $\frac{1}{12}$ and $\frac{1}{4}$ of the circumference of the circle.

4. Find the number of degrees in the angle subtended at the center of a circle by an arc 5 ft. 10 in. in length if the radius of the circle is 9 ft. 4 in.

5. If the length of the common chord of two intersecting circles is 16 ft. and the radii are 10 ft. and 17 ft., find the distance between the centers of the circles.

6. The angle of a sector is 72° and its arc is 44 in. Find the radius of the circle.

7. Prove that the shortest distance from an exterior point to a circle is the exterior segment of the secant which is drawn from that point through the center of the circle.

8. Prove that the longest secant from an exterior point is the secant which is drawn from that point through the center of the circle.

9. The shortest distance from a point to a circle is 6 in. and the greatest distance from the same point to the circle is 24 in. Find the length of the tangent from that point.

10. A circular pond 150 ft. in diameter is surrounded by a walk 7 ft. wide. Find the area of the walk.

11. The radius of a circle is 13 in. Through a point 5 in. from the center a chord is drawn. What is the product of the segments of this chord? What is the length of the shortest chord through this point?

12. Prove that if a chord and a tangent are drawn from a point on the circumference of a circle, the perpendiculars dropped on them from the midpoint of the subtended arc are equal.

13. An arch is built in the form of an arc of a circle and is subtended by a chord 30 ft. long. If a chord 17 ft. long subtends half that arc, what is the radius of the circle?

14. A, B, and C are points on the circumference of a circle. The minor arc, AB, contains 120°; C is the midpoint of the major arc, AB. Prove that the perpendicular from A to the chord BC passes through the center of the circle.

15. From an external point two secants, PAB and PCD, are drawn, one cutting the circle at A and B, the other cutting it at C and D. If $PB = 27$ in., $AB = 21$ in., and $PC = CD$, what is the length of PD?

16. An arch is built in the form of a circular arc with its highest point 9 ft. above the horizontal chord connecting its two ends. If the length of this chord is 30 ft., what is the radius of the arc?

17. A tangent and a secant are drawn from a point P outside a circle. The tangent is 6 in. long and the chord-part of the secant is 8 in. long. How long is the secant?

18. AB is a diameter of a circle whose radius is 17 in. and CD is a chord perpendicular to AB at P. If $PB = 9$ in., find the area of the quadrilateral $ABCD$.

19. A circle of radius 16 in. is cut by a chord 16 in. long. Find the area of the smaller segment of the circle.

20. AB is a fixed chord of a circle and P is any point in either arc. Show that the bisector of $\angle APB$ intersects the opposite arc at the same point no matter what the position of P is.

21. The radius of a circle is 10 in. AB, a chord of the circle, is 5 in. distant from the center of the circle. Find the length of the chord AB and of the arc AB.

22. Show that in two circles of different radii, angles at the center, subtended by arcs of equal length, are to each other inversely as their radii.

23. If A, B, C, and D are four points in order on the circumference of a circle and if the arcs AB, BC, CD, and DA are bisected, respectively, in E, F, G, and H, prove that EG is perpendicular to FH.

24. If P and Q are points on the circumferences of two concentric circles, prove that the angle included between the tangents at P and Q is equal to that subtended at the center by PQ.

25. If from a point within a circle more than two equal straight lines can be drawn to the circumference, prove that such a point is the center of the circle.

26. AB and AC are equal chords in a circle; any chord AD cuts BC in E. Prove that the $\triangle ABD$ and ABE are mutually equiangular.

27. Two tangents to a circle make an angle of 50° with each other. Find the lengths of the intercepted arcs if the radius of the circle is 10 in.

28. A triangle ABC is formed by the intersection of three tangents to a circle. Two of the tangents, AM and AN, are fixed in position, while BC touches the circumference at a variable point, P. Show that the perimeter of the $\triangle ABC$ is a constant and is equal to $2\,AN$.

29. An equilateral triangle is inscribed in a circle of radius R. Find expressions for the side and area of this triangle in terms of R.

30. C and D are two fixed points on the circumference of a circle. Through A, the midpoint of the arc CD, a chord AB is drawn,

intersecting the chord CD at M. For any position of B on the circumference prove that $\overline{AM} \times \overline{AB}$ is a constant.

31. Sea captains have an old rule: "The distance, d, in miles at which an object can be seen from the surface of the sea is $\sqrt{\dfrac{3h}{2}}$, where h is the height of the object in feet above the sea level." Prove that this rule is a very good approximation by showing that $d = \sqrt{\dfrac{3h}{2} + \left(\dfrac{h}{5280}\right)^2}$. Consider the earth to be spherical and to have a radius of 3960 miles.

32. A and B are points on the circumference of a circle of radius 8 in. and arc AB contains 120°. Find the distance from B to the diameter which passes through A.

33. If perpendiculars from the ends of any diameter be drawn upon a tangent, prove that the sum of the perpendiculars is equal to the diameter.

34. Two circles of diameters 12 in. and 27 in. are tangent externally. Find the lengths of their common external tangents.

35. Find the radius of the circle inscribed in a triangle whose sides are 5, 13, and 12 in. in length.

36. A circle is inscribed in a triangle whose sides are 36, 28, and 18 in. Find the lengths of the segments into which the sides are divided by the points of contact with the circle.

37. Find the area of the smaller segment subtended by one side of a regular hexagon which is inscribed in a circle of radius r.

38. Prove that the diameter of a circle inscribed in a right triangle is equal to the sum of the legs diminished by the hypotenuse.

39. Two circles intersect at points A and B; through B a line is drawn intersecting one circle at C and the other at D. Prove that the angle CAD is constant for all positions of the line CD.

40. From a point outside a circle two tangents are drawn, each 10 in. in length; the chord joining the points of tangency is 12 in. long. Find the radius of the circle.

41. Two circles, O and O', are tangent externally at A. PQ is a common external tangent touching circle O at P and circle O' at Q. A line through A cuts O again at R and O' again at S. RP and SQ, when produced, meet at X. Prove that the angle RXS is a right angle.

42. Two tangents to a circle are at right angles with each other. A point on the smaller arc of the circle between the two points

of contact is $4\frac{1}{2}$ in. from one tangent and 4 in. from the other. Find the radius of the circle.

43. A chord is perpendicular to a diameter of a circle at a point which divides the diameter into segments having the ratio 1 : 3. In what ratio does the chord divide the circumference?

44. Two equal circles are externally tangent to each other at A. Through A two chords, AB and AC, are drawn, one in each circle, at right angles with each other. Prove that BC is equal to the diameter of either circle and is parallel to the line of centers.

45. From a point P outside a circle of circumference 60 in., there are drawn two secants, PBA and PDC. Arc AC subtends an angle of 85° at the center of the circle. Chords AD and BC intersect at point X. What is the length of arc BD if angle BXD is four times as large as angle BPD?

46. Two parallel tangents are drawn to a circle whose center is O. A third tangent is drawn intersecting the first two at A and B. Prove that the circle constructed on AB as a diameter passes through O.

47. Find the radius of a circle if the difference between the areas of the inscribed and circumscribed regular triangles is 25 sq. in.

48. Prove that if from the midpoint A of an arc BC any two chords, AD and AE, are drawn cutting the chord BC at F and G, respectively, then the points D, E, F, and G lie on the circumference of a circle.

49. Find the area of a circle inscribed in a rhombus whose perimeter is 100 in. and whose longer diagonal is 40 in.

50. Prove that the common internal tangents of two unequal nonintersecting circles intersect on the line of centers.

51. A circle with center O has a chord AB equal in length to the radius r. A perpendicular from O to AB meets AB at M. A perpendicular from M to OA meets OA at D. Compute the area of triangle MDA in terms of r.

52. Three points, A, B, and C, lie on the circumference of a circle. $AC = 5$ in. and $AB = BC$. The distance from A to chord BC produced is one-half the length of chord BC. Find the lengths of arcs AB and BC.

53. Express the length of a side of an inscribed equilateral triangle in terms of the radius. Prove this expression true.

54. Express the length of a side of a circumscribed equilateral triangle in terms of the radius. Prove this expression true.

55. If two circles are internally tangent and their radii are in the ratio 2 : 1, prove that a chord of the larger circle drawn from the point of contact is bisected by the smaller circle.

56. If the chord NP extended meets the diameter MOX extended at A and if PA equals the radius, prove that the angle at A equals one-third the central angle MON.

57. If two straight lines are drawn through the point of tangency of two externally tangent circles and terminate in the circumferences of both circles, prove that the chords of the intercepted arcs are parallel.

58. Two circles are internally tangent at A; BC, a chord of the larger circle, is tangent to the smaller circle at D; prove that AD bisects the angle BAC.

59. Prove that if chords are drawn from a point A on the circumference of a circle and if they are cut by a secant which is parallel to the tangent at A, the product of a chord and its segment between the parallels is a constant.

60. The lines AB and AC are tangent to a circle at the points B and C; the lines AD and BD are drawn perpendicular to AB and BC, respectively. Prove that AD is equal to the radius of the circle.

61. If a tangent AD touches a circle at D and if DE is a diameter and if AE intersects the circle at F, prove that $\overline{AE} \times \overline{EF}$ is a constant, no matter where the point A is taken on the line AD.

62. Two equal circles are so drawn that the center of each is on the circumference of the other; their intersection points are A and B. Prove that, if from A any line is drawn cutting the circles in D and C, the triangle DBC is equilateral.

63. ABC and $A'BC$ are two triangles in a circle; $AC \parallel A'B$. The sides AB and $A'C$ intersect at D. If circles are described about $\triangle ADC$ and $A'BD$, prove that these circles are tangent to each other.

64. Two circles are externally tangent at O and are both tangent to a straight line at the points A and B; AO and BO are produced to meet the circles in P and Q, respectively. Prove that $AO : BO = BQ : AP$.

65. Let $\angle BAC$ be inscribed in the arc BC of a circle and let D and E be points on arcs AB and AC, respectively. Prove that the sum of angles ADB and AEC is a constant no matter where the point A be taken in the arc BC, and that this sum is equal to $\angle BAC + 180°$.

66. Prove that the center of a circle inscribed in a triangle does not coincide with the center of the circumscribed circle, except when the triangle is equilateral.

67. AB is the diameter of a circle; CD is a chord parallel to AB and equal to one-half of it; the tangent at B meets the line AC produced at E. Prove that AE equals $2 AB$.

68. Prove that the center of the circle circumscribed about a right triangle is the midpoint of the hypotenuse.

69. If one leg of a right triangle is the diameter of a circle, prove that the tangent at the point where the circumference intersects the hypotenuse bisects the other leg.

70. Two circles are tangent externally at A and a common external tangent touches them at B and C. The line segment BA is extended, meeting the second circle at D. Prove that CD is a diameter.

71. If the area of a square inscribed in a circle is 15 sq. in., what is the area of the square inscribed in a semicircle of the same circle?

72. A circle of 4 in. radius is tangent to a straight line. Two other circles of equal radii are drawn tangent to each other and each tangent to the given circle and to the given straight line. Find the radius of these circles.

73. PA, PB, and PC are chords of a circle such that PB bisects angle APC. Prove that AC is parallel to the tangent at B. Prove also that, if PA and PC when produced meet the tangent at Q and R, respectively, $QB : QA = RB : RC$.

74. The triangle DEF is inscribed in the triangle ABC; prove that the circles circumscribed about ADF, BDE, and EFC intersect at a common point.

75. If a circle is drawn through A, a corner of a square $ABCD$, and through the midpoints of AB and AD, prove that a tangent from C is equal to a side of the square.

76. The circumferences of three unequal circles, whose centers are A, B, and C, pass through a common point, O, from which lines are drawn through A, B, and C meeting the circumferences in A', B', and C'. Show that the sides of the triangle $A'B'C'$ pass through the other points of intersection of the circles and are respectively parallel to the sides of the triangle ABC.

77. If AB is the diameter and AP a chord of a circle and if a chord, AQ, bisects the angle BAP, prove that the tangent at Q is perpendicular to AP.

78. If an equilateral triangle is inscribed in a circle, prove that the chord drawn from any point in a subtended arc to the opposite vertex is equal to the sum of the chords drawn from the same point to the other two vertices.

79. Given that *POM* is a diameter and *A* is any point on it; prove that *AM* is less than any other line from *A* to the circumference and that *AP* is greater than any other line from *A* to the circumference. See Fig. 28.

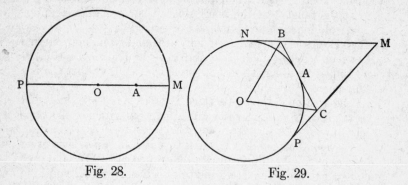

Fig. 28.   Fig. 29.

80. In Fig. 29, the △*MBC* is formed by the intersection of three tangents, two of which, *MN* and *MP*, are fixed lines, but *BC* is a variable tangent. Prove that, no matter where the point *A* lies, the angle *BOC* is a constant.

81. Prove that if a triangle is inscribed in a circle and if from any point on the circumference perpendiculars are drawn to the sides of the triangle, the feet of these perpendiculars lie in one straight line.

82. Given two points on a diameter equally distant from the center; prove that if from any point on the circumference lines are drawn to these points, the sum of the squares of these lines is a constant.

83. Prove that if two circles are externally tangent and if a common tangent is drawn, the part of the tangent between the points of contact is a mean proportional between the diameters of the circles.

84. If *a*, *b*, *c*, and *d* are four equidistant parallel chords in a circle, prove that $a^2 - d^2 = 3(b^2 - c^2)$.

85. *AB* is a chord and *AC* is a tangent to a circle and equal to *AB*. *CB* (produced, if necessary) cuts the circle again at *D*, and *M*

is the midpoint of the arc which is subtended by AB and lies opposite C. Prove that $ACDM$ is a parallelogram.

86. Prove that if two circles are externally tangent and if another circle is described having as its diameter that part of the common external tangent lying between the points of contact, this third circle will be tangent to the line of centers of the tangent circles.

87. If the circumference of circle A passes through the center of circle B and intersects circle B at the points C and D, prove that two chords in circle B drawn, one from C and the other from D, in such a way as to intersect on the circumference of circle A, are equal to each other.

88. The circumference of circle M passes through the center, O, of circle O; through A, one of the points of intersection, a diameter AB is drawn in circle M and meets circle O at C; prove that $\overline{AB} \times \overline{AC} = 2\,\overline{OC}^2$.

89. Prove that if three circles are tangent to one another, the tangents at the points of contact are concurrent at one point.

90. P is any point on the circumference of a circle whose center is O. Join OP and produce it to Q, making PQ equal to n times OP, and from Q draw a line tangent to the circle at R. Prove that the diameter of the circle described about the triangle PQR equals $(n + 1) \times \overline{PR}$.

CHAPTER V

PROBLEMS ON CONSTRUCTIONS

Before the student begins this chapter it is suggested that he review the special note on construction problems in Chapter II.

Example 1. Triangle ABC has $AB = 3$ in., $BC = 5$ in., and $AC = 6$ in. Point D is on AC and is 1 in. from C. By construction find the points which are equidistant from sides AB and BC (produced, if necessary) and $3\frac{1}{2}$ in. from D.
Solution.

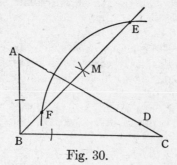

Fig. 30.

Given: $\triangle ABC$ with $AB = 3$ in., $BC = 5$ in., and $AC = 6$ in. Point D on AC and 1 in. from C.

To Find: Points equidistant from AB and BC and $3\frac{1}{2}$ in. from D.
Constructions.

1. Construct BM, the bisector of $\angle ABC$.
2. With D as center and a radius of $3\frac{1}{2}$ in. construct a circle.
3. The circle intersects BM at F and E which are the required points.

Proof.

1. BM is equidistant from AB and BC.	Bisector of $\angle ABC$ is equidistant from the sides.
2. F and E are equidistant from AB and BC.	Every point on BM is equidistant from AB and BC.
3. $DF = DE = 3\frac{1}{2}$ in.	Radii of constructed circle with radius $= 3\frac{1}{2}$ in.

Example 2. Construct a triangle, given its area equal to the square on a given line m, an angle equal to a given angle C, and the side opposite C equal to a given line n.

Solution.

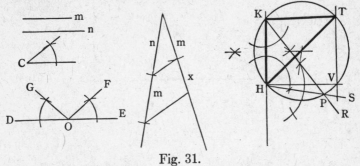

Fig. 31.

Given: The line segments m and n and the angle C.

To Construct: A triangle whose area equals the square on m, has one angle equal to C and the side opposite C equal to n.

Constructions.

1. Construct x such that $n : m = m : x$.
2. Draw any line DE and on it choose a point O.
3. Construct $\angle EOF = \angle C$.
4. Draw OG dividing $\angle DOF$ into any two parts.
5. Construct $KH = n$.
6. At K construct $\angle HKR = \angle DOG$.
7. At H construct $\angle KHS = \angle GOF$.
8. Let KR and HS intersect at P.
9. Circumscribe a circle about $\triangle KHP$.
10. At H construct $HV = 2\,x$ and $HV \perp KH$.
11. At V construct $VT \parallel HK$; VT intersects circle at T.
12. $\triangle HTK$ is the required triangle.

Proof.

1. $KH = n$.	Construction.
2. Area of $\triangle KTH = \frac{1}{2}\overline{KH} \times \overline{VH}$	Area of $\triangle = \frac{1}{2}$ base $\times$ alt.
$\quad = \frac{1}{2}\,n \times 2\,x$	Substitution of equals.
$\quad = nx = m^2$.	Construction of x.
3. $\angle KTH = \angle KPH$.	Both subtend arc KH.
4. $\angle KPH = \angle EOF = \angle C$.	Constructions (6) and (7) and $\angle DOE = 180°$.

Example 3. A right triangle is such that the difference between its acute angles is 45° and the radius of the inscribed circle is 1 in. Construct the triangle.

Solution.

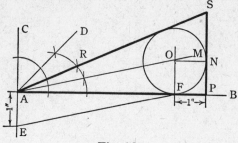

Fig. 32.

Given: The difference of the acute angles of a right triangle is 45°; the radius of the inscribed circle is 1 in.

To Construct: The right triangle.

Constructions.

1. Let x = one acute angle, then $x + x + 45° = 90°$ or $x = 22\frac{1}{2}°$.

2. Draw any line AB and construct $CA \perp AB$ at A.

3. Construct AD, the bisector of $\angle CAB$, and AR, the bisector of $\angle DAB$.

4. Construct AM, the bisector of $\angle RAB$.

5. Construct $AE \perp AB$ and $AE = 1$ in.

6. Construct $EF \parallel AM$; F is point of intersection with AB.

7. Construct $FO \perp AB$.

8. With O as center and OF as radius draw the circle.

9. Construct $ON \perp OF$ and ON = radius of circle.

10. Mark off $FP = ON = 1$ in.

11. Join P to N and extend it to intersect AR at S.

12. $\triangle APS$ is the required triangle.

Proof. [The student should supply the reasons for the following steps.]

1. $\angle RAB = 22\frac{1}{2}°$ = one angle of desired triangle.

2. The center of the inscribed circle will be on AM.

3. $AEFO$ is a $\square$ so that $OF = AE = 1$ in. = radius of inscribed circle.

4. $OFPN$ is a square; $\therefore PN \perp ON$ and tangent to circle at N.

5. $\therefore AR, AP,$ and PN are tangent to the circle of radius 1 in. and the circle is inscribed in $\triangle ASP$ which has $\angle RAB$ as one acute angle.

PROBLEMS

1. Construct an isosceles triangle, having given the sum of the equal sides and the vertex angle.
2. An isosceles triangle has a base 4 in. long and the radius of the circumscribed circle is 3 in. Construct the triangle and find the length of the equal sides.
3. Triangle ABC has sides AB 3 in. long, BC 5 in. long, and AC 6 in. long. Point D is on AC and is 1 in. from C. By construction find the points which are equidistant from sides AB and BC (produced, if necessary) and $3\frac{1}{2}$ in. from D.
4. Arrange three equal equilateral triangles to form a trapezoid.
5. Construct a triangle, being given two sides and the altitude to the third side.
6. Construct an equilateral pentagon that is not regular.
7. Given the diagonal of a square; construct the square.
8. Given in a circle a point which is the midpoint of a chord; construct the chord.
9. Given a triangle; construct a circle which shall be tangent to one side and to the other two sides produced.
10. Given two squares; construct a square equivalent to their sum.
11. Construct an isosceles triangle, being given the base and the radius of the inscribed circle.
12. Given $\angle A = 30°$, $AB = 3$ in., and $BC = 2$ in. Construct the triangle ABC.
13. Given a square 4 in. on a side; construct 4 equal circles, each tangent to exactly two of the others and also tangent to the midpoint of one of the sides of the square.
14. Given a quadrant of a circle whose radius is 6 in. In this quadrant inscribe a circle, that is, construct a circle which shall be tangent to the arc and to the two bounding radii of the quadrant.
15. Given an acute angle and the sum of the legs; construct the right triangle.
16. A point P is taken inside a circle of radius 5 units and at a distance of 3 units from the center. Construct a chord, 9 units in length, through P.
17. Given the base, a, the angle A opposite base a, and the altitude, p, upon one of the other sides; construct the triangle.
18. Construct a regular decagon in a given circle.
19. Construct a triangle equivalent to a given regular pentagon.

20. Divide a given triangle into two equivalent parts by a line parallel to the base.

21. Construct a triangle, given its area equal to the square on a given line m, an angle equal to a given angle C, and the side opposite C equal to a given line n.

22. Construct a line which shall be parallel to the base of a given triangle and whose length shall equal the sum of the segments of the sides intercepted between it and the base.

23. Construct a square such that it is inscribed in a given rhombus.

24. A straight line is given and two points on the same side of it. Construct through these points two lines which shall intersect on the given line and shall make equal angles with it.

25. A point is given within a given angle. Construct a line which shall be bisected by this point and shall terminate in the sides of the angle.

26. Given two straight lines and a point between them; construct a line which shall pass through the point and shall make equal angles with the straight lines.

27. Given a circle and a straight line outside the circle; construct a tangent whose intercept between the point of tangency and the straight line shall equal a given length.

28. Given a point within a circle; construct through this point a chord which shall equal a given length.

29. Given the base, one base angle, and the difference of the other two sides; construct the triangle.

30. Construct an isosceles triangle each of whose base angles is twice as great as the vertex angle.

31. Given two non-intersecting circles and two straight lines outside the circles; construct a straight line which shall cut both circles in such a way that the intercepted chords shall be respectively equal to the given straight lines.

32. In a given circle inscribe a triangle equiangular to a given triangle.

33. Given two circles internally tangent; construct in the large circle a chord which shall terminate in the point of tangency and whose intercept between the two circumferences shall equal a given straight line.

34. In a given circle describe a triangle having each of its base angles equal to one-third of the vertex angle.

35. Through a given point in the base of a given triangle construct a line which shall meet one of the sides (produced, if necessary)

to form a triangle bearing the ratio of $m : n$ to the given triangle; m and n are two given line segments.

36. Given two circles; construct a common external tangent.

37. Given two circles; construct a common internal tangent.

38. Two perpendicular lines, AB and CD, intersect at O. These lines are intersected by a fixed line EF which makes an angle of 30° with AB. Construct all possible squares which have one vertex in EF and one angle coinciding with one of the right angles at O.

39. Given triangle ABC, with AB equal to 6 in., BC equal to 8 in., and AC equal to 7 in.; point P is on AC, and AP is equal to 1 in. Construct a line through P that shall divide the triangle into two equivalent parts.

40. The distance between two points, P and Q, is c. A straight line is to be drawn so that its distance from P shall be a and its distance from Q shall be b. Draw figures showing all possible lines in the following cases: $c > a + b$; $c < a + b$; $c = a + b$.

41. Show how to inscribe a square in a given semicircle.

42. The angle at one vertex of a triangle is 60° and the altitude drawn from that vertex is 4 in. long. The base of the triangle is 5 in. long. Construct the triangle.

43. A right triangle is such that the difference between its acute angles is 45° and the radius of the inscribed circle is 1 in. Construct the triangle.

44. In a given circle find a point P on the arc subtended by chord AB such that the chord PA : chord $PB = 2 : 3$.

45. Construct a rectangle, given the difference in length of two sides equal to d and given angle A formed by the intersection of the two diagonals.

46. Construct a circle which shall be tangent to a given line and shall pass through two points which lie on the same side of the given line and which are at unequal distances from the given line.

47. Given an equilateral triangle inscribed in a circle of radius 1 in. Construct the altitude of an isosceles triangle whose area is one and one-half times that of the given triangle and whose base is the diameter of the given circle.

48. Construct a triangle, given two of its sides, p and q, and the median, m, to the third side.

49 Construct a right triangle having a perimeter equal to a given length p, and one acute angle equal to a given angle A.

50. Determine the point in the given line AB at which the given fixed line CD subtends the greatest angle. See Fig. 33.

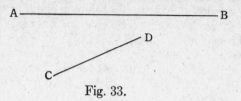

Fig. 33.

51. Given two non-parallel lines, whose intersection point cannot be obtained. Draw a line which, when extended, would pass through the intersection point and would bisect the angle at that point.

52. From the extension of a given chord of a circle construct a tangent which shall equal a given length.

53. Given a point outside a circle; construct through this point a line whose chord-intercept shall equal a given length.

54. Construct a triangle wherein one angle shall equal a given angle, the side opposite that angle shall equal a given length, and the area shall equal the area of a given square.

55. Divide a given circle into five equal parts by means of concentric circles.

56. Given a triangle and a point in one of its sides; trisect this triangle by means of straight lines drawn from this point.

57. Construct a circle passing through a given point, such that the tangent drawn to the circle from another given point shall be equal to a given straight line and also equal to the chord joining the first point with the point of tangency.

58. Find a point exterior to two concentric circles so that, if two tangents be drawn from this point, one to each circle, one tangent shall be twice as long as the other.

59. Given the perimeter, the vertex angle, and the altitude drawn from one extremity of the base; construct the triangle.

60. Given a, one side of a triangle, the opposite angle A, and the radius of the inscribed circle; construct the triangle.

61. Given two non-intersecting circles; construct in one circle a chord which shall equal a given length and, when extended, shall be tangent to the other circle.

CHAPTER VI

LOCI PROBLEMS

Before the student begins this chapter it is suggested that he review the special note on loci problems in Chapter II.

Example 1. Find the locus of the points of trisection of all chords which can be drawn from a fixed point on the circumference of a circle.

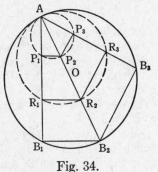

Fig. 34.

Given: A, a fixed point on circle O; AB_i, chords of circle O; P_i and R_i, trisection points of AB_i.

To Find: The locus of P_i and R_i.

Analysis.

1. Figure 34 shows the conditions of the problem in three positions.

2. The circle with center at O is the given circle and the point A is the given point fixed on the circumference of the circle, from which chords are to be drawn.

3. AB_1, AB_2, and AB_3 are three chords from the point A, and AB_2 is also the diameter of the circle.

4. The points of trisection of these chords are P_1 and R_1, P_2 and R_2, P_3 and R_3, respectively.

5. From the figure the probable shapes of the loci are two circles with AP_2 and AR_2 as diameters.

49

Proof.

6. AB_1B_2 is a semicircle.	AB_2 is the diameter of circle O.
7. $\therefore \angle AB_1B_2$ is a rt. $\angle$.	An angle inscribed in a semicircle is a right angle.
8. $AP_1 : AB_1 = AP_2 : AB_2.$ $AR_1 : AB_1 = AR_2 : AB_2.$	P_1 and R_1 are trisection points of AB_1; P_2 and R_2 are trisection points of AB_2.
9. $\therefore P_1P_2 \parallel R_1R_2 \parallel B_1B_2.$	If a line divides two sides of a triangle proportionally, it is parallel to the third side.
10. $\angle AP_1P_2 = \angle AR_1R_2$ $= \angle AB_1B_2.$	(9).
11. $\angle AP_1P_2$ and AR_1R_2 are rt. $\angle$.	$\angle AB_1B_2$ is a rt. $\angle$ by (7).

12. Similarly for the angles at P_2 and P_3.

13. Therefore the trisection points of all chords from A (except the diameter) will be the vertices of right angles formed by the lines from the trisection points to A and the corresponding trisection points of the diameter.

14. The loci are therefore two circles with AP_2 and AR_2 as diameters, except for the point A.

Example 2. The point P is variable in position but always lies on the semicircle which has MON for its diameter. If NA is drawn perpendicular to the tangent which touches at P, find the locus of the intersection of the chord MP and the perpendicular NA.

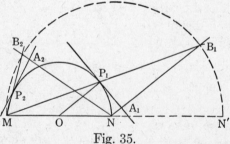

Fig. 35.

Given: The points P_i on the semicircle whose diameter is MON; NA_i perpendicular to the tangents at P_i.

To Find: The locus of the intersections of the chords MP_i and NA_i.

Constructions.

Draw the semicircle with MON as diameter. Choose two points P_1 and P_2 on the semicircle. Draw the tangents at P_1 and P_2. Construct the perpendiculars from N to these two tangents and let the points of intersection be A_1 and A_2. Draw the two chords MP_1 and MP_2. Extend NA_1 and NA_2, MP_1 and MP_2 till they intersect at B_1 and B_2, respectively.

Analysis.

From the figure thus constructed it appears as if the locus will be an arc of a circle.

Proof.

1. OP_1 and NA_1 are both $\perp A_1P_1$.	Given and Theorem.
2. $\therefore NB_1 \parallel OP_1$.	(1).
3. $\therefore \angle NB_1M = \angle MP_1O$ $= \angle P_1MO.$	(2) and $OM = OP_1 = $ radii of circle O.
4. $\therefore NB_1 = MN.$	(3).
5. Similarly $NB_2 = MN.$	

6. Therefore, the locus is a semicircle which has N as its center and MN as its radius, omitting the endpoints of its diameter, M and N'.

Example 3. If the base of a triangle is fixed and if the median to one side is constant in length though variable in direction, what is the locus of the vertex?

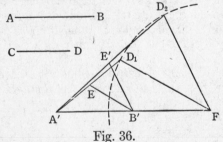

Fig. 36.

Given: AB, the base of a triangle; CD the median of the triangle.
To Find: The locus of the vertex of the triangle.
Constructions.

Draw $A'B' = AB$ and $B'E = CD$. Extend $A'E$ so that $A'E = ED_1$; $A'B'$ so that $A'B' = B'F$; and join D_1 and F. Draw $B'E' = CD$. Extend $A'E' = E'D_2$ and join D_2 and F.

Analysis. If the figure is carefully drawn it appears as if $D_1F = D_2F$ so that the locus may be a circle with F as the center. *Proof.*

1. $A'B' = B'F$ and $A'E = ED_1$.	Construction.
2. $\therefore D_1F = 2 EB' = 2 CD$.	A line segment connecting the midpoints of two sides of a triangle is equal to half of the third side.
3. $AE' = E'D_2$ and $A'B' = B'F$.	Construction.
4. $D_2F = 2 E'B' = 2 CD$.	Same as (2).
5. $\therefore D_1F = D_2F$.	(2) and (4).

6. Since D_i is always an equal distance from F, the locus is a circle with D_1F as the radius and F as the center, except for two points; namely, the two points where the circle intersects $A'B'$ extended, since in this case there would be no triangle.

PROBLEMS

1. Find the locus of the right angle vertices of right triangles which have a fixed hypotenuse.
2. Find the locus of the points of trisection of all chords drawn from a fixed point on the circumference of a circle.
3. The point C is the vertex of a 60 degree angle whose sides pass through two fixed points which are 8 in. apart. Show that the locus of C is an arc of a circle and find the radius of the circle.
4. Two circles of unequal radii are tangent externally. Find the locus of a point P, such that the tangents from P to the circles are equal.
5. From a given point A perpendiculars are drawn to all lines which pass through a given point B. Find the locus of the feet of these perpendiculars.
6. What is the locus of the vertex of a triangle that has a fixed base and a given area?
7. Show how to construct the locus of the vertex of a triangle that has a given base and a given vertex angle.
8. Find the locus described by a point P which divides a chord of given length in the ratio of $1 : 3$, as the chord takes all possible positions in the given circle.
9. A point moves so that it is always outside a square 3 ft. on a side and so that it is always 2 ft. from the nearest point of the

square. Find the area enclosed by the locus of this moving point.

10. From a fixed point A straight lines are drawn to a given line BC and are divided by a point M in the ratio of $c : d$, where c and d are two given line segments. Find the locus of M.

11. Find the locus of the midpoints of all chords that can be drawn from a fixed point in the circumference of a circle.

12. The angle ACB is inscribed in a segment of a circle. If AC is produced to a point P so that CP equals CB, what is the locus of P?

13. Find the locus of a point the difference of the squares of whose distances from two given points is a constant.

14. A triangle has a base 4 in. long and a vertex angle equal to the acute angle formed by the diagonals of a rectangle 3 in. long and 2 in. wide. Construct the locus of the center of the circle inscribed in this triangle when the base is kept fixed and the vertex takes all possible positions.

15. Find the locus of the intersections of the diagonals of all rhombuses which have a fixed line segment AB as one side.

16. Two rods, OA and OB, meet at right angles. A rod CD, 16 in. long, moves with one end always against OA and the other end always against OB. Find the locus of the midpoint of the rod CD.

17. Find the locus of the center of a circle which is tangent externally to each of two given non-intersecting equal circles.

18. Find the locus of the centers of circles which are tangent to two given straight lines.

19. If from an external point secants are drawn to a circle, find the locus of the midpoints of the intercepted chords.

20. If A is any point in the hypotenuse MO of the triangle MNO and if the perpendicular to MO at A meets MN (produced, if necessary) at B and ON (produced, if necessary) at C, find the locus of P, the intersecting point of MC and OB.

21. Find the locus of the midpoints of all the segments of chords that can be drawn from a fixed point P within a circle to the circumference.

22. From a fixed point A in the circumference of a circle a chord AB is drawn to a variable point B. On this chord (produced, if necessary) a point P is taken so that the product of AB and AP is a constant. Find the locus of P.

23. Find the locus of the vertex of a triangle that has a given fixed base and the difference of the squares of the other two sides equal to a given constant.

24. From the vertex A of the isosceles triangle ABC a line is drawn cutting the base at D. On AD produced a point P is taken so that $\overline{AD} \times \overline{AP} = \overline{AB}^2$. What is the locus of P as D moves along the base?

25. What is the locus of a point such that the two tangents from the point to a given circle form a given angle?

26. If the base of a triangle is fixed and if the vertex angle is constant in size but variable in position, find the locus of the intersecting point of the altitudes.

27. The point P is variable in position but always lies on the major arc MN. If the extension of the chord MP is always equal to PN, find the locus of the terminal point of the extension.

28. The point P is variable in position but always lies on the semicircle which has MON for its diameter. If NA is drawn perpendicular to the tangent which touches at P, find the locus of the intersection of the chord MP and the perpendicular NA.

29. Two intersecting straight lines are given. What is the locus of a point the sum of whose distances from the given lines is a given constant?

30. If the base of a triangle is fixed and if the median to one side is constant in length though variable in direction, what is the locus of the vertex?

31. Two lines, CD and EF, intersect at O. A third line is drawn, cutting these lines at A and B, respectively, so that OA equals OB. Prove that all points on this third line, except those in the segment AB, are on the locus of points the difference of whose distances from the lines CD and EF is a constant.

32. A straight line of given length moves so that it remains parallel to a given fixed line and touches a given circumference with one of its ends. Find the locus of the other end.

CHAPTER VII

PROBLEMS ON POLYGONS

Example 1. Prove that the diagonals of a trapezoid intersect at a point which divides them into proportional segments.
Solution.

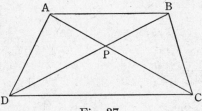

Fig. 37.

Given: The trapezoid *ABCD* and its diagonals *AC* and *BD* intersecting at *P*.
To Prove: $AP : PC = BP : PD$.
Proof.

1. $AB \parallel CD$.	Definition.
2. ∴ $\angle PAB = \angle PCD$ and $\angle ABP = \angle CDP$.	If two parallel lines are cut by a transversal, the alternate interior angles are equal.
3. ∴ $\triangle ABP \sim \triangle DPC$.	Two ⧍ are ∼, if two angles of one are equal, respectively, to two angles of the other.
4. ∴ $AP : PC = BP : PD$.	In similar ⧍ corresponding sides are proportional.

Example 2. *AX* and *BX* are two adjacent sides of a regular polygon. If angle *ABX* equals one-third of angle *AXB*, how many sides has the polygon?
Given: *AX* and *BX*, two adjacent sides of regular polygon; $\angle ABX = \frac{1}{3} \angle AXB$.
To Find: The number of sides in the polygon.

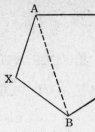

Fig. 38.

Solution.

1. $AX = XB$.	Regular polygon.
2. ∴ $\angle ABX = \angle XAB$.	∡ opp. = sides are =.
3. $\angle AXB = 3 \angle ABX$.	Given.
4. $\angle ABX + \angle XAB + \angle AXB = 180°$.	Sum of ∡ in a △.
5. $\angle ABX + \angle ABX + 3 \angle ABX = 5 \angle ABX$ $= 180°$.	Substitution of equals.
6. ∴ $\angle ABX = 36°$ and $\angle AXB = 108°$.	Solution of (5).
7. Angles of polygon are all equal.	The polygon is regular.
8. ∴ $108\,n = (n - 2)180$.	Sum of ∡ = $(n - 2)$ st. ∡.
9. ∴ $n = 5$.	Solution of (8).

Example 3. Prove that in a quadrilateral the lines which join the midpoints of the opposite sides and the line which joins the midpoints of the diagonals bisect one another at a common point.
Solution.

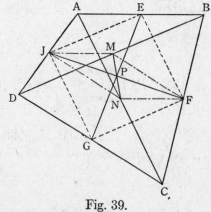

Fig. 39.

Given: $ABCD$, any quadrilateral; E, F, G, and J, the midpoints of the sides; M, the midpoint of BD; and N, the midpoint of AC.

To Prove: MN, EG, and JF intersect at P and P is the midpoint of MN, EG, and JF.

Proof:

1. $JEFG$ is a parallelogram.	See Prob. 13, Chap. VII.
2. JF and GE are the diagonals of $\square$.	(1).
3. $\therefore P$ is midpoint of EG and JF.	The diagonals of a parallelogram bisect each other.
4. Draw MJ and NF.	Construction.
5. $JM \parallel AB$ and $JM = \frac{1}{2} AB$.	JM joins midpoints of BD and AD.
6. $NF \parallel AB$ and $NF = \frac{1}{2} AB$.	NF joins midpoints of AC and BC.
7. $\therefore JM \parallel NF$ and $JM = NF$.	Substitution of equals.
8. $\therefore JMFN$ is a parallelogram.	Definition.
9. $\therefore JF$ and MN bisect each other.	Same as (3).
10. $\therefore MN$ passes through P.	P is midpoint of JF.
11. $\therefore P$ is midpoint of MN, EG, and JF.	(3) and (10).

PROBLEMS

1. The bases of a trapezoid are 15 in. and 9 in.; the altitude is 4 in. Find the altitudes of the triangles formed by producing the legs of the trapezoid.

2. Prove that if two adjacent angles of a quadrilateral are right angles, the bisectors of the other two angles are perpendicular to each other.

3. Prove that the diagonals of a trapezoid intersect in a point which divides them into proportional segments.

4. The interior angles of a polygon are in arithmetic progression; the least angle is 120° and the common difference is 5°. Find the number of sides of the polygon.

5. In the square $ABCD$ the points E, F, G, and H are the midpoints of the sides AB, BC, CD, and DA, respectively. Prove that the quadrilateral $EFGH$ is a square and that it is one-half the area of $ABCD$.

6. The area of *ABCDE* is 18 sq. in.; the area of a similar pentagon *A'B'C'D'E'* is 32 sq. in. The diagonal *AC* is 6 in.; find the length of *A'C'*.

7. Prove that the bisectors of the angles of a rectangle enclose a square.

8. Prove that the area of a rhombus is equal to one-half the product of the diagonals.

9. Through *A* a line *L* is drawn parallel to the diagonal *BD* of a rhombus *ABCD*. From any point *E* in *L* a line is drawn parallel to *AB* and intersects *AD* (or *AD* produced) at *F*. Prove that the triangle *AEF* is isosceles.

10. A rectangular lawn has an area of 126 sq. ft. Around it is a flower border 4 ft. wide whose area is 264 sq. ft. Find the dimensions of the lawn.

11. Prove that if the opposite angles of a quadrilateral are supplementary, a circle can be circumscribed around it.

12. Prove that the diagonals of a rhombus bisect the angles of the rhombus.

13. Prove that, if the midpoints of the adjacent sides of a quadrilateral are connected, a parallelogram is formed and that the perimeter of the parallelogram is equal to the sum of the diagonals of the quadrilateral.

14. Prove that if the midpoints of the sides of a quadrilateral are consecutively connected, the area of the new quadrilateral thus formed is equal to one-half that of the original quadrilateral.

15. Prove that if two diagonals of a regular pentagon intersect each other, the longer segments will be equal to the sides of the pentagon.

16. Prove that if two adjacent sides of a parallelogram make equal angles with either diagonal, the figure is a rhombus.

17. Prove that the sum of the alternate angles of any hexagon inscribed in a circle is equal to four right angles.

18. Upon the sides of a right triangle as corresponding sides three similar polygons are constructed. Show that the polygon upon the hypotenuse has an area equal to the sum of the areas of the polygons upon the legs.

19. *AX* and *BX* are two adjacent sides of a regular polygon. If angle *ABX* equals one-third of angle *AXB*, how many sides has the polygon?

20. Find the area of the parallelogram whose sides are 6 in. and 8 in. and whose longer diagonal is 12 in.

21. One base of a trapezoid is 10 ft. long, the altitude is 4 ft., and the area is 32 sq. ft. Find the length of a line parallel to and 1 ft. above the 10-ft. base and included between the legs of the trapezoid.

22. The bases of a trapezoid are 15 ft. and 9 ft., and the legs are each 5 ft. in length. Find the area of the triangle formed by the longer base and the segments of the diagonals which are adjacent to that base.

23. Prove that if two opposite angles of a quadrilateral are right angles, the bisectors of the other two angles are parallel.

24. Prove that the line joining the midpoints of the diagonals of a trapezoid is equal to one-half the difference of its bases.

25. The diagonals of a parallelogram are, respectively, 18 and 28 in., and one side is 20 in. long. Find the distance to this side from the intersection of the diagonals.

26. The bases of a trapezoid are 9 in. and 15 in.; the altitude is 7 in. Find the area of the quadrilateral formed by joining the midpoints of the adjacent sides of the trapezoid.

27. A regular hexagon has sides 4 ft. long. Find the area of the triangle formed by connecting alternate vertices.

28. Prove that the area of an inscribed regular octagon is equivalent to that of a rectangle whose dimensions are the sides of the inscribed and circumscribed squares.

29. Prove that two diagonals of a regular pentagon, not drawn from a common vertex, divide each other in extreme and mean ratio.

30. Two regular polygons of the same number of sides have sides 5 ft. and 12 ft. in length, respectively. What is the length of the side of another regular polygon of the same number of sides, if its area is equal to the sum of the other two?

31. A piece of paper, 24 in. long by 18 in. wide, is folded once in such a way that two diagonally opposite corners are made to coincide. What is the length of the crease?

32. Given that A and B are the midpoints of MN and PO in the parallelogram $MNOP$; prove that the diagonal MO is trisected by the lines AP and NB.

33. Prove that in the quadrilateral formed by the bisectors of the angles of a quadrilateral the opposite angles are supplementary.

34. On the sides AB and BC of a parallelogram $ABCD$ equilateral triangles, ABP and BCQ, are described with their vertices remote from the parallelogram. Prove that PQD is an equilateral triangle.

35. From AC, the diagonal of the square $ABCD$, cut off AE equal to one-fourth of AC and join B to E, and D to E. Prove that the figure $BADE$ equals twice the square on AE.

36. Prove that any polygons whatsoever described about a circle are to each other as their perimeters.

37. Let P be any point in the perimeter of a rectangle. Prove that the sum of the perpendiculars from P to the diagonals is a constant.

38. Find the area of a regular octagon whose perimeter is 40 ft. (Do this without the use of trigonometry.)

39. The diagonals of a rhombus are 30 in. and 50 in. Find the length of one side, the area of the rhombus, and the perpendicular distance between the bases.

40. The lengths of the parallel sides of an isosceles trapezoid are 8 and 18 in. What must be the lengths of the non-parallel sides if it is possible to inscribe a circle in the trapezoid? What is the altitude of the trapezoid?

41. The altitude of a trapezoid is 1 in.; its upper and lower bases are, respectively, 1 in. and 2 in. If a line parallel to the bases divides the trapezoid into areas having the ratio 7 : 20, find the distance of this line from the upper base.

42. Given the parallelogram $MNPA$ and a variable line from M cutting NP at B and AP at C; prove that $\overline{NB} \times \overline{AC}$ is a constant.

43. If on the sides of a parallelogram as hypotenuses there are described isosceles right triangles, all external to the parallelogram, prove that the vertices of the triangles, when connected, form a square.

44. $ABCD$ is a square; AC is a diagonal; AD is bisected at E; and the line BE cuts AC at F.

Prove: $\dfrac{\text{triangle } AEF}{1} = \dfrac{\text{triangle } CEF}{2} = \dfrac{\text{triangle } ABE}{3}$
$$= \dfrac{\text{triangle } BCF}{4}.$$

45. Prove that in a quadrilateral the lines which join the midpoints of the opposite sides and the line which joins the midpoints of the diagonals bisect one another at a common point.

46. Find the area of a trapezoid in which the bases are 17 ft. and 42 ft. and the legs are 15 ft. and 20 ft.

47. Prove that if a quadrilateral is inscribed in a circle, the product of the diagonals is equal to the sum of the products of the opposite sides.

48. The opposite sides of a quadrilateral inscribed in a circle are produced to meet at P and Q, and about the external triangles thus formed circles are drawn meeting again at R. Prove that the points P, R, and Q lie in one straight line. See Fig. 40.

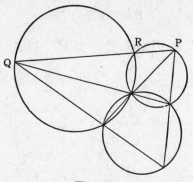

Fig. 40.

49. If the angles A and C of parallelogram $ABCD$ are trisected and the angles B and D are bisected, and if the bisector of D meets the trisectors of A at P and Q, and if the bisector of B meets the trisectors of C at R and S, prove that $PQRS$ is a parallelogram of which two sides are parallel to two sides of $ABCD$.

50. If $ABCD$ is a parallelogram and if E and F respectively bisect AB and DC and if the lines AF, BF, CE, and DE cut the two diagonals at P, Q, R, and S, respectively, prove that $PQRS$ is a parallelogram and that its area is one-ninth the area of $ABCD$.

CHAPTER VIII

PROBLEMS ON TRIANGLES

Example 1. If the sides of a triangle are 5 in., 9 in., and 12 in. in length, find the altitude to the 12-in. side.

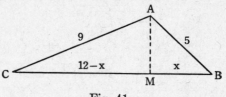

Fig. 41.

Given: $\triangle ABC$ with $AB = 5$ in., $AC = 9$ in., $BC = 12$ in.
To Find: Length of altitude to BC.
Solution:

1. Draw $AM \perp BC$; then $AM = h$ is the desired altitude by definition.

2. Let $BM = x$; then $CM = 12 - x$ since $BM + CM = BC = 12$.

3. In rt. $\triangle AMB$: $25 = x^2 + h^2$ by the Pythagorean Theorem.

4. In rt. $\triangle AMC$: $81 = (12 - x)^2 + h^2$ by the Pythagorean Theorem.

5. This gives two equations in the two unknowns x and h.

6. Solving:

$$h^2 = 25 - x^2.$$
$$81 = 144 - 24x + x^2 + 25 - x^2.$$
$$24x = 88, \text{ or } x = \tfrac{11}{3}.$$
$$h^2 = 25 - \tfrac{121}{9} = \tfrac{1}{9}(225 - 121) = \tfrac{4}{9}(26).$$
$$\therefore h = \tfrac{2}{3}\sqrt{26}.$$

Example 2. The base of a triangle is 10 in. and the angle opposite the base is 60°. Find to three decimals the radius of the circumscribed circle.

Given: $\triangle ABC$ with $AB = 10$ in. and $\angle ACB = 60°$.
To Find: The radius of the circumscribed circle.

62

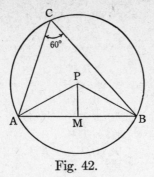

Fig. 42.

Solution:

1. Let P be the center of the circumscribed circle.
2. Since $\angle ACB = 60°$, arc $AB = 120°$ and $\angle APB = 120°$.
3. Draw $PM \perp AB$.
4. PM bisects $\angle APB$; $\therefore$ $\angle APM = 60°$ and $\angle PAM = 30°$.
5. PM bisects AB; $\therefore$ $AM = 5$ in.
6. In $\triangle APM$: It can be shown that $PM = \frac{1}{2} AP$ and $AM = \frac{\sqrt{3}}{2} AP$; see Prob. 11, Chap. VIII.

7. $\therefore$ $5 = \frac{\sqrt{3}}{2} AP$ or $AP = \frac{10}{\sqrt{3}} = \frac{10}{3} \sqrt{3} = (3.3333)(1.732) \Rightarrow 5.773$.

Example 3. Prove that the sum of the perpendiculars drawn from any point within an equilateral triangle to the three sides is a constant.

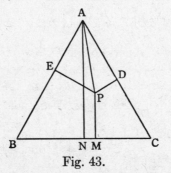

Fig. 43.

Given: P, any point in the equilateral $\triangle ABC$.

To Prove: The sum of the perpendiculars from P to the sides of $\triangle ABC$ is a constant.

Proof: [It is left for the student to supply the reasons for the following steps.]

1. Draw $PD \perp AC$, $PE \perp AB$, $PM \perp BC$, and $AN \perp BC$.
2. Area of $\triangle ABC$ = area of $\triangle PBC$ + area of $\triangle PAB$ + area of $\triangle PAC$

$$= \tfrac{1}{2}\,\overline{BC} \times \overline{PM} + \tfrac{1}{2}\,\overline{AB} \times \overline{PE} + \tfrac{1}{2}\,\overline{AC} \times \overline{PD}$$
$$= \tfrac{1}{2}\,\overline{BC} \times \overline{PM} + \tfrac{1}{2}\,\overline{BC} \times \overline{PE} + \tfrac{1}{2}\,\overline{BC} \times \overline{PD}$$
$$= \tfrac{1}{2}\,\overline{BC}(\overline{PM} + \overline{PE} + \overline{PD})$$
$$= \tfrac{1}{2}\,\overline{BC} \times \overline{AN}.$$

3. $\therefore PM + PE + PD = AN$ = constant.

Example 4. If the two sides AB and AC of the triangle ABC are bisected at D and E, respectively, and if BE and CD meet at F, prove that the areas of the quadrilateral $ADFE$ and the triangle FBC are equal.

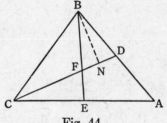

Fig. 44.

Given: $\triangle ABC$; D, midpoint of AB; E, midpoint of AC; DC and BE intersecting at F.

To Prove: Area of $ADFE$ = area of $\triangle FBC$.

Proof:

Let area of $\triangle BFD = K$; area of $\triangle BFC = M$; area of $\triangle BDC = R$; area of $\triangle ABC = P$.

1. BE and CD are medians of $\triangle ABC$.	Definition.
2. $FC = \tfrac{2}{3} CD$ and $DF = \tfrac{1}{3} CD$.	Medians intersect at $\tfrac{2}{3}$ point from vertex.
3. $\therefore FC : DF = 2 : 1$.	(2).
4. Draw $BN \perp CD$.	Construction.
5. BN is alt. of $\triangle BFC$ and BDF.	Definition.

6. $\therefore K : M = DF : FC = 1 : 2$.	Triangles having equal altitudes are to each other as their bases.
7. $\therefore M = 2 K$.	Product of means = product of extremes.
8. $\therefore R = 3 K$.	$R = M + K$.
9. $\triangle BDC$ and ABC have same alt.	Alt. is $\perp$ from C to AB.
10. $AB = 2 BD$.	D is midpoint of AB.
11. $\therefore P : R = AB : BD$.	Same as (6).
12. $\therefore P = 2 R = 6 K$.	(7), (10), and (8).
13. Similarly, area of $\triangle ABE = \frac{1}{2} P = 3 K$.	Steps similar to (1)–(12).
14. Quad. $ADFE = \triangle ABE - \triangle BDF$ $= 3 K - K = 2 K$ $= M$ $=$ area of $\triangle BFC$.	Postulate. Substitution of equals. Q.E.D.

Example 5. Two sides of a triangle are 8 and 18 in. in length and the bisector of the angle formed by them has a length of $\frac{60}{13}$ in. Find the length of the third side.

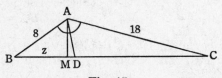

Fig. 45.

Given: $\triangle ABC$ with $AB = 8$ in., $BC = 18$ in., AD bisector of $\angle BAC$, and $AD = \frac{60}{13}$ in.

To Find: The length of BC.

Solution: [It is left for the student to supply the reasons for the following steps.]

1. Draw $AM \perp BD$.
2. Since $\angle BAD = \angle DAC$, $BD : DC = AB : AC = 8 : 18 = 4 : 9$.
3. Let $BD = 4 y$, $DC = 9 y$, and $BM = z$.
4. $\therefore MD = 4 y - z$.
5. In rt. $\triangle ADM$: $(\frac{60}{13})^2 - (4 y - z)^2 = \overline{AM}^2$.
6. In rt. $\triangle AMC$: $18^2 - (13 y - z)^2 = \overline{AM}^2$.
7. In rt. $\triangle AMB$: $8^2 - z^2 = \overline{AM}^2$.
8. $\therefore \frac{3600}{169} - (4 y - z)^2 = 64 - z^2$.
   $324 - (13 y - z)^2 = 64 - z^2$.

9. Solving these two simultaneous equations for y:

$$\begin{cases} 16\,y^2 - 8\,yz = -\frac{7216}{169}. \\ 169\,y^2 - 26\,yz = 260. \end{cases}$$

$$\begin{cases} 4\,y^2 - 2\,yz = -\frac{1804}{169}. \\ 13\,y^2 - 2\,yz = 20. \end{cases}$$

$$9\,y^2 = 20 + \frac{1804}{169} = \frac{4[169(5) + 451]}{169}.$$

$$y^2 = \frac{4(1296)}{9(169)} = \frac{4(144)}{169}.$$

$$y = \tfrac{24}{13}.$$

10. $$\therefore\ 13\,y = 24 = BC.$$

PROBLEMS

1. If a median of a triangle is drawn, prove that the perpendiculars from the other vertices upon this median are equal.

2. The captain of a ship at A, sailing in the direction ABC, observes a lighthouse, L, and finds the angle LAC to be $36°\,30'$. After sailing 5 miles to B, he observes angle LBC to be $73°$. How many miles is the position B from the lighthouse?

3. The bisector of angle A of the triangle ABC intersects BC at the point D. $AB = 27$ in.; $AC = 18$ in.; $BC = 37.5$ in. Find the lengths of BD and DC.

4. Let ABC be an equilateral triangle and let D, E, and F be points on AC, AB, and BC, respectively, so that $AD = BE = CF$. Prove that the triangle DEF is equilateral.

5. A triangular field containing 156,250 sq. ft. is represented to scale by a similar triangular plan whose sides are 12 in., 17 in., and 25 in. What distance on the field is represented by one foot on the plan?

6. Two triangles of equal area and equal bases stand with their bases on the same straight line but with their vertices on opposite sides of this line. Prove that the line joining the vertices of the triangles is bisected by the line on which their bases stand.

7. If the sides of a triangle are 5 in., 9 in., and 12 in. in length, find the altitude to the 12-in. side.

8. In the side AC of a triangle ABC any point D is taken, and the lines AD, DC, AB, and BC are bisected at the points E, F, G, and H, respectively; prove $EG = FH$.

9. If ABC is a right triangle with right angle at C and if BD is any line cutting AC at D, prove that $\overline{BD}^2 + \overline{AC}^2 = \overline{AB}^2 + \overline{DC}^2$.

10. In the triangle ABC, AB is greater than AC. A point P is taken on AB and a point Q on AC so that $BP = CQ$. Prove that BQ is greater than CP.

11. Prove that, if the hypotenuse of a 90°, 60°, 30° triangle is h in., the other two sides are $\dfrac{h}{2}$ in. and $\dfrac{h}{2}\sqrt{3}$ in.

12. Prove that the area of an equilateral triangle is equal to $\dfrac{s^2}{4}\sqrt{3}$, where s = length of one side.

13. Given an equilateral triangle inscribed in a circle of radius 1 in. Calculate the altitude of an isosceles triangle whose area is one and one-half times as great as that of the given triangle and whose base is the diameter of the given circle.

14. Prove that if in a right triangle the hypotenuse is twice one side, the acute angles are 30° and 60°.

15. Prove that in any right triangle the median from the vertex of the right angle to the hypotenuse is equal to one-half the hypotenuse.

16. If in a right triangle one acute angle is twice as great as the other acute angle, prove that the hypotenuse is twice as great as the shortest side.

17. If NO is the base of the isosceles triangle MNO and if the perpendicular from N to MO meets MO at A, prove that the angle ANO is equal to one-half the angle M.

18. Prove that, if from the intersection point of the bisectors of the base angles of an equilateral triangle lines parallel to the sides are drawn to the base, these lines trisect the base.

19. If one angle, C, of a triangle ABC is equal to the sum of the other two angles, prove that the side AB is equal to twice the line joining C with the midpoint of AB.

20. If the square described on one of the sides of a triangle is equal to the sum of the squares described on the other two sides, prove that the triangle is a right triangle.

21. If several triangles are described on the same base and have equal vertical angles, prove that the bisectors of the vertical angles are concurrent at one point.

22. If two triangles are equivalent and if one side and its adjacent angle in one triangle are equal, respectively, to one side and its adjacent angle in the other triangle, prove that the two triangles are congruent.

23. Prove that each side of a triangle is less than half the perimeter of the triangle.

24. The base of a triangle is 10 in. and the angle opposite the base is 60°. Find to three decimals the radius of the circumscribed circle.

25. If from any point in the base of an isosceles triangle perpendiculars are drawn to the equal sides, prove that the sum of these perpendiculars is equal to the altitude upon either of the equal sides.

26. The hypotenuse of a right triangle is divided into segments p and q by the perpendiculars from the vertex of the right angle. Find the area of the triangle in terms of p and q.

27. If two of the medians of a triangle are produced through the respective sides to which they are drawn, each to its own length, prove that the line joining their external extremities will pass through one of the vertices of the triangle.

28. The base of a triangle is 12 in. and the median drawn to the base is 5 in. The area of the triangle is 24 sq. in. Find the lengths of the other two sides.

29. The angle C of triangle ABC is a right angle; $AC = 8$ in., $BC = 15$ in. BA is produced through A to D, making $AD = 5$ in. CA is produced through A to E, so that the triangle AED is equivalent to triangle ABC. Find the length of AE.

30. The base AB of a triangular sheet of paper is 12 in. long. The paper is folded down over the base, the crease being parallel to the base. The area of the part of the triangle that projects below the base is .36 of the triangle ABC. Find the length of the crease.

31. Triangle ABC has sides $AB = AC = 5$ in.; $BC = 7$ in. From point D on BC such that $BD = 3$ in., DE and DF are drawn respectively parallel to AC and AB. Find the perimeter of the quadrilateral $AEDF$.

32. In a given triangle, if lines are drawn from the center of the inscribed circle to the extremities of the base, prove that the angle so formed equals 90° plus one-half the angle of the triangle opposite the base.

33. Prove that the sum of the three lines drawn from any point within a triangle to the vertices is less than the sum of the three sides and greater than half their sum.

34. Prove that the sum of the perpendiculars drawn from any point within an equilateral triangle to the three sides is a constant.

35. Prove that the feet of the altitudes drawn to two sides of a triangle are equidistant from the midpoint of the third side.

36. The hypotenuse of a right triangle is 25 in. The altitude on the hypotenuse is 12 in. What are the lengths of the other two sides of the triangle?

37. The sides of a right triangle are in arithmetic progression. The radius of the circumscribed circle is 25 in. Find the lengths of the three sides.

38. Prove that, if from any point in the base of an isosceles triangle lines parallel to the sides are drawn, a parallelogram is formed whose perimeter is a constant.

39. The three medians of the triangle MNO meet at P. The median from N to MO meets MO at A. If PA is extended to its own length to B, prove that the sides of the triangle POB are respectively two-thirds the lengths of the medians.

40. In the triangle MNO, NO is the base and if the bisectors of angle N and of the exterior angle at O meet at A, prove that angle A equals one-half angle M.

41. Prove that the product of two sides of a triangle is equal to the product of the diameter of the circumscribed circle and the altitude upon the third side.

42. Prove that the area of a triangle is equal to the product of the three sides divided by twice the diameter of the circumscribed circle.

43. ABC is an equilateral triangle. From D, the midpoint of BC, DE is drawn perpendicular to AB. Prove that BE is one-fourth of AB.

44. If the two sides AB and AC of the triangle ABC are bisected in D and E, respectively, and if BE and CD meet in F, prove that the areas of the quadrilateral $ADFE$ and the triangle FBC are equal.

45. If a straight line, terminated by two sides of a triangle, is bisected, prove that no other line terminated by the same sides can be bisected at the same point.

46. Prove that in any triangle the line bisecting an angle and the line which is the perpendicular bisector of the opposite side intersect at one point on the circumscribed circle.

47. The sides AB and AC of the triangle ABC are 16 in. and 9 in. respectively, and the median from angle C is 11 in. Find the side BC.

48. The sides of a right triangle are 3 ft., 4 ft., and 5 ft. in length. A point is taken on the hypotenuse at a distance of 2 ft. from the vertex adjacent to the 4-ft. side. Find the distance from this point to the vertex of the right angle.

49. A point within an equilateral triangle, whose perimeter is 30 ft., is 2 ft. from one side and 3 ft. from another side. Find its distance from the third side.

50. Find the length of the bisector of the least angle of the triangle whose sides are 7 ft., 15 ft., and 20 ft. in length.

51. The sides of a triangle are a, b, and c. Derive a formula in terms of a, b, and c for the median to side c.

52. Two sides of a triangle are 5 in. and 10 in. in length, and the median to the third side is $6\frac{1}{2}$ in. Compute the area of the triangle.

53. Find the areas of the two triangles into which triangle ABC is divided by the bisector of angle A, if $AB = BC = 40$ ft., and $AC = 10$ ft.

54. In triangle ABC, M is the midpoint of AB and P is any point in AM. Line MD meeting BC at D is parallel to PC. Prove that the triangle BPD has half the area of triangle ABC.

55. Find the sides of a right triangle whose perimeter is 56 ft. and whose area is 84 sq. ft.

56. Find the area of the square inscribed in an isosceles triangle whose base is 60 ft. long and whose equal sides are each 50 ft. long. Let two vertices lie on the base of the triangle.

57. Two sides of a triangle are each 17 in. long and the altitude to the third side is 15 in. Find the radius of the inscribed circle.

58. In triangle ABC, AD is the bisector of angle A. $AD = 8$ in., $AB = 7$ in., and $BD = 3$ in. Find the lengths of AC and BC.

59. The lengths of the three sides of a triangle are 4, 6, and 8 in. Find the length of the median to the 8-in. side.

60. The legs of a right triangle are 5 in. and 12 in. Find the distance from the intersection of the bisectors of the acute angles to the shorter leg.

61. The bisector of angle A of triangle ABC is 6 in. and it divides the opposite side into segments of lengths 4 in. and 3 in. Find the lengths of AB and AC.

62. Prove that the median to a side of a triangle is less than one-half the sum of the other two sides.

63. Prove that the median to a side of a triangle is greater than the difference between one-half the sum of the other two sides and one-half the third side.

64. Prove that the sum of the three medians of a triangle is less than the perimeter of the triangle.

65. Prove that the sum of the three medians of a triangle is greater than one-half the perimeter of the triangle.

66. If from two points external to a given straight line and lying on the same side of the given line, straight lines are drawn to a point in the given line so that they make equal angles with the given line, prove that the sum of these two straight lines is less than the sum of any other two straight lines drawn from the same external points but meeting the given line at a different point.

67. If from the vertex of a triangle a perpendicular to the base is drawn, prove that the angle between this perpendicular and the bisector of the vertex angle equals one-half the difference between the base angles of the triangle.

68. AD is perpendicular to AB, the hypotenuse of the right triangle ABC, and is equal to AC. Prove that CD is parallel or perpendicular to the bisector of angle ABC.

69. Prove that if A is the right angle of a given right triangle and if O is the intersection point of the diagonals of the square constructed on the outer side of the hypotenuse, then AO bisects angle A.

70. Let ACB and ADB be two right triangles having a common hypotenuse AB. If the line CD is produced in both directions and to it the perpendiculars AE and BF are drawn from A and B, prove that $\overline{CE}^2 + \overline{CF}^2 = \overline{DE}^2 + \overline{DF}^2$.

71. A and B are two towns on the same side of a straight railroad and C and D are the points on the railroad nearest to A and B respectively. If $AC = 1$ mile, $BD = 4$ miles, and $CD = 12$ miles, find the length of the shortest road that can be built from A to B and at the same time touch the railroad at one point. Find also the exact location of this point.

72. The sides of a triangle are 10, 17, and 21 in. in length. Find the length of the altitude to the longest side and the diameter of the circumscribed circle.

73. In triangle ABC, AD and BE are medians intersecting at F. Prove that the quadrilateral $CDFE$ is one-third the area of the triangle ABC.

74. Compute the length of the shortest median in a triangle having sides 5, 7, and 11 in.

75. Two sides of a triangle are 8 and 18 in. in length, and the bisector of the angle formed by them has a length of $\frac{60}{13}$ in. Find the length of the third side.

76. If E and D are the points of trisection of the sides AC and AB of a triangle and if F is the point of intersection of CD and BE, prove that the triangle BFC is one-half the triangle ABC and

that the quadrilateral $ADFE$ is equivalent to either of the triangles CFE or BDF.

77. Prove that in an oblique triangle the square of a side opposite an acute angle is equal to the sum of the squares of the other two sides diminished by twice the product of one of those sides and the projection of the other side on it.

78. If ABC is a right triangle with right angle at A and if from B and C bisectors of AC and AB are drawn, meeting the line through A drawn parallel to BC at points D and E, prove that $\overline{BD}^2 + \overline{CE}^2 = 5\,\overline{BC}^2$.

79. Prove that the area of a triangle is equal to $\sqrt{s(s-a)(s-b)(s-c)}$ where $s = $ one-half the perimeter and a, b, and c represent the lengths of the sides.

80. Given a straight line AB, divided by points, M and N, in such a way that $\overline{AB} \times \overline{AM} = \overline{AN}^2$; prove that if a line AP is drawn equal to AN, PN bisects the angle MPB.

PROBLEMS ARRANGED ACCORDING TO THE "BOOKS" ON WHICH THEY DEPEND

This arrangement should be of benefit to teacher and self-taught student. When a class has finished a "Book," the following arrangement permits the teacher (or student) to select those problems which require no more knowledge than that acquired from the particular "Book" finished. *By "Book," we refer to the traditional division of Geometry into five Books since the time of Euclid.*

CIRCLES

BOOK 1. BOOK 2 — 2, 3, 7, 8, 12, 14, 20, 23, 24, 25, 26, 27, 29, 37, 40, 42, 44, 45, 47, 49, 51, 56, 57, 58, 59, 61, 63, 64, 66, 67, 68, 69, 70, 71, 75, 76, 77, 78, 82, 83, 85, 86, 87. BOOK 3 — 1, 5, 9, 11, 13, 15, 17, 31, 32, 33, 34, 35, 36, 39, 41, 43, 54, 55, 60, 62, 65, 72, 73, 74, 79, 80, 81, 84, 88, 89, 90. BOOK 4 — 18, 30, 48, 50, 52. BOOK 5 — 4, 6, 10, 19, 21, 22, 28, 38, 46, 53.

CONSTRUCTIONS

BOOK 1 — 1, 4, 5, 7, 12, 15, 22, 23, 24, 25, 26, 29, 38, 45, 51, 54, 60. BOOK 2 — 3, 8, 9, 11, 13, 14, 16, 17, 28, 32, 36, 37, 40, 42, 43, 48, 53, 55, 58, 61, 62. BOOK 3 — 2, 10, 18, 21, 27, 30, 31, 33, 34, 41, 44, 46, 49, 50, 52. BOOK 4 — 19, 20, 35, 39, 47, 57, 59. BOOK 5 — 6, 56.

LOCI

BOOK 1 — 18, 31. BOOK 2 — 1, 4, 5, 7, 9, 11, 12, 14, 15, 16, 17, 19, 20, 21, 26, 27, 28, 30, 32. BOOK 3 — 2, 3, 8, 10, 13, 22, 23, 24, 25. BOOK 4 — 6, 29. BOOK 5.

POLYGONS

BOOK 1 — 2, 4, 7, 9, 12, 13, 16, 19, 23, 24, 32, 33, 34, 37, 43, 45, 49. BOOK 2 — 11, 17, 48. BOOK 3 — 1, 3, 5, 40, 42, 47. BOOK 4 — 6, 8, 10, 14, 18, 20, 21, 22, 25, 26, 27, 28, 30, 31, 35, 36, 39, 41, 44, 46, 50. BOOK 5 — 15, 29, 38.

TRIANGLES

Book 1 — 1, 2, 4, 8, 10, 14, 15, 16, 17, 18, 19, 23, 27, 31, 32, 33, 35, 38, 39, 40, 45, 61, 62, 63, 64, 65, 66. Book 2 — 21, 46, 68. Book 3 — 3, 7, 9, 13, 20, 24, 36, 37, 41, 43, 47, 50, 51, 54, 55, 58, 59, 60, 67, 69, 70, 71, 74, 75, 77, 78, 80. Book 4 — 5, 6, 11, 12, 22, 25, 26, 29, 30, 34, 42, 44, 48, 49, 52, 53, 56, 57, 72, 73, 76, 79.

Part Two

SOLUTIONS OF THE PROBLEMS

INTRODUCTION

In presenting the answers to the problems stated in Part I the authors assume that the student knows the regular book theorems and book constructions. The solutions therefore will not be given in a model form since the statements of the theorems will not be given in full. Nevertheless, the student should supply the statements of the theorems used and he should present his solutions in a good form; he is referred to the examples given in Part I. Sufficient information is given so that the reader will have no difficulty in supplying the complete statements of the reasons.

Some of the problems reduce to problems that have already been solved or are given in other chapters; in these cases a reference is made to the solved problems. The reader should, of course, supply the proof of the reference problem in order to have a complete solution. Since the problems are given, more or less, in order of their difficulty it is suggested that they be studied in order. Problems 11, 12, and 13 of Chapter VIII are referred to extensively and for this reason it may be advantageous to skip over and study these in the early part of the study.

Each figure of this Part is numbered to correspond to the problem to which it refers. Thus the figure numbered "Fig. 1" refers to Problem 1 of the particular section in which it occurs.

ANSWERS TO THE REVIEW OF BOOK THEOREMS

[Chapter III, pp. 18–28]

Figure numbers refer to the figures in Chapter III.

I. Questions Pertaining to Figure 14.

1. $\angle ABC = \angle ACB$.
2. $AB = AC$.
3. $\angle ABC = \angle ACB = \angle BAC = 60°$.
4. $90°$; $1 : 1$.
5. $1 : 1 : 1$.
6. No.
7. $180°$.
8. Yes.
9. Yes.
10. Yes.
11. Yes.
12. Yes.
13. Yes; yes.
14. Yes.
15. Yes.
16. Yes.
17. $\angle ABC > \angle ACB$.
18. $AC > BC$.
19. Yes.
20. Yes.
21. Yes.
22. Yes.
23. Yes.
24. $BF > FC$.
25. $\angle BAF > \angle FAC$.
26. $AC > AB$.
27. $FC > BF$.
28. $BF : FC = AB : AC$.
29. $\frac{1}{2} \overline{AF} \times \overline{BC}$.
30. $\sqrt{s(s-a)(s-b)(s-c)}$.
31. Point of intersection of the bisectors of the angles.
    Point of intersection of the perpendicular bisectors of the sides.
32. At a point two-thirds of the distance from any vertex to the midpoint of the opposite side.

II. Questions Pertaining to Figure 15.

1. $\angle ABC + \angle BAC$. 2. $\angle ECD$. 3. Equal. 4. Yes.
5. The length of the perpendicular from the point to the line.
6. Yes. 7. AK, if extended, is the perpendicular bisector of BC.
8. $PQ \parallel BC$; $PQ = \frac{1}{2} BC$.
9. $AR : RC$; $AR : AC$; $NB : RC$ or $AB : AC$; $AN : AR$.
10. Q is the midpoint of AC. 11. $AR : RQ$; $RQ : QC$.
12. Parallel.
13. (a) $\triangle AFT$ and FTC;
    (b) $\triangle FTC$ and AFC;
    (c) $\triangle AFT$ and AFC;
    (d) $TC : FT = FT : TA$;
    (e) $TC : FC = FC : AC$;
    (f) $AC : AF = AF : AT$;
    (g) $\overline{AF}^2 + \overline{FC}^2 = \overline{AC}^2$.

77

14. Yes.   **15.** The ratio of any two corresponding sides.

16. $\overline{NR}^2 : \overline{BC}^2$ or $\overline{AN}^2 : \overline{AB}^2$ or $\overline{AR}^2 : \overline{AC}^2$.   **17.** $\frac{1}{2}\overline{ZF}(\overline{PQ} + \overline{BC})$.

18. Parallel.   **19.** Parallel.   **20.** Equal; supplementary.

III. Questions Pertaining to Figure 16.

1. Yes.   **2.** Equal; supplementary.   **3.** Yes.   **4.** Equal.

5. BG is the bisector of $\angle ABC$.

6. $(a) = (b) = (c) =$ parallelogram.

7. (a) They bisect each other.   (b) Equal and parallel.
   (c) Equal and parallel.   (d) Equal.
   (e) Supplementary.   (f) Supplementary.

8. Equal.

9. If the triangles are mutually equiangular.
   If two sides of one are proportional to two sides of the other
      and the included angles are equal.
   If the corresponding sides are proportional.

10. $\overline{BC} \times \overline{AF}$.   **11.** $AW : WX$.   **12.** $NO : NR$.

13. $\overline{AX} \times \overline{NR} : \overline{AF} \times \overline{BC}$.   **14.** $\frac{1}{2}\overline{AC} \times \overline{BG}$.   **15.** Parallel.

16. Perpendicular.

IV. Questions Pertaining to Figure 17.

1. $SB : SC = AB : AC$.   **2.** $AZ : AF$.

3. $BC : SB$.   **4.** $\overline{AZ} \times \overline{PQ} : \overline{AF} \times \overline{SB}$.

V. Questions Pertaining to Figure 18.

1. Any diameter.   **2.** Equal.   **3.** Equal; equal.

4. $\overset{\frown}{AC} > \overset{\frown}{CD}$.   **5.** Equal; $\overset{\frown}{AC} > \overset{\frown}{CD}$.   **6.** $AC > CD$.

7. Equal; equal; equal.   **8.** CE is $\perp$ bis. of AD.

9. The center O.

10. Equal; distance of $AD <$ distance of JE.

11. Equal; $AD < JE$.   **12.** $\angle AOC : \angle DOB = AC : DB$.

13. $\overset{\frown}{AC}$.   **14.** $\frac{1}{2}\overset{\frown}{JC}$; $\frac{1}{2}(\overset{\frown}{ED} + \overset{\frown}{DC})$.

15. 90°.   **16.** One.   **17.** $\overline{EP} \times \overline{PC}$.

18. $CP : PD = PD : PE$; $CP : CD = CD : CE$; $PE : ED = ED : CE$.

19. Equal.   **20.** Circumference $= 2\pi\overline{OA}$.   **21.** $(\angle OAC)\dfrac{2\pi\overline{OA}}{360}$.

22. $\pi\overline{OA}^2$.   **23.** $(\angle AOD)\dfrac{\pi\overline{OA}^2}{360}$.   **24.** Yes; yes.

VI. Questions Pertaining to Figure 19.

1. $OE \perp FE$.

2. FE is tangent to the circle.

3. JL passes through O.

4. OW passes through J.

5. Equal; equal.

6. Equal; equal; equal.

7. CE passes through O.

8. $\frac{1}{2}$(arc JDE — arc JAE).

9. $ND : NJ = NJ : NV$.

$\frac{1}{2}$(arc DE — arc BV).

$\frac{1}{2}$ arc EAJ.

$\frac{1}{2}$(arc DEJ — arc VBJ).

VII. Questions Pertaining to Figure 20.

1. $OO' \perp$ bis. of AD.

2. OS passes through T.

3. Circumference of O : circumference of $O' = OA : O'D$.

4. Area of O : area of $O' = \overline{OA}^2 : \overline{O'D}^2$;

Area of O : area of $O' = \overline{CE}^2 : (2\ \overline{O'D})^2$.

5. $CP : PE$.   **6.** $\overline{CP} \times \overline{PA} : \overline{PD} \times \overline{PE}$.   **7.** $\overline{CP} \times \overline{AP}$.

VIII. Questions Pertaining to Figure 21.

1. $180(n - 2)°$ or $540°$.

2. $180\ n° - [180(n - 2)°]$ or $360°$.

3. $\dfrac{180(n - 2)°}{n}$ or $108°$.

4. Yes; yes.

5. $\dfrac{360}{n}$ or $72°$.

6. $\dfrac{1}{2} p \times \overline{OM}$.

IX. Questions Pertaining to Figure 22.

1. Similar; similar; similar.   **2.** Similar.   **3.** Yes.

4. $\overline{AB}^2 : \overline{A'B'}^2$, or $\overline{BC}^2 : \overline{B'C'}^2$, etc.

5. $AB : A'B'$, or $BC : B'C'$, etc.

6. $r : r'$, where r and r' represent the radii, respectively, of the inscribed circles.

$R : R'$, where R and R' represent the radii, respectively, of the circumscribed circles.

SOLUTIONS OF THE PROBLEMS ON CIRCLES

[Chapter IV, pp. 33–41]

1. Let $AO = x$; then $BO = 5 - x$.

Since the products of the segments of chords drawn through one point is a constant, we have

$x(5 - x) = (1)(6)$ or $5x - x^2 = 6$; $x = 2$ or 3.

∴ $AO = 2$ or 3 and $BO = 3$ or 2.

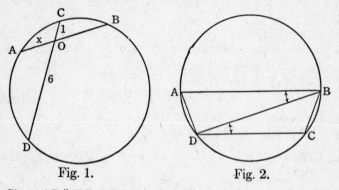

Fig. 1.   Fig. 2.

2. Since $AB \parallel DC$, $\angle BDC = \angle ABD$ and arc $AD = $ arc BC.

∴ $AD = BC$ and the trapezoid is isosceles.

3. $\angle BAD = \frac{1}{2}($arc $CE - $ arc $BD)$.

Arc $CE = \frac{1}{4}(360°) = 90°$ and arc $BD = \frac{1}{12}(360°) = 30°$.

∴ $\angle BAD = \frac{1}{2}(90°) - \frac{1}{2}(30°) = 45° - 15° = 30°$.

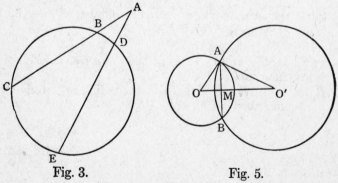

Fig. 3.   Fig. 5.

4. See Example 1, Chapter IV.

5. Since $AO = OB =$ radius of circle O, $OO' \perp$ bis. of AB.

 $\therefore AM = 8$ ft. and $\triangle AOM$ and $AO'M$ are rt. $\triangle$.

 $\therefore \overline{AO}^2 = \overline{AM}^2 + \overline{OM}^2$ or $10^2 = 8^2 + \overline{OM}^2$ and $OM = 6$.

 $\overline{AO'}^2 = \overline{AM}^2 + \overline{O'M}^2$ or $17^2 = 8^2 + \overline{O'M}^2$ and $O'M = 15$.

 $\therefore OO' = OM + O'M = 6 + 15 = 21$ ft.

6. Since $\angle AOB = 72°$, $\overparen{AB} = 72° = \frac{72}{360}$ (circumference)
   $= \frac{1}{5}(2\pi r)$.

 $\therefore 44 = \frac{2}{5}\pi r$ and $r = \frac{220}{2\pi} = 35.014$ in.

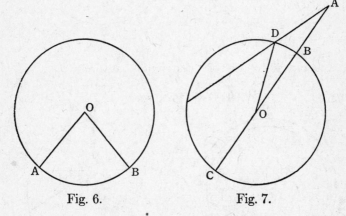

Fig. 6.   Fig. 7.

7. In Fig. 7 it is required to prove that $AB < AD$.

 Draw DO and since the shortest distance between 2 pts. is a st. line, $AB + BO < AD + DO$.

 But since $BO = DO =$ radii of circle, this inequality reduces to $AB < AD$.

8. Given the circle O and the exterior point A. Draw the secant AC through O and any other secant AE. It is required to prove $AC > AE$.

 Draw EO; then $AO + EO > AE$.

 Since $EO = OC$, then $AO + OC > AE$.

 Since $AO + OC = AC$, we have $AC > AE$.

9. Given $AC = 24$ and $AB = 6$. Let AD be tangent from A.

 Since the tangent is a mean proportional between AC and AB,

 $\overline{AD}^2 = (\overline{AC})(\overline{AB}) = (24)(6) = 144$.

 $\therefore AD = 12$.

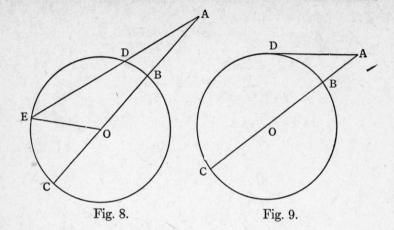

Fig. 8.　　　　　　　　　Fig. 9.

10. Area of walk = area of outer circle − area of inner circle
$$= \pi\,82^2 - \pi\,75^2 = \pi(82^2 - 75^2)$$
$$= 1099\,\pi = 3452.6 \text{ sq. ft.}$$

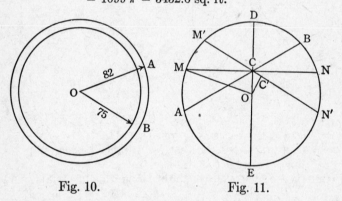

Fig. 10.　　　　　　　　　Fig. 11.

11. Given the circle O with $r = 13$ in. The point C is 5 in. from O.
Let AB be any chord through C and DE, the diameter through C.

Since $OD = 13$ and $OC = 5$, then $DC = 8$ and $CE = 18$.
The product of the segments is a constant.
$\therefore \overline{AC} \times \overline{CB} = \overline{DC} \times \overline{CE} = 8 \times 18 = 144.$
Draw $MN \perp OC$; then $\triangle MCO$ is a rt. $\triangle$.
$\therefore \overline{MO}^2 = \overline{MC}^2 + \overline{OC}^2$ or $169 = 25 + \overline{MC}^2$.
$\therefore MC = 12$ and $MN = 24$.

To complete the problem it remains to prove that *MN* is the
shortest chord.

Draw any other chord *M'N'* and *OC'* ⊥ *M'N'*.

Since *OC'* ⊥ *M'N'*, *OC* > *OC'*.

Since the chord at the greater distance from the center is the
smaller chord, *MN* < *M'N'*.

12. *Given:* Circle *O*; tangent *CB*; chord *AB*; and *M*, midpoint
of *AB*.

From *M* draw *MN* ⊥ *BC* and *MP* ⊥ *AB*.

To Prove: MN = MP.

⦤*MNB* and *MBP* are rt. ⦤.	Definition.
∠*MBP* = $\frac{1}{2}$ arc *MA*.	Theorem.
∠*MBN* = $\frac{1}{2}$ arc *MB*.	Theorem.
Arc *MA* = arc *MB*.	*M* is midpoint of arc *AB*.
∠*MBP* = ∠*MBN*.	From above steps.
MB = *MB*.	Identity.
∴ △*MNB* ≅ △*MBP*.	Hyp. and ∠ = hyp. and ∠.
∴ *MN* = *MP*.	Corr. parts of ≅ ⦤.

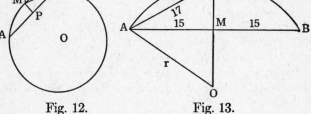

Fig. 12.   Fig. 13.

13. Construct Fig. 13 to represent the given.

OC ⊥ bis. of *AB*.

∴ $17^2 = 15^2 + \overline{CM}^2$ and *CM* = 8.

OM = *r* − 8.

∴ $r^2 = 225 + (r-8)^2$ or *r* = 18 ft. $\frac{3}{4}$ in.

14. In Fig. 14, major arc *AB* = 360° − 120° = 240°.

Since *C* is midpoint of major arc, arc *BC* = arc *AC* = 120°.

∴ minor arc *AB* = minor arc *CA* and chord *AB* = chord *AC*.

∴ *A* is equidistant from *B* and *C*; the same is true for *O*.

∴ *AOM* ⊥ bis. of *BC* since 2 pts. equally distant from ends
of a line determine the ⊥ bis. of the line.

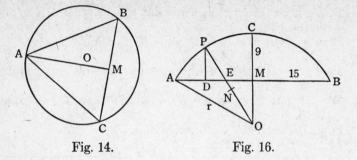

Fig. 14.   Fig. 16.

15. See Example 2, Chapter IV.
16. Let AB be the horizontal chord and C, the highest point above AB.

    We shall first prove that C is the midpoint of arc AB.

    Take any point P in arc AB and draw $PD \perp AB$.

    Let C be the midpoint of arc AB, then $CM \perp AB$ and $OM \perp AB$.

    Therefore OM is shorter than any other line from O to AB.

    Draw OP intersecting AB at E. $OE > OM$.

    On OE measure off $ON = OM$.

$PE < PN$	since	$OE > OM$.
$PE < OP - ON$	since	$PN = OP - ON$.
$PD < OP - ON$	since	$PD < PE$.
$PD < r - ON$	since	$OP = r$.
$PD < r - OM$	since	$ON = OM$.
$PD < CM$	since	$CM = r - OM$.

    Now since C is the midpoint of arc AB, $OC \perp$ bis. of AB.

    $\therefore \triangle AMO$ is a rt. $\triangle$.

    $\therefore r^2 = 15^2 + (r - 9)^2$ or $r = 17$.

17. Let $PA = x$. Since the tangent is a mean proportional between the secant and the exterior segment of the secant, we have $x : 6 = 6 : (x - 8)$ or $x = 4 + 2\sqrt{13}$.

18. $AP = AB - BP = 34 - 9 = 25$.

    Since $\angle ACB$ is inscribed in a semicircle, it is a right angle.

    The perpendicular from the vertex of a right angle is a mean proportional between the segments of the hypotenuse.

    $\therefore \overline{CP}^2 = \overline{AP} \times \overline{PB} = 25 \times 9 = 225$ and $CP = 15$.

    Area of $\triangle ABC = \frac{1}{2}(34)(15)$.

    Since $PD = CP$, area of $\triangle ABD$ = area of $\triangle ABC$.

    $\therefore$ area of $ACBD = 2$ area $\triangle ABC = (34)(15) = 510$ sq. in.

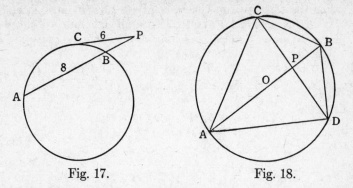

Fig. 17.   Fig. 18.

19. Since $CD = 16 = OC = OD$, $\triangle OCD$ is equilateral and $\angle COD = 60°$.

Then area of sector $OCMD = \frac{60}{360}\pi r^2 = \frac{1}{6}\pi(16)^2$.

Area of $\triangle COD = \frac{8^2}{4}\sqrt{3} = \frac{16^2}{4}\sqrt{3}$. [See Prob. 12, Chap. VIII.]

Area of segment $MCD = \frac{1}{6}\pi(16)^2 - \frac{1}{4}\sqrt{3}(16)^2$

$$= (16)^2\left(\frac{\pi}{6} - \frac{\sqrt{3}}{4}\right)$$

$$= \frac{64}{3}(2\pi - 3\sqrt{3}) = 23.1936 \text{ sq. in.}$$

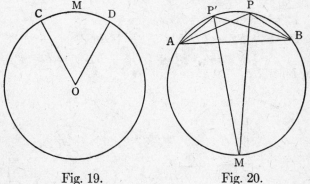

Fig. 19.   Fig. 20.

20. Take two positions for P, say P and P'. $\measuredangle AP'B$ and APB are both measured by $\frac{1}{2}$ major arc AB. The bisector of $\angle APB$ must intersect the major arc AB at its midpoint M since the two equal angles into which the bisector divides $\angle APB$ must be measured by equal arcs.

For the same reason the bisector of $\angle AP'B$ must intersect the major arc AB at M. Hence all bisectors will meet at one point. Similar reasoning applies when P lies on the major arc AB.

21. $\triangle AOC$ is a 90°, 60°, 30° $\triangle$. [See Prob. 14, Chap. VIII.]

$\therefore AC = 5\sqrt{3}$. [See Prob. 11, Chap. VIII.]

$\therefore AB = 10\sqrt{3}$.

$\angle AOB = 120°$ since $\angle AOC = \angle COB = 60°$.

$\therefore AB = \frac{120}{360}(2\pi r) = \frac{2}{3}\pi(10) = 20.944$.

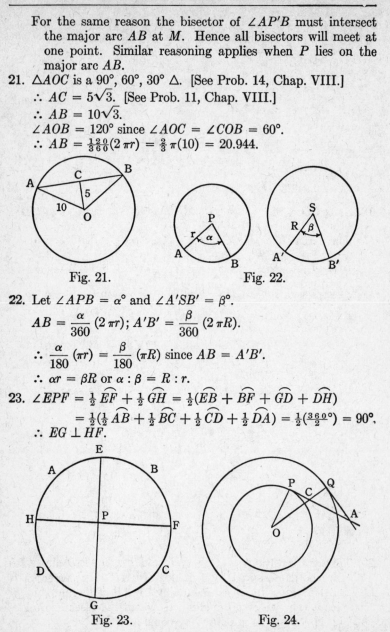

Fig. 21.   Fig. 22.

22. Let $\angle APB = \alpha°$ and $\angle A'SB' = \beta°$.

$$AB = \frac{\alpha}{360}(2\pi r); \; A'B' = \frac{\beta}{360}(2\pi R).$$

$$\therefore \frac{\alpha}{180}(\pi r) = \frac{\beta}{180}(\pi R) \text{ since } AB = A'B'.$$

$$\therefore \alpha r = \beta R \text{ or } \alpha : \beta = R : r.$$

23. $\angle EPF = \frac{1}{2}\overset{\frown}{EF} + \frac{1}{2}\overset{\frown}{GH} = \frac{1}{2}(\overset{\frown}{EB} + \overset{\frown}{BF} + \overset{\frown}{GD} + \overset{\frown}{DH})$

$= \frac{1}{2}(\frac{1}{2}\overset{\frown}{AB} + \frac{1}{2}\overset{\frown}{BC} + \frac{1}{2}\overset{\frown}{CD} + \frac{1}{2}\overset{\frown}{DA}) = \frac{1}{2}(\frac{360°}{2}) = 90°$,

$\therefore EG \perp HF$.

Fig. 23.   Fig. 24.

24. Let the two tangents intersect at A; it is then required to prove that $\angle PAQ = \angle POQ$. Let C be intersection of OQ and AP.

Since $OQ \perp AQ$, $\angle PAQ$ is the complement of $\angle ACQ$.

Since $\angle ACQ = \angle OCP$, $\angle PAQ$ is the complement of $\angle OCP$.

Since $OP \perp AP$, $\angle POQ$ is the complement of $\angle OCP$.

$\therefore \angle PAQ = \angle POQ$.

25. Given $OP = OQ = OR$. To prove that O is the center of the circle.

Since $OP = OQ$, the $\perp$ bis. of PQ passes through O.

Since $OR = OQ$, the $\perp$ bis. of QR passes through O.

Since the center of a circle lies on the $\perp$ bis. of a chord, it must lie on the intersection of the $\perp$ bis. of PQ and QR which is O.

$\therefore O$ is the center of the circle.

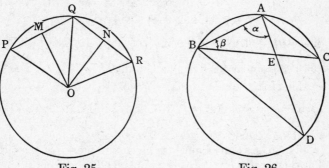

Fig. 25. Fig. 26.

26. Since $AC = AB$, arc $AC = $ arc AB.

$\therefore \angle \beta = \angle BDA$ since they are measured by equal arcs.

$\angle \alpha = \angle \alpha$.

$\therefore$ 2 $\angle$ of $\triangle ABE = $ 2 $\angle$ of $\triangle ABD$ and consequently the third angles are equal.

27. $\angle ADC = 50° = \frac{1}{2}(\text{arc } ABC - \text{arc } AC)$
$= \frac{1}{2}[\text{arc } ABC - (360° - \text{arc } ABC)]$
$= \text{arc } ABC - 180°$.

$\therefore$ arc $ABC = 230°$ and arc $AC = 130°$.

Arc $ABC = \frac{230}{360}(2\pi r) = \frac{23}{18}(10\pi) = 40.1427$ in.

Arc $AC = \frac{130}{360}(2\pi r) = \frac{13}{18}(10\pi) = 22.6893$ in.

28. See Example 3, Chapter IV.

29. Given the equilateral $\triangle ABC$ inscribed in circle O with radius R. Draw $OM \perp AB$ and $ON \perp BC$.

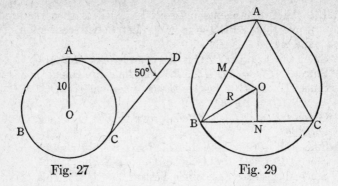

Fig. 27   Fig. 29

Since equal chords are equidistant from the center, $OM = ON$.
Further, since $OB = OB$, $\triangle OBM \cong \triangle OBN$.

$\therefore \angle MBO = \angle NBO$ and since $\angle ABC = 60°$, $\angle OBN = 30°$.

$\therefore \triangle OBN$ is a 90°, 60°, 30° triangle.

Since $OB = R$, $NB = \dfrac{R}{2}\sqrt{3}$. [See Prob. 11, Chap. VIII.]

Since $\perp$ from center bisects a chord, $BC = 2\,NB = R\sqrt{3}$.

$\therefore$ side of the equilateral $\triangle = R\sqrt{3}$.

Area of equilateral $\triangle = \dfrac{s^2}{4}\sqrt{3}$. [See Prob. 12, Chap. VIII.]

$\therefore$ area of $\triangle ABC = \frac{1}{4}(R\sqrt{3})^2\sqrt{3} = \frac{3}{4}R^2\sqrt{3}$.

30. In Fig. 30, B is any point on the circumference of the circle.
The diameter $AP \perp CD$ since a diameter which bisects an arc
is also the $\perp$ bis. of the chord.

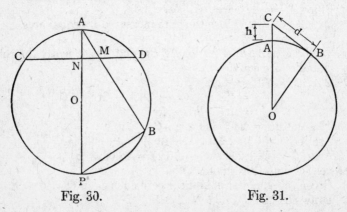

Fig. 30.   Fig. 31.

$\angle ABP$ is a rt. $\angle$ since it is inscribed in a semicircle.

$\angle PAB$ is common to $\triangle AMN$ and APB.

$\therefore \triangle AMN \sim \triangle APB$.

$\therefore AM : AP = AN : AB$ or $\overline{AM} \times \overline{AB} = \overline{AP} \times \overline{AN}$.

Since B is any point on the circumference, $\overline{AM} \times \overline{AB}$ will always be equal to $\overline{AP} \times \overline{AN}$, a constant.

31. $OA = OB = 3960$ miles; 1 mile = 5280 ft.

$\triangle OCB$ is a rt. $\triangle$ since BC is tangent to O.

$$d^2 = (\overline{OA} + h)^2 - \overline{OB}^2 = \left(3960 + \frac{h}{5280}\right)^2 - 3960^2$$

$$= \frac{3}{2}h + \left(\frac{h}{5280}\right)^2.$$

But h is very small in comparison with 5280; therefore the second term may be disregarded.

$\therefore d = \sqrt{\frac{3}{2}h}$ approximately.

32. Since AOC is a diameter, arc $ABC = 180°$, and arc $AB = 120°$.

$\therefore \angle BOM = 60°$. $BM \perp AC$.

$\therefore \triangle BOM$ is a 90°, 60°, 30° triangle.

Since $OB = 8$, $BM = 4\sqrt{3}$. [See Prob. 11, Chap. VIII.]

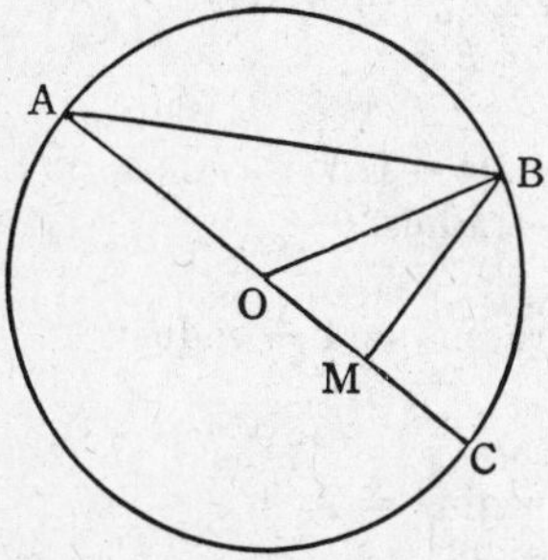

Fig. 32. 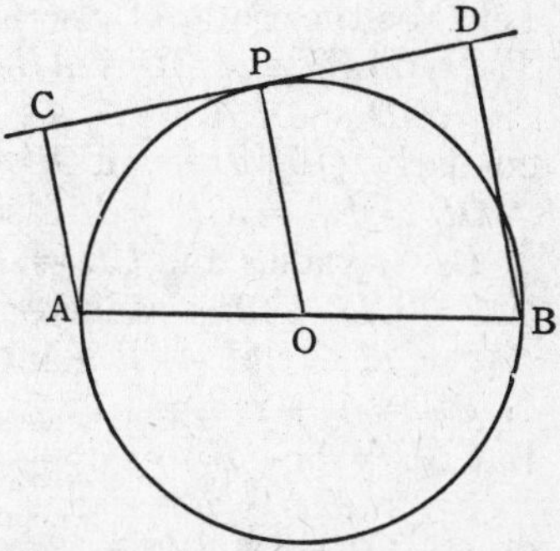   Fig. 33.

33. *Given:* AB, diameter of circle O; CD, tangent to circle at P; $AC \perp CD$; and $BD \perp CD$.

To Prove: $AC + BD = AB = 2\,OP$.

$AC \parallel BD$, since both are $\perp CD$.

$OP \perp CD$ since a radius $\perp$ the tangent to circle.

$\therefore OP \parallel AC \parallel BD$.

$CP = PD$ since $AO = OB$ and if parallels cut off equal seg-

ments on one transversal they cut off equal segments on any
other transversal.

∴ OP is a median of trapezoid $ABDC$.

∴ $OP = \frac{1}{2}(AC + BD)$ or $AC + BD = 2\,OP =$ diameter.

34. In Fig. 34, $AO \perp AB$ and $O'B \perp AB$ and ∴ $OA \parallel O'B$.

Draw $ON \perp O'B$; then $ON \parallel AB$ and $ABNO$ is a $\square$.

∴ $ON = AB$, $OA = BN = 6$, $O'B = 13.5$.

∴ $O'N = 13.5 - 6 = 7.5$. $OM + MO' = 6 + 13.5 = 19.5$.

$\triangle ONO'$ is a rt. $\triangle$ and $(19.5)^2 = \overline{ON}^2 + (7.5)^2$ or $ON = 18$.

Since $ON = AB$, $AB = 18$ in.

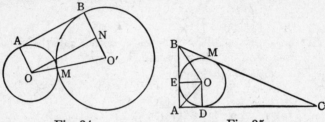

Fig. 34.   Fig. 35.

35. Since $(13)^2 = 5^2 + (12)^2$, $\triangle ABC$ is a rt. $\triangle$.

Let O be the center of inscribed circle.

The radii OE and $OD \perp AB$ and AC, respectively.

Since OD and EA are $\perp AC$, $OD \parallel EA$.

Similarly, $OE \parallel DA$ and $ODAE$ is a $\square$.

∴ $OD = EA = OE = DA$, since $OD = OE =$ radii of circle O.

∴ $DA =$ radius and $CD = 12 -$ radius.

$CM = CD = 12 -$ radius.

$BM = 13 - CM = 13 - 12 +$ radius $= 1 +$ radius.

∴ $BE = 1 +$ radius.

But $BE = 5 - EA = 5 -$ radius.

∴ $1 +$ radius $= 5 -$ radius, or radius $= 2$.

36. *Given*: $AB = 36$, $BC = 18$, $AC = 28$.

Let $AD = x$; then $BD = 36 - x$.

$BE = BD = 36 - x$.

$CE = 18 - BE = 18 - 36 + x = x - 18$.

$CF = CE = x - 18$.

$AF = 28 - CF = 28 - x + 18 = 46 - x$.

$AD = AF = 46 - x = x$. ∴ $x = 23 = AD = AF$.

∴ $BE = 13 = BD$; $CE = CF = 5$.

37. Since there are 6 equal chords, there are 6 equal arcs and each
arc contains 60°; therefore $\angle AOB = 60°$.

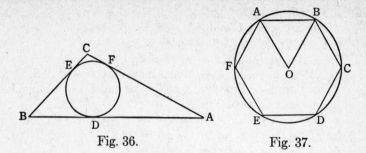

Fig. 36.   Fig. 37.

$\therefore\ \angle OAB + \angle OBA = 180° - 60° = 120°.$

Since $OA = OB$, $\angle OAB = \angle OBA = 60°$.

$\therefore\ \triangle OAB$ is equiangular and equilateral.

Area of sector $OAB = \frac{60}{360}(\pi r^2) = \frac{1}{6}\pi r^2.$

Area of $\triangle OAB = \frac{1}{4}\sqrt{3}\,r^2.$ [See Prob. 12, Chap. VIII.]

$\therefore$ area of segment $AB = \frac{1}{6}\pi r^2 - \frac{1}{4}r^2\sqrt{3} = \dfrac{r^2}{12}(2\pi - 3\sqrt{3}).$

38. In Fig. 38, $OD = EA = OE = DA = r.$ [See Prob. 36, this section.]

$DC = AC - r$ and $CM = CD = AC - r.$

$BE = BA - EA = BA - r$ and $BM = BE = BA - r.$

$\therefore\ BM + CM = BA - r + AC - r = BA + AC - 2r = BC.$

$\therefore\ BA + AC - BC = $ diameter.

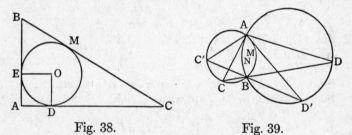

Fig. 38.   Fig. 39.

39. Fig. 39 shows two positions of the line CD.

$\angle ACD = \frac{1}{2}$ arc AMB for all positions of C and D.

$\angle ADC = \frac{1}{2}$ arc ANB for all positions of C and D.

$\therefore$ in $\triangle ACD$ and $AC'D'$: $\angle ACD = \angle AC'D'$ and $\angle ADC = \angle AD'C'.$

$\therefore\ \angle C'AD' = \angle CAD = $ a constant for all positions of C and D.

40. $AO = OC$ and $AB = BC$.

$\therefore BO \perp$ bis. of AC and $AM = 6$.

In rt. $\triangle AMB$: $100 = 36 + \overline{BM}^2$ or $BM = 8$.

$OA \perp AB$, since radius $\perp$ tangent at pt. of tangency.

$\therefore AM$ is the mean proportional between OM and MB, since the $\perp$ from vertex of rt. $\angle$ to hyp. is mean proportional between segments of hyp.

$\therefore OM : AM = AM : MB$ or $OM : 6 = 6 : 8$ or $OM = \frac{36}{8}$.

In rt. $\triangle AMO$: $\overline{AO}^2 = 36 + (\frac{36}{8})^2 = 36[1 + \frac{36}{64}] = \frac{36}{64}(100)$.

$AO = \frac{6}{8}(10) = 7.5$ inches.

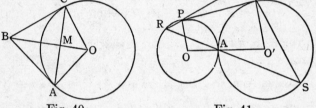

Fig. 40.   Fig. 41.

41. $OP \perp PQ$ and $O'Q \perp PQ$. $\therefore \angle OPQ + \angle O'QP = 180°$.

$\therefore \angle POO' + \angle QO'O = 180°$ since sum of $\angle$ of quad. $= 360°$.

$\therefore PA + QA = 180°$ since they measure $\angle POO'$ and $QO'O$.

$\angle PRA = \frac{1}{2}\widehat{PA}$ and $\angle ASQ = \frac{1}{2}\widehat{QA}$.

$\therefore \angle PRA + \angle ASQ = \frac{1}{2}(\widehat{PA} + \widehat{AQ}) = 90°$.

$\therefore$ in $\triangle XRS$; $\angle RXS = 90°$ since sum of $\angle = 180°$.

42. Since $CA \perp AB$ and $OB \perp AB$, $OB \parallel AC$.

Similarly, $OC \parallel AB$.

$\therefore ACOB$ is a $\square$ and $OB = AC$.

Since $OB = OC$, we have $OB = OC = AC = AB$.

Since opposite $\angle$ of $\square$ are equal, $\angle BOC = \angle BAC$.

$\therefore ACOB$ is a square.

E is 4 in. from AC and $4\frac{1}{2}$ in. from AB.

Draw $EG \perp AC$ and extend it to M; draw $EF \perp AB$.

Since $EG \perp AC$, $GM \perp BO$ and $EM = GM - 4$.

Since $\angle$s between $\parallel$s are equal, $GM = AB = OC = r$.

$\therefore EM = r - 4$ and $EF = BM = 4\frac{1}{2}$.

$\therefore MO = r - 4\frac{1}{2}$.

In rt. $\triangle OEM$: $\overline{OE}^2 = (r - 4)^2 + (r - 4\frac{1}{2})^2 = r^2$.

$$4 r^2 - 68 r + 145 = 0.$$

$$r = \frac{5}{2} \text{ and } \frac{29}{2}.$$

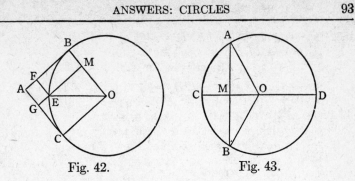

Fig. 42.   Fig. 43.

43. In Fig. 43, $MD = 3\,CM$.

∴ $CM + 3\,CM = 4\,CM = $ diameter $= CD$.

∴ $CM = \frac{1}{4}\,CD = \frac{1}{2}\,r$.

In rt. $\triangle OMA$: $OA = r$ and $OM = \dfrac{r}{2}$.

∴ $\triangle OMA$ is a 90°, 60°, 30° △. [See Prob. 14, Chap. VIII.]

∴ $\angle AOM = 60°$ and arc $AC = 60°$.

∴ AB divides circumference into arcs of 120° and 240° or in the ratio of $1 : 2$.

44. Draw PA tangent to circle at A.

Then $\angle BAP = \frac{1}{2}$ arc AB and $\angle PAC = \frac{1}{2}$ arc AC.

∴ $\angle BAP + \angle PAC = \frac{1}{2}$(arc AB + arc AC).

Since $AB \perp AC$, $\angle BAC = 90° = \angle BAP + \angle PAC$.

∴ $\frac{1}{2}(\widehat{AB} + \widehat{AC}) = 90°$ or $\widehat{AB} + \widehat{AC} = 180°$.

$\angle BOA + \angle AO'C = \widehat{AB} + \widehat{AC} = 180°$.

If two lines are cut by a transversal such that the two interior ∡ = 180°, the lines are ∥. ∴ $BO \parallel O'C$.

Since $BO = O'C$, $BOO'C$ is a ▱.

∴ $BC \parallel OO'$ and $BC = OO'$.

Since $OO' = 2\,r = $ diameter, $BC = $ diameter of circle.

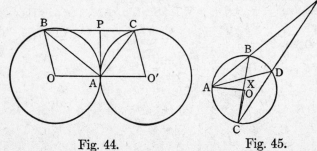

Fig. 44.   Fig. 45.

45. Since arc $AC = 85°$, $\angle BPD = \frac{1}{2}(85° - \text{arc } BD)$.

$\angle BXD = 4 \angle BPD = \frac{1}{2}(85° + \text{arc } BD)$.

Adding, we get $5 \angle BPD = 85°$ or $\angle BPD = 17°$.

Since $\angle BPD = \frac{1}{2}(85° - \overarc{BD}) = 17$, arc $BD = 51°$.

Arc $BD = \frac{51}{360}(2\pi r) = \frac{51}{360}(60) = \frac{51}{6} = 8.5$ in.

46. Since $AD \parallel BC$, $\angle DAB + \angle ABC = 180°$.

Since the line from center of circle to point where tangents meet bisects the angle formed by the tangents, we have

$\angle OAB = \frac{1}{2} \angle DAB$ and $\angle ABO = \frac{1}{2} \angle ABC$.

$\therefore \angle OAB + \angle ABO = 90°$. $\therefore \angle AOB = 90°$.

$\therefore$ a circle having AB as its diameter must pass through O.
[See Prob. 1, Chap. VI.]

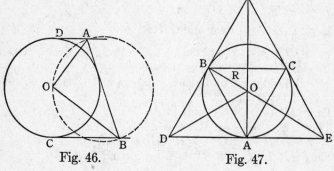

Fig. 46. Fig. 47.

47. Let R be the radius of the circle.

Since the $\triangle$ are regular polygons they are equilateral.

Area of $\triangle ABC = \frac{3}{4} R^2\sqrt{3}$. [See Prob. 29, this section.]

Since the center of the inscribed circle lies on the bisector of the angles, OE bisects $\angle DEF$.

$\therefore \angle AEO = 30°$.

$OA \perp AE$. $\therefore \triangle AEO$ is a 90°, 60°, 30° $\triangle$.

Since $OA = R$, $AE = R\sqrt{3}$. [See Prob. 11, Chap. VIII.]

Similarly, it may be proved that $DA = R\sqrt{3}$.

$\therefore DE = 2R\sqrt{3}$.

Area of $\triangle DEF = \dfrac{\overline{DE}^2}{4}\sqrt{3} = \dfrac{12 R^2}{4}\sqrt{3} = 3 R^2\sqrt{3}$. [See Prob. 12, Chap. VIII.]

$\therefore 3 R^2\sqrt{3} - \frac{3}{4} R^2\sqrt{3} = 25$ or $3 R^2\sqrt{3}(4 - 1) = 100$.

$R^2 = \dfrac{100}{9}\left(\dfrac{\sqrt{3}}{3}\right)$. $R = \dfrac{10}{3}\sqrt{\dfrac{\sqrt{3}}{3}} = 2.533$.

48. $\angle DFG = \frac{1}{2}(\text{arc } AB + \text{arc } CED)$ and $\angle DEG = \frac{1}{2} \text{arc } ABD$.

$\therefore \ \angle DFG + \angle DEG = \frac{1}{2}(\text{arc } AB + \text{arc } CED + \text{arc } DBA)$

$\qquad\qquad\qquad\quad = \frac{1}{2}(\overset{\frown}{AB} + \overset{\frown}{CE} + \overset{\frown}{ED} + \overset{\frown}{DB} + \overset{\frown}{BA})$

[Since $\overset{\frown}{AB} = \overset{\frown}{AC}$]: $= \frac{1}{2}(\overset{\frown}{AC} + \overset{\frown}{CE} + \overset{\frown}{ED} + \overset{\frown}{DB} + \overset{\frown}{BA})$

$\qquad\qquad\qquad\quad = \frac{1}{2}(360°) = 180°$.

$\therefore$ the opposite angles of the quadrilateral are supplementary
and a circle can be drawn through $DEFG$. [See Prob. **11**,
Chap. VII.]

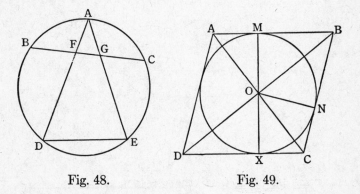

Fig. 48.   Fig. 49.

49. Since $ABCD$ is a rhombus, $AB \parallel CD$ and $AB = BC = CD = AD$.

$\therefore \ \angle ABD = \angle BDC = \angle DBC$.

$\therefore \ BD$ is the bisector of $\angle ABC$.

$OM = ON$ since they are radii of circle O.

$\therefore \ BD$ passes through O since all points on the bisector are
equally distant from the sides.

Similarly, AC can be proved to pass through O.

Since the diagonals of a rhombus bisect each other at right
angles, $OB = 20$ and $CO \perp BO$.

$\therefore$ in rt. $\triangle BOC$: $25^2 = 20^2 + \overline{CO}^2$ or $CO = 15$ and $AC = 30$.

$\therefore$ area of rhombus $ABCD = \frac{1}{2}(40)(30) = 600$.

Extend MO to intersect CD at X.

Since $MO \perp AB$ and $AB \parallel CD$, then $MO \perp DC$ and X must
be the point of tangency of CD to circle O.

$\therefore \ MOX = 2\,r$.

Area of rhombus $ABCD = \overline{DC} \times \overline{MOX} = 25\,MOX = 600$.

$\therefore \ MOX = 24$ and $MO = 12 = r$.

$\therefore$ area of circle $O = \pi r^2 = 144\,\pi = 452.39$.

50. Let P be the point of intersection of the tangents AB and CD.
Connect O with P and O' with P.
Since AP and PC are tangent to circle O, the line OP bisects
the angle included between them.
∴ $\angle OPC = \frac{1}{2}\angle APC$.
Similarly, $\angle DPO' = \frac{1}{2}\angle DPB$.
Then, since $\angle APC = \angle DPB$, $\angle OPC = \angle DPO'$.
$\angle OPC + \angle OPA + \angle APD = 180°$ since CD is a st. line.
∴ $\angle DPO' + \angle OPA + \angle APD = 180°$ and OPO' form a st.
line.

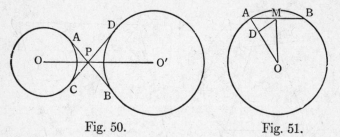

Fig. 50.   Fig. 51.

51. Since OM bisects AB and $AB = r$, $AM = \frac{1}{2}r$.
In rt. $\triangle AMO$: $MD \perp AO$, the hypotenuse.
Therefore either side is the mean proportional between the
hypotenuse and the segment of the hypotenuse adjacent to
it.
∴ $AO : AM = AM : AD$ or $r : \frac{1}{2}r = \frac{1}{2}r : AD$ or $AD = \frac{1}{4}r$
In rt. $\triangle AMO$: the $\perp MD$ is the mean proportional between
the segments of the hypotenuse.
∴ $AD : MD = MD : DO$ or $\frac{1}{4}r : MD = MD : (r - \frac{1}{4}r)$.
∴ $\overline{MD}^2 = \frac{r}{4}\left(\frac{r}{4}\right)$ (3) and $MD = \frac{1}{4}r\sqrt{3}$.

Area of $\triangle AMD = \frac{1}{2}(\overline{AD})(\overline{MD}) = \frac{1}{2}\left(\frac{r}{4}\right)\left(\frac{r}{4}\sqrt{3}\right) = \frac{r^2}{32}\sqrt{3}$.

52. Let AX be $\perp BC$ produced; then $AX = \frac{1}{2}BC = \frac{1}{2}AB$.
∴ in rt. $\triangle AXB$: $AX = \frac{1}{2}$ hypotenuse and $\angle ABX = 30°$.
[See Prob. 14, Chap. VIII.]
∴ $\angle ABC = 150°$ and $\angle ABO = 75°$.
Since $OA = OB$, $\angle OAB = \angle ABO = 75°$.
In $\triangle AOB$ we then have $\angle AOB = 30°$ and $\angle AOC = 60°$.
Since $OA = OC$, $\angle OAC = \angle OCA = 60°$.
∴ $AO = OC = AC = 5$.

Since $\angle AOB = 30°$, arc $AB = 30°$.

$\therefore$ arc $AB = \frac{30}{360}(2\pi r) = \frac{5}{6}\pi =$ arc BC since $AB = BC$.

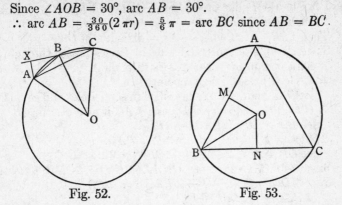

Fig. 52.   Fig. 53.

53. Given the equilateral $\triangle ABC$ and the circumscribed circle O.
Draw $OM \perp AB$ and $ON \perp BC$.
Since equal chords are equally distant from center, $OM = ON$.
$\therefore$ since $OB = OB$, rt. $\triangle OBM \cong$ rt. $\triangle OBN$.
$\therefore \angle OBM = \angle OBN$ and $\therefore \angle OBN = 30°$.
$\therefore \triangle OBN$ is a 90°, 60°, 30° $\triangle$.

Then, since $OB = r$, $BN = \frac{r}{2}\sqrt{3}$. [See Prob. 11, Chap. VIII.]

But $BC = 2 BN$; $\therefore BC = r\sqrt{3}$.

54. Given the equilateral $\triangle ABC$ and the inscribed circle O.
Since center of O lies on bis. of the $\angle$, $\angle MBO = 30°$.
Since $MO \perp AB$, $\triangle MOB$ is a 90°, 60°, 30° $\triangle$.
Since $MO = r$, $MB = r\sqrt{3}$. [See Prob. 11, Chap. VIII.]
In $\triangle MOA$: $\angle MAO = 30°$ and since $\angle OMA = 90°$, $\angle MOA = 60°$,
$\triangle AMO \cong \triangle OMB$.

$\therefore AM = MB = r\sqrt{3}$ and $AB = 2r\sqrt{3}$.

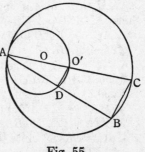

Fig. 54.   Fig. 55.

55. Let r be the radius of smaller circle O and R be the radius of the larger circle O'.

Then $r : R = 1 : 2$ or $R = 2r =$ diameter of O.

Since the line of centers of tangent circles passes through the point of tangency, OO' passes through A.

$\therefore$ circle O passes through point O'.

$\therefore \angle ADO'$ and ABC are inscribed in semicircles and equal 90°.

$\therefore O'D \parallel BC$ and since $O'D$ bisects AC it also bisects AB.

56. Since $PA = OP$, $\angle PAO = \angle POA$.

$\angle OPN = \angle POA + \angle PAO = 2 \angle PAO$.

Since $OP = ON$, $\angle ONP = \angle OPN = 2 \angle PAO$.

Since $\angle MON$ is ext. $\angle$ of $\triangle ONA$, $\angle MON = \angle ONP + \angle PAO$.

$\therefore \angle MON = 2 \angle PAO + \angle PAO = 3 \angle PAO$.

$\therefore \angle PAO = \frac{1}{3} \angle MON$.

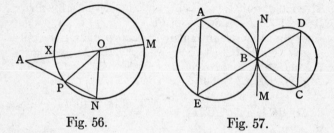

Fig. 56.   Fig. 57.

57. Draw NBM tangent to both circles.

$\angle EBM = \frac{1}{2}$ arc EB and $\angle EAB = \frac{1}{2}$ arc EB.

$\therefore \angle EAB = \angle EBM$.

Since $\angle EBM = \angle NBD$, $\therefore \angle EAB = \angle NBD$.

$\angle NBD = \frac{1}{2}$ arc $BD = \angle BCD$. $\therefore \angle EAB = \angle BCD$.

$\therefore AE \parallel CD$.

58. Draw the tangent at A.

$\angle NAM = \frac{1}{2}$ arc AM and $\angle NAB = \frac{1}{2}$ arc AB.

Since $\angle NAM = \angle NAB$, arc $AM =$ arc AB.

$\therefore \angle ACB = \angle ADM$ since they are measured by equal arcs AM and AB.

$\angle AMD = \angle ADC$ since they are both measured by $\frac{1}{2}$ arc AD.

$\therefore$ Since $2 \angle$ in $\triangle AMD = 2 \angle$ in $\triangle ADC$, the third $\angle$ must be equal.

$\therefore \angle MAD = \angle DAC$ and AD bisects $\angle BAC$.

59. Since $MN \parallel BD$, $\angle ABD = \angle MAC$ (alt. int. $\angle$ of $\parallel$s).

$\angle MAC = \angle AEC$ since they are both measured by $\frac{1}{2}$ arc AC.

$\therefore \angle ABD = \angle AEC$.

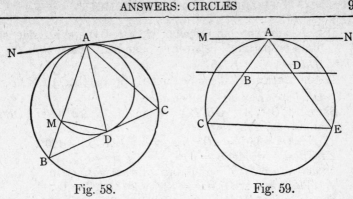

Fig. 58.   Fig. 59.

Similarly, $\angle ADB = \angle NAE = \angle ACE$.

$\therefore \triangle ABD \sim \triangle ACE$.

$\therefore AB : AE = AD : AC$ or $\overline{AB} \times \overline{AC} = \overline{AE} \times \overline{AD}$.

For all positions of chord ADE, $\overline{AE} \times \overline{AD} = \overline{AC} \times \overline{AB}$.

$\therefore$ the product of the chord and segment is a constant.

60. Since $AD \perp AB$ (given) and $BO \perp AB$ (radius $\perp$ tangent),

$AD \parallel OB$.

Since $AB = AC$ and $OB = OC$, $AO \perp$ bis. of BC.

Since $BD \perp BC$ (given), $BD \parallel AO$.

$\therefore DAOB$ is a $\square$; $\therefore DA = BO = r$.

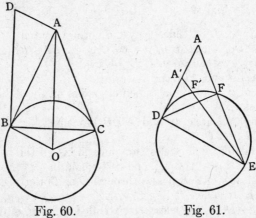

Fig. 60.   Fig. 61.

61. Fig. 61 shows two positions of the conditions of the problem.

Since $DE \perp AD$, $\triangle ADE$ is a rt. $\triangle$.

$\angle DFE$ is inscribed in a semicircle; $\therefore \angle DFE$ is a rt. $\angle$.

If a ⊥ is drawn from vertex of rt. ∠ to hyp., either side is **a** mean proportional between hyp. and adj. side.

∴ $\overline{DE}^2 = \overline{AE} \times \overline{EF}$.

If A be taken at A', it can be similarly proved that $\overline{A'E} \times \overline{EF'} = \overline{DE}^2$; ∴ $\overline{AE} \times \overline{EF}$ is a constant.

62. Since OA, OO', AO', OB, BO' are equal radii, △AOO' and OBO' are equilateral.

∴ ∠$AOO' = 60° = ∠O'OB$ and ∴ arc $AO'B = 120°$.

∠$ACB = \frac{1}{2}$ arc $AO'B = 60°$.

Similarly, arc $AOB = 120°$ and ∴ arc $AMB = 240°$.

∴ ∠$ADB = \frac{1}{2}$ arc $AMB = 120°$ and ∠$CDB = 60°$.

Since 2 △ in △$CDB = 60°$, ∠$DBC = 60°$.

∴ △DCB is equilateral.

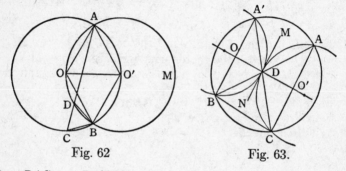

Fig. 62   Fig. 63.

63. ∠$BAC = ∠BA'C$ since they are both measured by $\frac{1}{2}$ arc BC. Since $AC \parallel A'B$, ∠$BA'C = ∠DCA = ∠BAC$. ∴ $AD = DC$. Similarly, we can prove $A'D = BD$.

∴ △$A'DB$ and ADC are isosceles.

The center of a circumscribed circle lies on the ⊥ bisectors of the sides.

∴ center of circle around $A'DB$ lies on ⊥ bis. of $A'B$; call this center O.

Since △$A'DB$ is isosceles and since ⊥ bis. of the base of isosceles △ passes through the vertex and bisects the vertex ∠, the ⊥ bis. of $A'B$ passes through D and bisects ∠$A'DB$.

If OD is extended, it bisects ∠ADC.

Since △ADC is isosceles, OD extended is ⊥ bis. of AC.

∴ center of circle around △ADC lies on OD extended; call this center O'.

If at D, MN is drawn ⊥ ODO', M will be tangent to both circles since it is perpendicular to a radius at its extremity.

∴ since both circles are tangent to the same line at the same point, they are tangent to each other.

64. Draw MN tangent at O; then $\angle AOM = \angle PON$.

$\angle AOM = \frac{1}{2}$ arc AO and $\angle PON = \frac{1}{2}$ arc OP; ∴ $\overarc{AO} = \overarc{PO}$.

∴ $\angle BAO = \angle OBP$ since they are measured by equal arcs.

$\angle ABO = \angle OPB$, both measured by $\frac{1}{2}$ arc BO.

∴ $\triangle AOB \sim \triangle BPO$ and $AO : BO = AB : BP$.

$\angle AQO = \frac{1}{2}$ arc $AO = \angle PAB$.

$\angle ABQ = \frac{1}{2}$ arc $BO = \angle APB$.

∴ $\triangle ABQ \sim \triangle ABP$ and $BQ : AP = AB : BP$.

∴ $AO : BO = BQ : AP$.

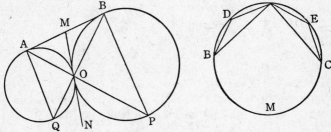

Fig. 64.   Fig. 65.

65. $\angle ADB = \frac{1}{2}$ arc $BMCA$ and $\angle AEC = \frac{1}{2}$ arc $ADBMC$.

∴ $\angle ADB + \angle AEC = \frac{1}{2}$(arc $BMCA$ + arc $ADBMC$)
$$= \frac{1}{2}(\text{arc } BMC + \text{arc } CA + \text{arc } ADB$$
$$+ \text{arc } BMC)$$
$$= \frac{1}{2}(\text{arc } BMC + 360°)$$
$$= \frac{1}{2}(\text{arc } BMC) + 180°$$
$$= \angle BAC + 180°.$$

Since $\angle BAC$ is always inscribed in the same arc, it is a constant and 180° is a constant.

∴ $\angle ADB + \angle AEC$ is a constant.

66. See Example 4, Chapter IV.

67. $CD = \frac{1}{2} AB = r = OC = OD.$

∴ $\triangle OCD$ is equilateral and $\angle OCD = 60°$.

Since $CD \parallel AB$, $\angle AOC = \angle OCD = 60°$.

In $\triangle ACO$: $AO = CO; \angle OAC = \angle OCA$.

$\angle AOC = 60°$; ∴ $\angle OAC = 60°$.

$\angle ABE = 90°$; ∴ $\triangle AEB$ is a 90°, 60°, 30° $\triangle$.

∴ $AE = 2 AB.$ [See Prob. 11, Chap. VIII.]

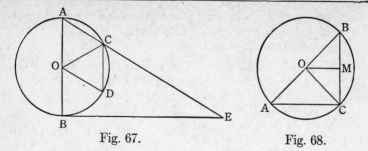

Fig. 67.   Fig. 68.

68. Let O be midpoint of hyp. and M, midpoint of BC.
    Then $CM \parallel AC$ and $\angle OMB = \angle ACB = 90°$.
    In $\triangle OMB$ and OMC: $OM = OM$; $MB = MC$; $\angle OMB = \angle OMC$.
    $\therefore \triangle OMB \cong \triangle OMC$ and $OC = OB$.
    Since $OB = OA$, $OA = OC$.
    $\therefore$ circle with O as center will pass through A, B, and C.
69. Let BC be the diameter of the circle O.
    Since $AC \perp BC$, AC is tangent to circle O.
    Since NM and NC are tangents from same point, $NM = NC$.
    Since $PMN \perp OM$, $\angle PMB$ is complement of $\angle BMO$.
    Since $MO = BO$, $\angle BMO = \angle OBM$.
    $\therefore \angle PMB$ is the complement of $\angle OBM$.
    Since $\angle PMB = \angle AMN$, $\angle AMN$ is complement of $\angle OBM$.
    In rt. $\triangle ABC$: $\angle BAC$ is complement of $\angle OBM$.
    $\therefore \angle BAC = \angle AMN$ and $AN = NM$.
    Since $NC = NM$, $AN = NC$.

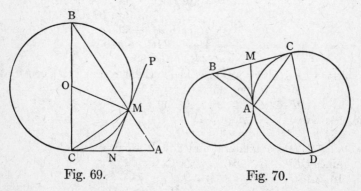

Fig. 69.   Fig. 70.

70. Draw tangent MA.
    $MA = MB$ and $MA = MC$, being tangents from same point.

∴ $\angle ABC = \angle MAB$ and $\angle MCA = \angle MAC$.

Since $\angle ABC + \angle MAB + \angle MAC + \angle MCA = 180°$, we have

$2 \angle MAB + 2 \angle MAC = 180°$ and ∴ $\angle MAB + \angle MAC = 90°$.

∴ $\angle CAD = 90°$ and CD is a diameter.

71. If a square is inscribed in a circle, $\overline{AO}^2 + \overline{BO}^2 = \overline{AB}^2$.

∴ $r^2 + r^2 = 15$ or $r = \frac{1}{2}\sqrt{30}$.

If the square $A'B'C'D'$ is inscribed in a semicircle,

$B'A' : A'O = NM : MO = 2 : 1$. [See Prob. 41, Chap. V.]

Since $\overline{B'A'}^2 + \overline{A'O}^2 = \overline{B'O}^2$, $\overline{B'A'}^2 + (\frac{1}{2} \overline{B'A'})^2 = r^2 = \frac{15}{2}$.

∴ $\overline{B'A'}^2 = 6$.

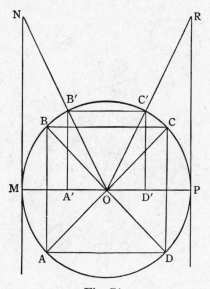

Fig. 71.

72. $ODC = O'EC = r + r$. Draw $PM \perp OO'$.

MP is the $\perp$ bis. of OO' and ∴ MP extended must pass through C.

Since $OA = O'B$ and $OA \parallel O'B$ (both are $\perp AB$), $ABO'O$ is a $\square$.

∴ $OO' \parallel AB$ and MP extended $\perp AB$.

Then since MP passes through C it meets AB at N, the point of tangency.

∴ $ANPO$ is a $\square$. ∴ $NP = AO = r$ and $CP = r - 4$.

Then in rt. $\triangle COP$:
$$\overline{CO}^2 = \overline{CP}^2 + \overline{OP}^2 \text{ or } (r+4)^2 = (r-4)^2 + r^2 \text{ and } r = 16.$$

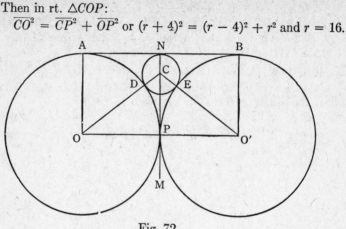

Fig. 72.

73. $\angle PEC = \frac{1}{2}$ arc $PC + \frac{1}{2}$ arc $AB = \frac{1}{2}$ arc $PC + \frac{1}{2}$ arc $BC = \frac{1}{2}$ arc PCB.

Since $\angle PBR = \frac{1}{2}$ arc PCB, $\angle PEC = \angle PBR$ and $AC \parallel QR$.

Since PB is bis. of $\angle APC$, $QB : BR = PQ : PR$.

Then since $AC \parallel QR$, $AQ : CR = PQ : PR$.

$\therefore QB : BR = AQ : CR$ or $QB : AQ = BR : CR$.

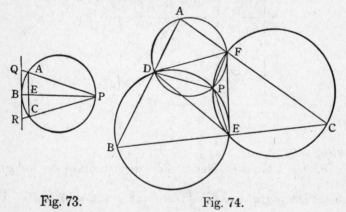

Fig. 73.   Fig. 74.

74. Let the circles about ADF and DBE intersect at P.

Draw the lines DP, PE, and PF.

Since $BDPE$ is an inscribed quadrilateral,
$$\angle DPE + \angle DBE = 180°.$$

Similarly, $\angle DPF + \angle DAF = 180°$.

$\therefore \angle DPE + \angle DBE + \angle DPF + \angle DAF = 360°$.

Since $\angle DPE + \angle DPF + \angle EPF = 360°$,

$$\angle EPF = \angle DBE + \angle DAF.$$

Since $\angle ACB$ is the supplement of $\measuredangle BAC$ and ABC,

$\angle ACB$ is the supplement of $\angle EPF$.

Therefore a circle can be circumscribed about quadrilateral $CFPE$ and circle about CFE passes through P.

75. Let CM be the tangent.

Since $AB = BC$ and $\angle ABC = 90°$, $\angle BAC = \angle BCA = 45°$.

$\therefore \angle DAC = 45°$.

Since $\angle EAN = 90°$, EN must be a diameter.

Since $AN = AE$ and AO bisects $\angle EAN$, AO is $\perp$ bis. of EN.

$\therefore O$ is center of circle and $\angle AEP = 90°$.

$\therefore EP \parallel DC$ and since EP bisects AD it bisects AC.

$\therefore CP = \frac{1}{2} AC$.

Since CM is a tangent and AC is a secant,

$$\overline{CM}^2 = \overline{AC} \times \overline{PC} = \overline{AC} \times \tfrac{1}{2} \overline{AC} = \tfrac{1}{2} \overline{AC}^2.$$

Now $\overline{AC}^2 = \overline{AB}^2 + \overline{BC}^2 = 2\overline{AB}^2$.

$\therefore \frac{1}{2} \overline{AC}^2 = \overline{AB}^2$ and $\overline{CM}^2 = \overline{AB}^2$ or $CM = AB$.

76. See Example 5, Chapter IV.

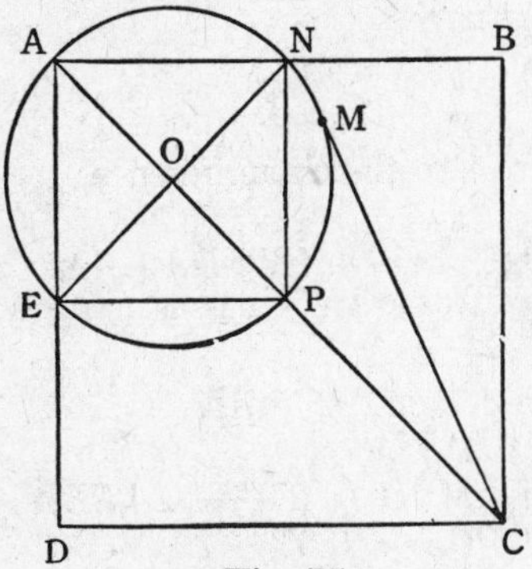

Fig. 75. 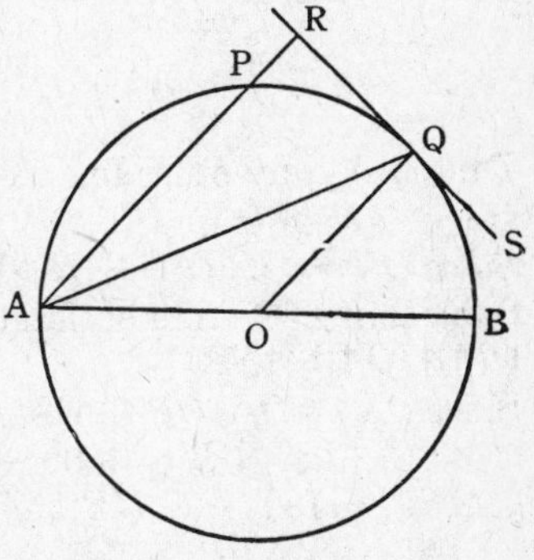   Fig. 77.

77. Draw OQ, the radius to point of tangency.

Since $\angle PAQ = \angle QAB$, $\overset{\frown}{PQ} = \overset{\frown}{QB} = \frac{1}{2} \overset{\frown}{PB}$.

$\angle PAB = \frac{1}{2} \overset{\frown}{PB}$ and $\angle QOB = \overset{\frown}{QB}$.

$\therefore \angle PAB = \angle QOB$ and $APR \parallel QO$.

$\therefore \angle ARQ = \angle OQS$.

Then, since $\angle OQS = 90°$, $\angle ARQ = 90°$.

78. Since arc ABC > arc BC, chord AC > chord BC.
   Measure off $CM = BC$ on AC.
   Since arc $AB = 120°$, $\angle BCM = 60°$.
   Since $CM = BC$, $\angle CMB = \angle CBM$.
   $\therefore \angle CMB = 60° = \angle CBM$ and $\angle AMB = 120°$.
   $\angle BCD = \frac{1}{2}$ arc $BAD = 120°$. $\therefore \angle AMB = \angle BCD$.
   $\angle MAB = \angle BDC$ since both are measured by $\frac{1}{2}$ arc BC.
   Thus 2 △ of $\triangle AMB$ = 2 △ of $\triangle BCD$.
   $\therefore \angle CBD = \angle MBA$ and $AB = BD$.
   $\therefore \triangle ABM \cong \triangle BCD$ and $AM = CD$.
   $\therefore AM + MC = BC + CD$ or $AC = BC + CD$.

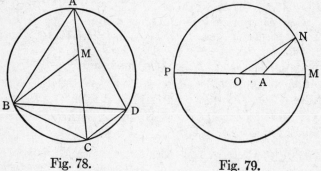

Fig. 78.   Fig. 79.

79. Draw AN, any other line from A to the circumference.
   $OA + AN > ON$.
   Since $ON = OM$, $OA + AN > OM$ or $OA + AN > OA + AM$.
   Subtracting OA from both sides, we get $AN > AM$ or $AM < AN$.
   $ON + OA > AN$.
   Since $ON = OP$, $OP + OA > AN$ or $PA > AN$.

80. $\angle MBC + \angle MCB = 180° - \angle BMC$.
   $\angle MBC = 180° - \angle NBC$ and $\angle MCB = 180° - \angle PCB$.
   $\therefore 180° - \angle NBC + 180° - \angle PCB = 180° - \angle BMC$;
   or $\angle NBC + \angle PCB = 180° + \angle BMC$
   and $\frac{1}{2}\angle NBC + \frac{1}{2}\angle PCB = 90° + \frac{1}{2}\angle BMC$.
   Since a line to the center bisects $\angle$ formed by tangents,
      $\angle OBC = \frac{1}{2}\angle NBC$ and $\angle OCB = \frac{1}{2}\angle PCB$.
   $\therefore \angle OBC + \angle OCB = 90° + \frac{1}{2}\angle BMC$.
   Since $\angle OBC + \angle OCB = 180° - \angle BOC$,
      $180° - \angle BOC = 90° + \frac{1}{2}\angle BMC$.
   $\therefore \angle BOC = 90° - \frac{1}{2}\angle BMC$.

Since 90° is a fixed number and ∠BMC is a constant, ∠BOC is a constant.

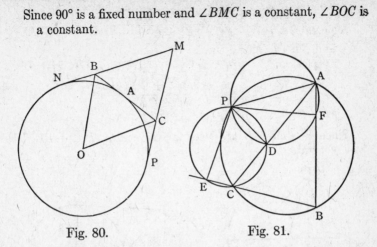

Fig. 80.   Fig. 81.

81. Let ABC be the inscribed △ and PD, PF, and PE the ⊥s dropped to the sides. Connect E with D and with F. It is required to prove that ED and DF form a st. line.

Since ∠PDC + ∠PEC = 90° + 90° = 180°, a circle can be circumscribed about the quadrilateral $PDCE$.

∴ ∠EDC = ∠EPC since both are measured by $\frac{1}{2}$ arc EC.

Since △PDA and PFA are rt. ⧍, a circle can be circumscribed about P, D, F, and A having PA as its diameter. [See Prob. 68, this section.]

∴ ∠FPA = ∠ADF.

Since quad. $APCB$ is inscribed in a circle, ∠PAF is the supplement of ∠PCB.

Since ∠PCE is the supplement of ∠PCB, ∴ ∠PAF = ∠PCE.

In rt. △PFA: ⧍FPA and PAF are complementary.

∴ ⧍FPA and PCE are complementary.

Since ∠FPA = ∠ADF, ⧍ADF and PCE are complementary.

In rt. △PEC: ⧍EPC and PCE are complementary.

∴ ∠EPC = ∠ADF.

Since ∠EPC = ∠EDC, ∠EDC = ∠ADF.

Since CDA is a st. line, ∠EDC + ∠EDP + ∠PDA = 180°.

∴ ∠ADF + ∠EDP + ∠PDA = 180° and, consequently, ED and DF form a st. line.

82. Let A and B be the given points with $OA = OB$.

Draw $PX \perp AB$.

Then $\overline{PA}^2 = \overline{PX}^2 + \overline{AX}^2$ and $\overline{PB}^2 = \overline{PX}^2 + \overline{XB}^2$.

$$\therefore \overline{PA}^2 + \overline{PB}^2 = 2\,\overline{PX}^2 + \overline{AX}^2 + \overline{BX}^2.$$

Now $\overline{PX}^2 = \overline{PO}^2 - \overline{XO}^2$; $\overline{AX}^2 = (\overline{AO} - \overline{XO})^2$;

and $\overline{XB}^2 = (\overline{XO} + \overline{OB})^2$.

$$\begin{aligned}
\therefore \overline{PA}^2 + \overline{PB}^2 &= 2\,\overline{PO}^2 - 2\,\overline{XO}^2 + \overline{AO}^2 - 2(\overline{AO})(\overline{XO}) \\
&\qquad + 2\,\overline{XO}^2 + 2\,\overline{XO}(\overline{OB}) + \overline{OB}^2 \\
&= 2\,\overline{PO}^2 + \overline{AO}^2 + \overline{OB}^2 \\
&= 2\,\overline{PO}^2 + 2\,\overline{AO}^2.
\end{aligned}$$

Since PO and AD are constant quantities, $\overline{PA}^2 + \overline{PB}^2$ is **a** constant.

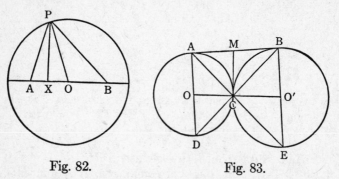

Fig. 82.   Fig. 83.

83. Draw the line of centers OO'; it passes through C.

Connect B with C, A with C, D with C, and E with C.

$OA \parallel O'B$ since both are $\perp AB$.

$\therefore \angle AOC + \angle CO'B = 180°$ and arc $AC +$ arc $BC = 180°$.

Draw CM, the common internal tangent.

$\angle ACM = \frac{1}{2}$ arc AC and $\angle MCB = \frac{1}{2}$ arc CB.

$\therefore \angle ACM + \angle MCB = \frac{1}{2}\,\widehat{AC} + \frac{1}{2}\,\widehat{CB} = \frac{1}{2}(180°) = 90°.$

$\therefore \angle ACB = 90°.$

$\angle ACD = 90°$ since it is inscribed in a semicircle.

$\therefore DCB$ is a st. line.

Similarly, ACE is a st. line.

In $\triangle ADB$ and ABE: $\angle DAB = \angle ABE$ (both rt. $\angle$s); $\angle ABD = \angle AEB$ since both are measured by $\frac{1}{2}$ arc BC.

$\therefore \triangle ABD \sim \triangle ABE$ and $AD : AB = AB : BE$.

84. Draw $OR \perp a$; then $OR \perp b$, c, and d and OR bisects a, b, c, and d.

Let $OS = p$ and let the distances between the chords be m

In rt. $\triangle OAR$: $\overline{AR}^2 = \overline{OA}^2 - \overline{OR}^2$ or $(\frac{1}{2}\,a)^2 = r^2 - (3\,m + p)^2.$

Similarly, $\overline{DS}^2 = \overline{OD}^2 - p^2$ or $(\frac{1}{2} d)^2 = r^2 - p^2.$

$\therefore \frac{1}{4}(a^2 - d^2) = -9\,m^2 - 6\,mp - p^2 + p^2$

or $\qquad a^2 - d^2 = -36\,m^2 - 24\,mp.$

Similarly, $(\frac{1}{2} b)^2 = r^2 - (2\,m + p)^2$ and $(\frac{1}{2} c)^2 = r^2 - (p + m)^2.$

$\therefore b^2 - c^2 = -12\,m^2 - 8\,mp$ or $3(b^2 - c^2) = -36\,m^2 - 24\,mp.$

$\therefore 3(b^2 - c^2) = a^2 - d^2.$

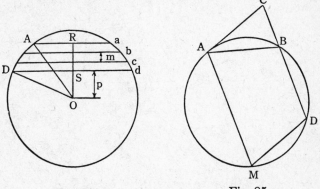

Fig. 84.   Fig. 85.

85. Since $AC = AB$, $\angle ACB = \angle ABC$.

$\angle ABC$ is supplement of $\angle ABD$ and $\angle AMD$ is supplement of $\angle ABD$.

$\therefore \angle AMD = \angle ABC = \angle ACB$.

$\angle MDB = \frac{1}{2}$ arc BAM and $\angle CAM = \frac{1}{2}$ arc ABM.

Since arc BAM = arc ABM, $\angle MDB = \angle CAM$.

In quad. $ACDM$: $\angle ACB + \angle CDM + \angle DMA + \angle MAC = 360°$.

$\therefore 2\,\angle DMA + 2\,\angle CDM = 360°$ or $\angle DMA + \angle CDM = 180°$.

$\therefore AM \parallel CD$.

Similarly, $\angle DMA + \angle CAM = 180°$ and $MD \parallel AC$.

$\therefore ACDM$ is a parallelogram.

86. Let OO' be the line of centers. Connect A with P, B with P, O with A, and O' with B.

$OA \parallel O'B$ since both are $\perp AB$.

$\therefore \angle AOP + \angle PO'B = 180°$ and $\overset{\frown}{AP} + \overset{\frown}{PB} = 180°$.

$\angle BAP = \frac{1}{2} \overset{\frown}{AP}$ and $\angle ABP = \frac{1}{2} \overset{\frown}{BP}$.

$\therefore \angle BAP + \angle ABP = \frac{1}{2}(180°) = 90°$.

$\therefore \angle APB = 90°$ and $\triangle ABP$ is a rt. $\triangle$.

$\therefore$ circle with AB as diameter will pass through P. [See Prob. 68, Chap. IV.]

Draw $PX \perp OO'$.

Since $XP = AX$ and $XP = XB$ (tangents from external point), $AX = XB$.

$\therefore$ X is center of circle passing through A, B, and P and XP is a radius. Since $OO' \perp XP$ at its extremity P, OO' is tangent to circle.

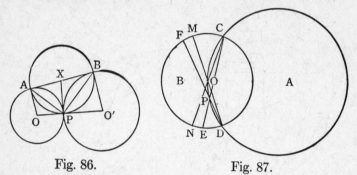

Fig. 86.   Fig. 87.

87. It is required to prove that $DPF = CPE$.

Draw the diameters DOM and CON.

$\measuredangle DFM$ and CEN are rt. $\measuredangle$ since they are inscribed in semi-circles.

$\angle OCP = \angle ODP$ since they are both measured by $\frac{1}{2}$ arc OP.

$CN = MD$ since both are diameters of circle O.

$\therefore$ rt. $\triangle DFM \cong$ rt. $\triangle CEN$ and $DPF = CPE$.

88. Extend CO to D and connect D with A.

Since AB is a diameter, $\angle AOB$ is a rt. $\angle$.

Since COD is a diameter, $\angle CAD$ is a rt. $\angle$.

$OA = OC$ since they are radii of circle O.

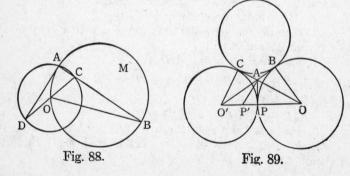

Fig. 88.   Fig. 89.

$\therefore \angle OAC = \angle OCA$.

In rt. $\triangle AOB$: $\angle ABO$ is complement of $\angle OAC$.

In rt. $\triangle DAC$: $\angle ADC$ is complement of $\angle OCA$.

$\therefore \angle ADC = \angle ABO$ and rt. $\triangle DAC \sim$ rt. $\triangle OAB$.

$\therefore AB : DC = OA : AC$ or $AB : 2\,OC = OC : AC$.

$\therefore \overline{AB} \times \overline{AC} = 2\,\overline{OC}^2$.

89. Let the tangents at B and C meet at A.

Draw the line of centers OPO'. The aim is to prove that the line AP is tangent to circles O and O'.

$\overline{OA}^2 = \overline{OB}^2 + \overline{BA}^2$ and $\overline{O'A}^2 = \overline{O'C}^2 + \overline{AC}^2$.

$\therefore \overline{OA}^2 - \overline{O'A}^2 = \overline{OB}^2 - \overline{O'C}^2$ since $AB = AC$.

Since $OB = OP$ and $O'P = O'C$, $\overline{OA}^2 - \overline{O'A}^2 = \overline{OP}^2 - \overline{O'P}^2$.

Now assume that AP is not $\perp O'O$ and draw $AP' \perp O'O$.

Then $\overline{P'A}^2 = \overline{OA}^2 - \overline{OP'}^2$ and $\overline{P'A}^2 = \overline{O'A}^2 - \overline{O'P'}^2$.

$\therefore \overline{OA}^2 - \overline{OP'}^2 = \overline{O'A}^2 - \overline{O'P'}^2$ or $\overline{OA}^2 - \overline{O'A}^2 = \overline{OP'}^2 - \overline{O'P'}^2$.

$\therefore \overline{OP}^2 - \overline{O'P}^2 = \overline{OP'}^2 - \overline{O'P'}^2$ or

$(\overline{OP} + \overline{O'P})(\overline{OP} - \overline{O'P}) = (\overline{OP'} + \overline{O'P'})(\overline{OP'} - \overline{O'P'})$.

Since $OP + O'P = OO' = OP' + O'P'$, we have

$OP - O'P = OP' - O'P'$ or $OP + O'P' = O'P + OP'$.

But this is absurd unless $P = P'$.

$\therefore AP \perp OO'$ and AP is tangent to O and O'.

90. Extend OR to S and connect S with Q.

Since $\angle ORQ = 90°$, $\angle QRS = 90°$.

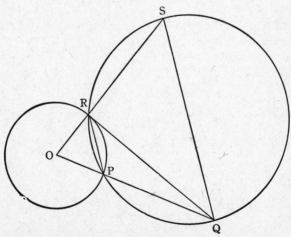

Fig. 90.

$\therefore$ SQ is a diameter of the circle about P, R, and Q.

Since $PQSR$ is an inscribed quadrilateral, $\angle RSQ$ is the supplement of $\angle RPQ$.

Since $\angle RPO$ is the supplement of $\angle RPQ$, $\angle RPO = \angle RSQ$.

Since $OR = OP$, $\angle ORP = \angle RPO$.

$\therefore$ $\angle ORP = \angle RSQ$ and $SQ \parallel RP$.

Since $\angle RSQ = \angle ORP$ and $\angle SQO = \angle RPO$, $\triangle ORP \sim OSQ$.

$\therefore$ $SQ : PR = OQ : OP$.

$OQ = OP + PQ = OP + n(OP) = OP(n + 1)$.

$\therefore$ $SQ : PR = OP(n + 1) : OP$ or $SQ : PR = (n + 1) : 1$.

$\therefore$ $SQ = (n + 1)PR$.

SOLUTIONS OF THE PROBLEMS ON CONSTRUCTIONS

[Chapter V, pp. 45–48]

When indefinite angles and line segments are given, the student should draw an arbitrary angle or line segment and then proceed to the constructions; there he should duplicate the already chosen angles and line segments. For example, in Problem 1 below, first draw the line AB of arbitrary length and $\angle C$ also arbitrary; then in the constructions duplicate $\angle C$ in $\angle DOE$, etc.

The letters r and R will be used to denote radii of circles and arcs and in many cases will replace the word "radius." In the case of the "easier" problems the proofs of the constructions have been omitted; however, the student should supply these proofs in order to have the complete solutions.

1. Bisect the given line AB at M.

Construct $\angle DOE =$ given $\angle C$.

Mark off $OF = AM$ and $OG = MB = AM$.

$\triangle OFG$ is the required triangle.

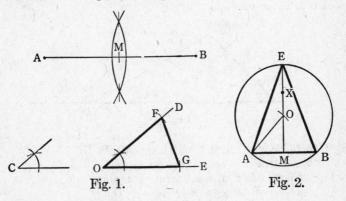

Fig. 1.   Fig. 2.

2. Draw $AB = 4$ units and construct $MX \perp$ bis. of AB.

With A as center and $r = CD = 3$ units draw arc cutting MX at O.

With O as center and $r = OA$ draw a circle.

Extend MX to E and connect E with A and with B.

113

△*AEB* is the required triangle.

In rt. △*OAM*: $\overline{OM}^2 = 9 - 4 = 5$ and $OM = \sqrt{5}$.

In rt. △*AEM*: $\overline{AE}^2 = \overline{ME}^2 + \overline{AM}^2 = (\sqrt{5}+3)^2 + 4 = 18 + 6\sqrt{5}$.

∴ $AE = \sqrt{18 + 6\sqrt{5}}$.

3. See Example 1, Chapter V.

4. Given 3 equal equilateral △*ABC*, *DEF*, and *MNO*.

Place △*DEF* so that *DE* coincides with *AC*.

The new figure *ABCF* has *AF* ∥ *BC* since ∠*ACB* = 60° = ∠*CAF*.

Place △*MNO* so that *MN* coincides with *FC*.

Then *AFOB* is the required trapezoid.

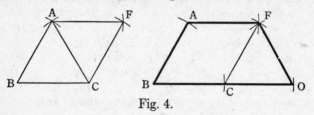

Fig. 4.

5. Given the two sides *a* and *b*, and the altitude *c*.

Construct *AB* = *c* and at *B* construct *MN* ⊥ *AB*.

With *A* as center and *r* = *a*, draw arc cutting *MN* at *C*.

With *A* as center and *r* = *b*, draw arc cutting *MN* at *D*.

△*ACD* is the required triangle.

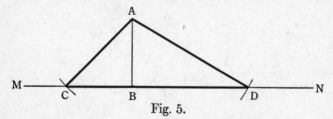

Fig. 5.

6. With *BC* as a side construct the square *BCDE*.

With *BE* as a base construct equilateral △*BEA*.

Figure *ABCDE* is an equilateral pentagon.

It is not regular since ∠*BAE* ≠ ∠*BCD*.

7. Given *AB*, the diagonal of a square.

Construct *NC* ⊥ bis. of *AB*. Mark off *MN* = *AM* and *MC* = *MB*.

Connect the points *A*, *N*, *B*, and *C*.

ANBC is the required square.

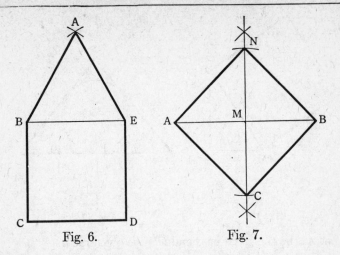

Fig. 6. Fig. 7.

8. Let *P* be the given point in the circle *O*.
   Draw *OP* and construct *AB* ⊥ *OP* at *P*.
   AB is the required chord.

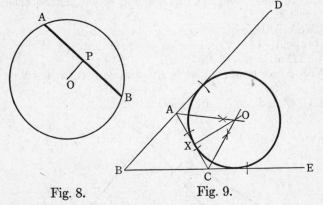

Fig. 8. Fig. 9.

9. Given the △*ABC*.
   Extend *BA* to *D* and *BC* to *E*.
   Construct the bisectors of ∡*DAC* and *ACE*; they meet at *O*.
   Construct *OX* ⊥ *AC*.
   With *O* as center and *r* = *OX* draw the circle.
10. Let *ABCD* and *EFGH* be the given squares.
    Construct *MN* = *DC* and *NP* = *HG* and ⊥ *MN*.
    Construct a square on *MP*. This is the required square.

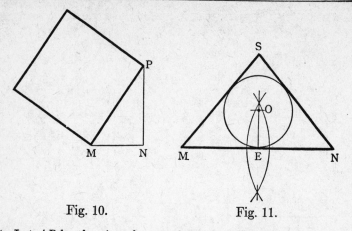

Fig. 10.   Fig. 11.

11. Let AB be the given base and CD the given radius.
    Construct $MN = AB$.
    Construct $OE \perp$ bis. of MN such that $OE = CD$.
    With O as center and $r = OE$ draw the circle.
    Construct the tangents from M and N and extend them to meet at S.
    $\triangle MSN$ is the required triangle.

12. At a point A construct $\angle NAD =$ given $\angle A$.
    On AD measure off $AB' = AB$.
    With B' as center and $r = BC$ draw arc cutting AN at C' and C''.
    $\triangle AB'C'$ and $AB'C''$ are the required $\triangle$.

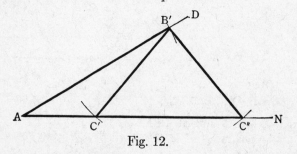

Fig. 12.

13. Given the square $ABCD$.
    Draw the diagonals AC and BD meeting at O.
    Inscribe circles in $\triangle AOB$, AOD, DOC, and COB.
    These circles are the required circles.

Proof: $\triangle AOB$ is an isosceles rt. $\triangle$.

∴ the bis. of $\angle AOB$ is also $\perp$ bis. of AB.

∴ center of inscribed $\odot$ lies on MO and a radius lies on MO.
Since $MO \perp AB$, the $\odot$ is tangent to AB at its midpoint.
Similarly for the other circles.
Let P be point of tangency of inscribed $\odot$ of $\triangle AOB$ to AO.
Then $AP = AM = \frac{1}{2} AB$.
Let P' be point of tangency of inscribed $\odot$ of $\triangle AOD$ to AO.
Then $AP' = AN = \frac{1}{2} AD = \frac{1}{2} AB$.

∴ P and P' coincide and $\circledS$ inscribed in $\triangle AOB$ and AOD are
tangent to AO at the same point.

Similarly for the other circles.

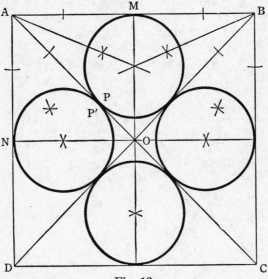

Fig. 13.

14. Let AOB be the given quadrant.

Construct OM, the bisector of $\angle AOB$.

At M construct a $\perp OM$ meeting OA and OB (extended) at C
and D, respectively.

Inscribe a circle in $\triangle OCD$. This is the required circle.

15. See Example 7, Chapter I.

16. Let O be the center of given circle and P be 3 units from O.
Construct chord $AB = 9$ units and $OM \perp AB$.

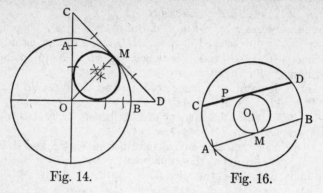

Fig. 14.   Fig. 16.

With O as center and $r = OM$ draw a circle.

From P draw a tangent to this inner circle.

The tangent CD is the required chord.

[Chords equidistant from center are equal; $\therefore CD = AB = 9$.]

17. Draw $CD = a$ and with CD as diameter draw a semicircle.

    From D draw chord $DM = p$ and connect C with M.

    At D construct $\angle CDN = 180° - (\angle C + \text{given } \angle A)$.

    $\triangle CDN$ is the required triangle.

    In order to construct $\angle CDN$ proceed as follows:

        Pick any point O on a line EF.

        Draw $\angle EOS = \angle C$ and $\angle SOR = \text{given } \angle A$.

        Then $\angle ROF = \angle CDN$ and $\angle MND = \angle A$.

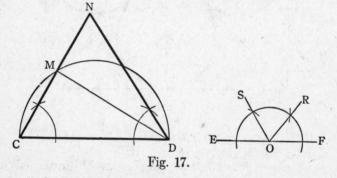

Fig. 17.

18. In circle O draw any radius OA.

    Divide OA into extreme and mean ratio at B as follows:

        At A construct $PA = \frac{1}{2} OA$ and $\perp OA$.

    Draw circle with P as center and $r = PA$.

    Draw secant $OB'PD$ and mark off $OB = OB'$ on OA.

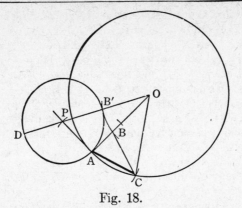

Fig. 18.

[Prove that $OA : OB = OB : BA$; start with $OD : OA = OA : OB'$.]

Draw chord $AC = OB$.

AC is the side of the required decagon.

Proof:

Since $AC = OB$ and $OA : OB = OB : BA$, $OA : AC = AC : BA$.

Since $\angle OAC$ is common to $\triangle ABC$ and OAC, $\triangle ABC \sim \triangle OAC$.

Since $\triangle OAC$ is isosceles, $\triangle ABC$ is isosceles and $AC = BC = OB$.

$\angle ABC = \angle BOC + \angle BCO$ or $\angle ABC = 2 \angle BOC = \angle CBA$.

Then since $AO = OC$, $\angle CAB = \angle ACO$ and in $\triangle OAC$,

$\angle AOC + 2 \angle AOC + 2 \angle AOC = 180°$.

∴ $\angle AOC = 36°$ and there will be 10 arcs in the circle each equal to arc AC. Consequently, there will be 10 equal chords and a regular decagon.

19. Given the pentagon $ABCDE$. Connect A with C.

From B construct $BM \parallel CA$, meeting AE extended at M.

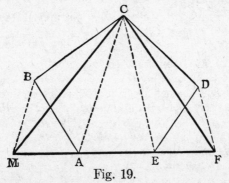

Fig. 19.

The 4-sided figure $CMED$ is equivalent to $ABCDE$.

Proof: Polygon $CMED$ = fig. $AEDC + \triangle ACM$.

Polygon $ABCDE$ = fig. $AEDC + \triangle ABC$.

$\triangle ACM$ and ABC have the same base, AC.

They also have equal altitudes since $BM \parallel CA$.

$\therefore$ $\triangle ACM$ is equivalent to $\triangle ABC$. Q.E.D.

Next, connect C with E and construct $DF \parallel CE$.

Then $\triangle CMF$ is equivalent to $CMED$ is equivalent to $ABCDE$.

The proof is similar to that given above.

20. Given $\triangle ABC$. Construct $AD \perp BC$.

With AD as a side draw the square $ADEF$.

At G, the midpoint of AD, construct $GH \parallel DE$.

$\square AGHF = \frac{1}{2} \square ADEF$.

Construct the mean proportional, MN, between AF and AG.

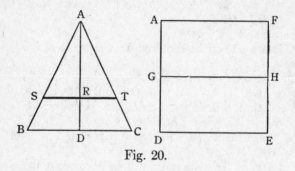

Fig. 20.

In $\triangle ABC$: mark off $AR = MN$ on AD.

Through R construct $ST \parallel BC$. ST is the required line.

Proof: Since $ST \parallel BC$, $\triangle AST \sim \triangle ABC$.

$\therefore$ $\triangle AST : \triangle ABC = \overline{AR}^2 : \overline{AD}^2$.

But $\overline{AR}^2 = \overline{MN}^2 = \overline{AF} \times \overline{AG} = \frac{1}{2}$ square $ADEF = \frac{1}{2} \overline{AD}^2$.

$\therefore$ $\triangle AST : \triangle ABC = \frac{1}{2} \overline{AD}^2 : \overline{AD}^2 = 1 : 2$.

21. See Example 2, Chapter V.

22. Given $\triangle ABC$. Construct the bisectors of $\angle ABC$ and ACB
    and let them meet at D.

    Through D construct $EF \parallel BC$; EF is the required line.

    Proof: $\angle EDB = \angle DBC = \angle EBD$; $\therefore$ $ED = EB$.

    Similarly, $DF = FC$. $\therefore$ $ED + DF = EB + FC$.

23. Let $ABCD$ be the given rhombus.

    Draw BD and AC.

    Bisect $\angle AOB$ and DOC by EF.

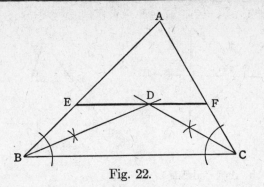

Fig. 22.

Bisect ∠ BOC and AOD by HG.
The figure EGFH is the required square.
Proof: ∠AOB is a rt. ∠; ∴ ∠EOB = 45°.
Similarly, ∠BOG = 45°; ∴ ∠EOG = 90°.
Similarly, ∠GOF = 90° = ∠HOF = ∠HOE.
In △EOB and BOG:
   ∠EOB = ∠BOG, ∠EBO = ∠OBG, and OB = OB.
∴ △EOB ≅ △BOG and EO = OG.
Similarly, OG = OF = OH and EGFH is a square.

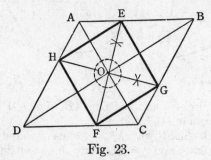

Fig. 23.

24. Given the line AB and the points C and D.
   Construct DM ⊥ AB and extend it to N making **DM = MN.**
   Draw CN cutting AB at O. Draw DO.
   DO and CO are the required lines.
   [∠DOM = ∠NOM = ∠COA.]
25. Given the ∠C and the point A.
   Construct AE ∥ CD and measure off **EF = EC.**
   Connect F with A and extend to G.

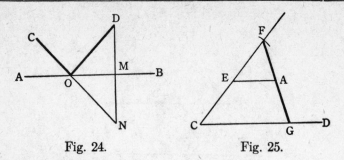

Fig. 24.   Fig. 25.

FG is the required line.

[*EA* ∥ *CD* and bisects *FC*; ∴ *EA* bisects *FG*.]

26. Given the lines *AB* and *CD* and the point *O*.
    Extend *AB* and *CD* to meet at *P*.
    Construct *PM*, the bisector of ∠*APC*.
    Construct *ON* ⊥ *PM* and extend to *E* and *F*.
    EF is the required line.

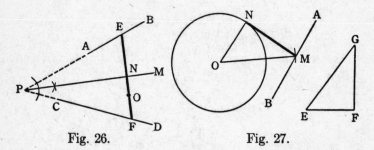

Fig. 26.   Fig. 27.

27. Given the circle *O* and the line *AB*. Let *CD* represent the
    given length of the intercepts.
    Construct rt. △*EFG* with *EF* = radius of *O* and *FG* = *CD*.
    With *O* as center and *r* = *EG* draw an arc cutting *AB* at *M*.
    From *M* draw tangent *MN*; this is the required tangent.
    $[\overline{MN}^2 = \overline{OM}^2 - \overline{ON}^2 = \overline{EG}^2 - \overline{EF}^2 = \overline{FG}^2 = \overline{CD}^2; \therefore MN = CD.]$

28. See Example 5, Chapter II.

29. Given the base *AB*, the base angle *C*, and *DE*, the difference
    of the other two sides.
    Draw *MN* = *AB* and at *M* construct ∠*NMO* = ∠*C*.
    At *N* draw *NP* ∥ *MO* and equal to *DE*.
    Connect *M* and *P*.
    With *N* as center and *r* = *NP*, draw arc cutting *MP* at *S*.

Connect N with S and extend to T.

Triangle NTM is the required triangle.

Proof: $\angle NPS = \angle SMT$ and $\angle NSP = \angle MST$;

  $\therefore \angle MST = \angle SMT.$

$\therefore MT = TS; NT - MT = NT - TS = SN = NP = DE.$

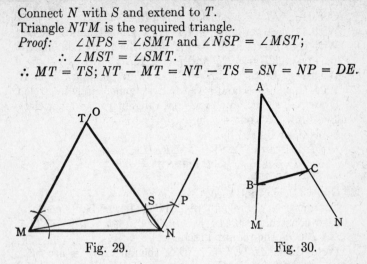

Fig. 29.   Fig. 30.

30. Let x = vertex angle; then $2x + 2x + x = 180°$ and $x = 36°$
Construct $\angle MAN = 36°$. [See Prob. 18, this section.]
Mark off equal distances AB and AC on AM and AN.
$\triangle ABC$ is the required triangle.

31. Given the circle O (radius OP), the circle O' (radius $O'R$), and
the straight lines AB and CD.

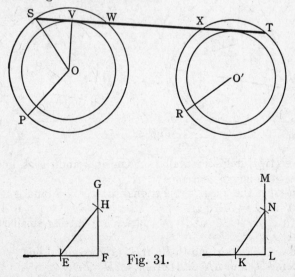

Fig. 31.

Construct $EF = \frac{1}{2} AB$ and $FG \perp EF$.

With E as center and $r = OP$ draw arc cutting FG at H.

With O as center and $r = FH$ draw inner circle in circle O.

Construct $KL = \frac{1}{2} CD$ and $LM \perp KL$.

With K as center and $r = O'R$ draw arc cutting LM at N.

With O' as center and $r = LN$ draw inner circle in circle O'.

Draw ST, the common external tangent to the inner circles.

[See Prob. 36, this section.]

ST is the required line.

Proof: Prove that $\triangle SVO \cong \triangle EFH$.

Then $SV = EF = \frac{1}{2} AB$ and $SW = AB$.

Similarly, $XT = CD$.

32. Given circle O and $\triangle ABC$.

Circumscribe a circle about $\triangle ABC$. Let O' be its center.

At O construct $\angle B'OC' = \angle BO'C$ and $\angle C'OA' = \angle CO'A$.

$\triangle A'B'C'$ is the required triangle.

Proof: Since $\angle B'OC' = \angle BO'C$, then arc $B'C' =$ arc BC.

$\therefore \angle B'A'C' = \angle BAC$.

Similarly for the other angles.

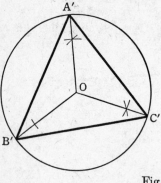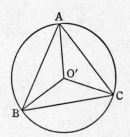

Fig. 32.

33. Given two circles internally tangent at A and the st. line BC.

Draw the line of centers $AO'ON$.

Construct the fourth proportional to MN, BC, and AM.

$[MN : BC = AM : x.]$

With A as center and $r = x$ draw arc cutting smaller circle at D.

Draw AD and extend to E. AE is the required line.

Proof: MD and $EN \perp ADE$. $\therefore MD \parallel EN$.

Then $AM : AD = MN : DE$ or $AM : x = MN : DE$.

Since $AM : x = MN : BC$, $MN : DE = MN : BC$ and $DE = BC$.

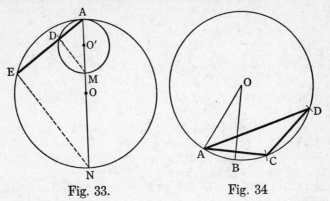

Fig. 33.   Fig. 34

34. Let $x =$ vertex angle; then $x + \frac{1}{3}x + \frac{1}{3}x = 180°$ or $\frac{1}{3}x = 36°$.

In the given circle construct $\angle AOB = 36°$. [See Prob. 18, this section.]

Measure off arc $BC =$ arc $AB = 36°$.

Draw chord AC and chord $CD =$ chord AC.

$\triangle ACD$ is the required triangle.

[$AC = 72° = CD$; $\therefore \angle DAC = \angle ADC = 36°$.]

35. Given $\triangle ABC$, the point D on AB, and two line segments m and n.

Construct the mean proportional x; $AB : x = x : BC$.

Draw two lines ES and EF at any angle.

Mark off $EK = x$, $EG = n$, and $GH = m$.

Join G to K and construct $HT \parallel GK$.

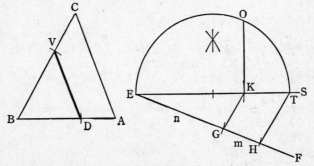

Fig. 35.

Construct semicircle on ET as diameter and $KO \perp ET$.

$EG : GH = EK : KT = \overline{EK}^2 : \overline{EK} \times \overline{KT} = \overline{EK}^2 : \overline{OK}^2$ or
  $n : m = x^2 : \overline{OK}^2$.

Construct a third proportional y such that $BD : OK = OK : y$.

Mark off $BV = y$; then DV is the required line.

Proof: $\overline{OK}^2 = \overline{BD} \times \overline{BV}$; $x^2 = \overline{AB} \times \overline{BC}$;
  $n : m = \overline{AB} \times \overline{BC} : \overline{BD} \times \overline{BV}$.

Since $\triangle ABC : \triangle BVD = \overline{AB} \times \overline{BC} : \overline{BD} \times \overline{BV}$,

$\therefore \triangle ABC : \triangle BVD = n : m$.

36. Let the given circle have radii OA and $O'B$.

Construct CD, the difference between OA and $O'B$.

With O as center and CD as radius draw inner circle.

Construct $O'M$ tangent to inner circle.

Draw OM and extend it to N. Construct $O'P \perp O'M$.

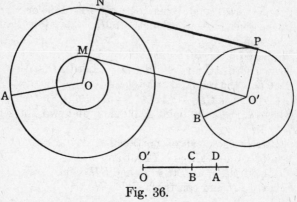

Fig. 36.

NP is the required tangent.

A similar tangent can be drawn on the lower parts of the circles.

Proof: Since $MN \perp O'M$, $MN = O'P$, and $MN \parallel O'P$,

$\therefore MO'PN$ is a $\square$ and $NP \parallel MO'$.

Also $NP \perp NO$ and $NP \perp PO'$.

$\therefore NP$ is a tangent.

37. Let OA and $O'B$ be the radii of the given circles.

Construct $CD = OA + O'B$.

With O' as center and $r = CD$ draw the outer circle.

Construct OM, tangent from O to the outer circle.

Draw $O'M$ cutting the inner circle at P.

Construct $ON \perp OM$ and connect N with P.

NP is the required tangent.

Another internal tangent may be drawn in a similar manner. The proof is similar to that in the preceding problem.

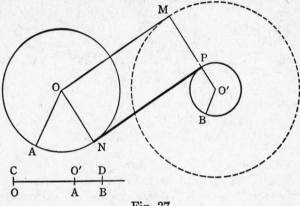

Fig. 37.

38. Construct *GOH*, the bisector of $\angle COB$ and *AOD*.

Since $\angle COB$ must be one angle of the square and the bisector of an angle of a square is the diagonal of the square, then one vertex of all possible squares in the first and third quadrants must lie on *GOH*.

Construct a perpendicular to *OB* at *M*, meeting *OH* at *K*.

Construct $JK \perp KM$. At *N* construct $NP \perp OD$ and the square *NPRO*.

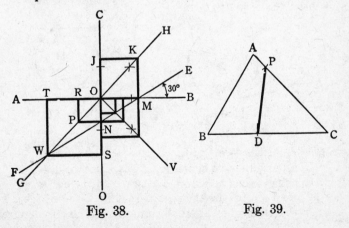

Fig. 38.   Fig. 39.

At W construct $WS \perp OD$ and the square $SWTO$.

Similarly, construct OV, the bisector of $\angle BOD$, and the three squares shown in Fig. 38 that have OV as a diagonal.

$\therefore$ there are six squares.

39. Construct the fourth proportional so that $2\,PC : AC = BC : x$ On CB mark off $CD = x$. PD is the required line.

Proof: Since $\angle PCD$ is common to $\triangle PCD$ and ABC,

$$\triangle PCD : \triangle ABC = \overline{PC} \times \overline{DC} : \overline{AC} \times \overline{BC}$$
$$= \overline{PC} \times \overline{DC} : 2\,\overline{PC} \times \overline{DC} = 1 : 2.$$

40. Given two points P and Q such that $PQ = c$ and two distances a and b.

To construct a straight line so that its distance from P shall be a and its distance from Q shall be b.

Case I: $c > a + b$.

Construct a circle with P as center and $r = a$.

Construct a circle with Q as center and $r = b$.

Construct two internal tangents and two external tangents. [See Probs. 36 and 37, this section.]

These four tangents are the required lines.

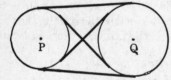

Case I   Case III

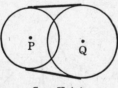

Case II (a)   Case II (b)

Fig. 40.

Case II: $c < a + b$.

Construct the two circles as in Case I.

Construct the two external tangents to the circles.

These tangents are the required lines.

If the circles are internally tangent the external tangents

degenerate into a common tangent at the point of tangency
of the circles.

Case III: $c = a + b.$

Construct the two circles as in Case I; these circles will now
be externally tangent since $c = a + b.$

Construct the two external tangents and the one internal
tangent to the circles. These three tangents are the
required lines.

41. Given the semicircle with AB as diameter.

Construct $AC \perp AB$ and $AC = AB.$

Draw CO cutting semicircle at $M.$

Construct $MN \perp AB$ and mark off $OP = ON.$

Construct $PR \perp AB$; then $MNPR$ is the required square.

Proof: $MN \parallel AC$ since both are $\perp AB.$

$\therefore AC : AO = MN : NO = 2 : 1$ since $AC = AB = 2\,AO.$

Then, since $NO = \frac{1}{2}\,MN$ and $NO = OP,$ $NP = MN.$

Since $\overline{MO}^2 - \overline{NO}^2 = \overline{OR}^2 - \overline{OP}^2,$ $\overline{MN}^2 = \overline{RP}^2$ or $MN = RP.$

$MN \parallel RP$ since both are $\perp AB;$ $\therefore MR = NP.$

We thus have $MN = NP = MR = RP$ and $MNPR$ is a
square.

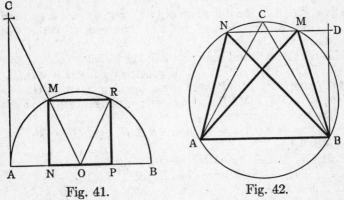

Fig. 41.   Fig. 42.

42. Construct $AB = 5$ units.

Construct the equilateral $\triangle ABC$; then $\angle ACB = 60°.$

Circumscribe a circle about $\triangle ABC.$

At B construct $BD \perp AB$ and $BD = 4$ units.

At D construct $DMN \perp DB.$

The $\triangle AMB$ and ANB are the required triangles.

43. See Example 3, Chapter V.

44. Given the chord AB in the circle O.

Divide AB in the ratio $2 : 3$ so that $AM : MB = 2 : 3$.

Construct the $\perp$ bis. of chord AB and extend to N.

Join N to M and extend to P. P is the required point.

Proof: N is the midpoint of major arc AB; $\therefore$ $AN = NB$.

Then $\angle APM = \angle MPB$.

$\therefore$ $AM : MB = AP : PB = 2 : 3$.

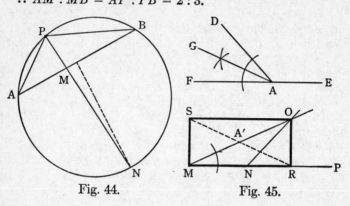

Fig. 44.   Fig. 45.

45. Given $BC = d$, the difference of two sides of a rectangle, and $\angle DAE =$ angle formed by the intersection of the two diagonals.

Extend EA to F and construct AG, the bis. of $\angle DAF$.

Construct $MN = BC$ and at M construct $\angle NMO = \angle DAG$.

At N construct $\angle ONP = 45°$, thus locating the point O.

Construct $OR \perp MNP$ and complete rectangle $MROS$; this is the required rectangle.

Proof: Since $\angle ONR = 45°$ and $OR \perp NP$, $\angle NOR = 45°$ and $NR = OR$.

$\therefore MN = MR - NR = MR - OR = d$.

Draw diagonal SR intersecting MO at A'.

In $\triangle MA'R$: $\angle A'MR + \angle A'RM + \angle MA'R = 180°$.

Since SR and MO are diagonals of a rectangle,

$$MA' = A'R \text{ and } \angle A'MR = \angle A'RM.$$

$\therefore 2 \angle A'MR + \angle MA'R = 180°$.

$\angle FAE = 180° = 2 \angle DAG + \angle DAE$.

Then, since $\angle A'MR = \angle DAG$, $\angle MA'R = \angle DAE$.

$\therefore$ rectangle $MROS$ satisfies the given data.

46. Given the line CD and the points A and B.

Join B to A and extend BA to M on the line CD.

Construct the mean proportional MN to MB and MA.

Pass a circle through A, B, and N. This is the required circle.

[Since a tangent is the mean proportional between the external segment and the whole secant, MN (and $\therefore$ CD) is tangent to the circle.]

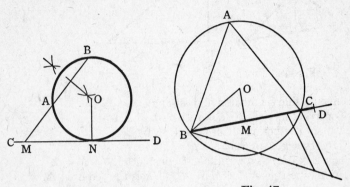

Fig. 46.   Fig. 47.

47. Given the circle O with $r = 1$ in. and the inscribed equilateral triangle ABC.

Construct $OM \perp BC$. $\triangle OMB$ is a 30°, 60°, 90° $\triangle$.

$OB = r = 1$; $OM = \frac{1}{2}$; and $BM = \frac{1}{2}\sqrt{3}$. $\therefore BC = \sqrt{3}$.
[See Prob. 11, Chap. VIII.]

Area of $\triangle ABC = \frac{1}{4}s^2\sqrt{3}$ (where s = one side) = $\frac{3}{4}\sqrt{3}$. [See Prob. 12, Chap. VIII.]

$\therefore$ area of desired isos. $\triangle = (\frac{3}{2})(\frac{3}{4})\sqrt{3} = \frac{9}{8}\sqrt{3}$
$$= \frac{1}{2}(\text{base})(\text{altitude}) = \frac{1}{2}(2)(h) = h.$$

$\therefore$ altitude $= \frac{9}{8}\sqrt{3} = \sqrt{3} + \frac{1}{8}\sqrt{3} = BC + \frac{1}{8}BC$.

Divide BC into 8 equal parts and add one part to BC, thus obtaining the altitude, BD.

48. Given the line segments p, q, and m.

Construct $AB = 2q$ and let O be its midpoint.

With O as center and $r = p$ draw an arc.

With A as center and $r = 2m$ draw an arc intersecting first arc at C.

Join O and A to C and from O construct $OD \parallel AC$.

$\triangle OCB$ is the required $\triangle$ and OD is the median.

[Since $OD \parallel AC$ and O is midpoint of AB, D is midpoint of BC and $CD = \frac{1}{2} AC = \frac{1}{2}(2m) = m$.]

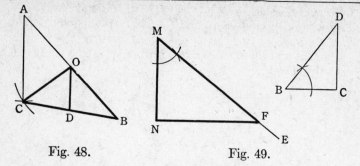

Fig. 48.   Fig. 49.

49. Given a line segment p and an angle A.
    Construct any rt. $\triangle BCD$ with $\angle B = \angle A$.
    Denote the perimeter of this rt. $\triangle$ by p'.
    Construct x such that $p' : p = BC : x$.
    Construct $MN = x$ and at M construct $\angle NME = \angle A$.
    At N construct $NF \perp MN$. $\triangle MNF$ is the required $\triangle$.
50. Given the lines AB and CD.
    Extend CD to intersect AB at M.
    Construct x such that $MC : x = x : MD$.
    Mark off $MN = x$; N is the required point.
    Proof: Draw a circle through N, C, and D. This circle will
      be tangent to AB since $MC : MN = MN : MD$.
    $\therefore \angle CND >$ any other angle, say $\angle CPD$.

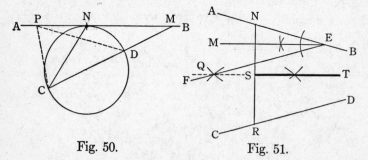

Fig. 50.   Fig. 51.

51. Given the two lines AB and CD.
    Construct $EF \parallel CD$ and intersecting AB at E.
    Construct EM, the bisector of $\angle AEF$.
    From N, any point on AE, construct $NR \perp ME$.
    Construct ST, the $\perp$ bis. of NR. ST is the required line.
    Proof: Let X_1 be the point of intersection of ST and AB.

Let X_2 be the point of intersection of ST and CD.

Since $ME \perp NR$ and $ST \perp NR$, $ME \parallel ST$.

$\therefore \angle NEM = \angle NX_1S$ and $\angle MES = \angle EQS$.

Since $FE \parallel CD$, $\angle EQS = \angle SX_2R = \angle MES$.

But, since $\angle NEM = \angle MES$, then $\angle NX_1S = \angle SX_2R$.

In rt. $\triangle NSX_1$ and RSX_2: $NS = RS$ and $\angle NX_1S = \angle SX_2R$.

$\therefore \triangle NSX_1 \cong \triangle RSX_2$ and $RX_2 = NX_1$.

But then, since X_1 and X_2 both lie on ST, the $\perp$ bis. of NR, we have $X_1 = X_2 = X$.

$\therefore ST$ passes through the point of intersection of AB and CD and since $\angle NXS = \angle SXR$, it bisects $\angle NXR$.

52. Given the chord AB in circle O and a length t.

At any point on circumference draw tangent $MN = t$.

With O as center and $r = ON$ draw a circle meeting extension of AB at D.

Draw tangents ED and DF; these are the required lines.

Proof: $OD = ON =$ radius of larger circle.

$$CD = OD - OC = ON - OP = PN.$$
$$\overline{DF}^2 = \overline{CD} \times \overline{OD} = \overline{PN} \times \overline{ON} = \overline{MN}^2 = t^2.$$
$$\therefore \qquad DF = t.$$

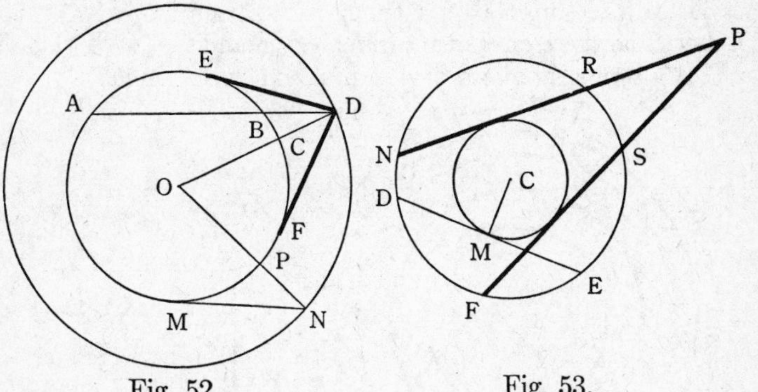

Fig. 52.   Fig. 53.

53. Given circle C, the point P, and a length AB.

Construct chord $DE = AB$ and $CM \perp DE$.

With C as center and $r = CM$ draw inner circle.

Construct PN and PF tangent to inner circle.

These are the required lines.

[$NR = FS = DE = AB$ since they are equidistant from center.]

54. Given $\angle A$, side BC, and square $DEFG$.

Construct $\angle HJK = \angle A$ and extend JK to M.

Divide $\angle MJH$ into any two parts by the line NJ.
At B construct $\angle PBC = \angle NJM$; at C construct
$$\angle PCB = \angle NJH.$$
Then $\angle PBC = \angle A$.

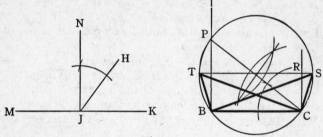

Fig. 54.

Circumscribe a circle about $\triangle BCP$.
Construct y such that $BC : 2\,DG = DG : y$.
At C construct $y = RC \perp BC$.
At R construct $TSR \perp RC$.
The $\triangle BSC$ and BTC are the required triangles.

55. Let C be the center of the given circle and $CA = r$, its radius.
Let y represent the radius of first concentric circle.

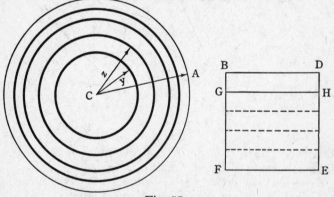

Fig. 55.

Then $\pi y^2 = \frac{1}{5}\pi r^2$ or $y^2 = \frac{1}{5}r^2$.
Construct a square having $BD = CA$ as a side.
Then the area of this square equals $\overline{BD}^2 = \overline{CA}^2 = r^2$.

Measure $BG = \frac{1}{5} BF$ and construct $GH \parallel BD$.

Then $BDHG = \frac{1}{5} r^2 = \overline{BD} \times \overline{BG} = y^2$.

Construct the mean proportional between BD and BG; this mean proportional is y.

Let z be the radius of the second concentric circle, then $z^2 = \frac{2}{5} r^2$ and we may obtain z in the same manner as we did y.

Similarly for the other three concentric circles.

56. Given the $\triangle ABC$ and D, a point on AC.

Construct y such that $3\, AD : AC = AB : y$.

Mark off $AE = y$.

Then $3 \overline{AD} \times \overline{AE} = \overline{AB} \times \overline{AC}$ or $\dfrac{1}{3} = \dfrac{\overline{AD} \times \overline{AE}}{\overline{AB} \times \overline{AC}} = \dfrac{\triangle ADE}{\triangle ABC}$

since two $\triangle$ having an $\angle$ of one $=$ an $\angle$ of the other are to each other as the products of the sides containing the equal angles.

Similarly, construct CF such that $3\, DC : CA = CB : CF$.

DE and DF are the required lines.

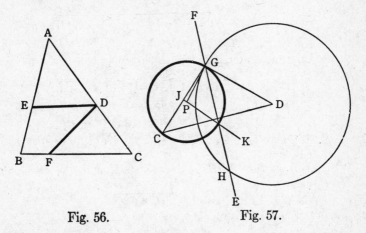

Fig. 56.   Fig. 57.

57. Let C be the given point through which circle must pass.

Let D be the given point from which tangent is to be drawn.

Let AB be the given straight line.

Connect C with D and draw $EF \perp$ bis. of CD.

With D as center and $r = AB$ draw circle cutting EF at G and H.

Construct $JK \perp$ bis. of CG and at G construct $GP \perp GD$ cutting JK at P.

With P as center and $r = CP$ draw the required circle.

Proof: Since P lies on $\perp$ bis. of CG, $CP = PG$ and circle passes through G.

Since $GP \perp GD$, GD is tangent to the circle and it equals AB.

58. Let the given concentric circles have P as the common center. This problem will be done by the backward method and thus will be analyzed first. Suppose A is the required point, then $AB = 2AC$.

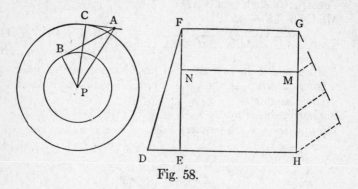

Fig. 58.

Now $\overline{AP}^2 - \overline{BP}^2 = \overline{AB}^2 = 4\,\overline{AC}^2$.

$\overline{AP}^2 - \overline{PC}^2 = \overline{AC}^2$ or $4\,\overline{AP}^2 - 4\,\overline{PC}^2 = 4\,\overline{AC}^2$.

$\therefore \quad \overline{AP}^2 - \overline{BP}^2 = 4\,\overline{AP}^2 - 4\,\overline{PC}^2$

or $\qquad 3\,\overline{AP}^2 = 4\,\overline{PC}^2 - \overline{BP}^2 = (2\,\overline{PC})^2 - \overline{BP}^2$.

Construct rt. $\triangle DEF$ with $DF = 2PC$ and $DE = BP$;

$\therefore \overline{FE}^2 = 3\,\overline{AP}^2$.

Construct square $FGHE$, $GM = \frac{1}{3}GH$, and the rectangle $FGMN$.

$\therefore FGMN = \frac{1}{3}\overline{FE}^2 = \overline{AP}^2 = \overline{FG} \times \overline{GM}$.

$\therefore AP$ is the mean proportional between FG and GM.

Construct this mean proportional and A, the required point, lies at a distance from P equal to this mean proportional.

59. Let AB be the perimeter, $\angle C$, the given vertex angle, and DE, the given altitude.

Construct $\angle FGH = \angle C$.

At G construct $GJ \perp GH$ and $GJ = DE$.

At J construct $JK \perp JG$ meeting GF at K.

From K construct $KM \perp GH$.

On MH mark off $MN = AB - (GK + GM)$.

Connect K with N and construct $\angle NKP = \angle PNK$.
$\triangle GKP$ is the required triangle.

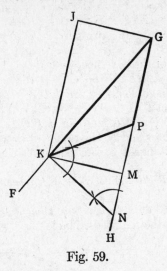

Fig. 59.

Proof: $\angle KGP = \angle FGH = \angle C$.
Altitude $= KM = JG = DE$.
Perimeter $= KG + GP + KP = KG + GP + PM + MN$
$$= KG + GM + AB - (GK + GM) = AB.$$

60. Let us first analyze the problem. Suppose $\triangle DBC$ is the required triangle with $BC = a$, $\angle BDC = \angle A$, and the inscribed circle has a radius equal to r and center at P.

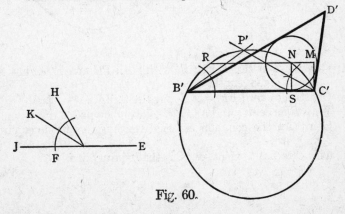

Fig. 60.

$$\angle BPC = 180° - \tfrac{1}{2}(\angle DBC + \angle DCB) = 180° - \tfrac{1}{2}(180° - \angle BDC)$$
$$= 90° + \tfrac{1}{2} \angle BDC = 90° + \tfrac{1}{2} \angle A.$$

We can now proceed with the construction.

Draw any line JFE and construct $\angle HFE = 90° + \tfrac{1}{2} \angle A$.

Divide $\angle HFJ$ into any two parts by KF.

Construct $B'C' = a$, $\angle B' = \angle JFK$, and $\angle C' = \angle KFH$.

Let the sides of these ⊿ meet at P'.

∴ $\angle B'P'C' = \angle HFE = 90° + \tfrac{1}{2} \angle A$.

Circumscribe a circle about $\triangle B'P'C'$.

At C' construct $C'M \perp B'C'$ and $C'M = r$.

Construct $MNR \perp MC'$ and $NS \perp B'C'$.

With N as center and NS as radius draw a circle.

This circle is tangent to $B'C'$ since $NS \perp B'C'$; its radius = $C'M = r$.

$\angle B'NC' = \angle B'P'C'$ since both are measured by major arc $B'C'$.

From B' and C' draw tangents to this circle meeting at D'.

∴ $\triangle B'C'D'$ is the required triangle.

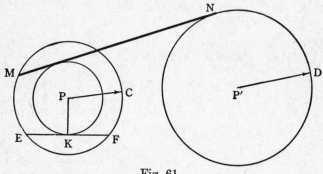

Fig. 61.

61. Given two circles P and P' with radii PC and $P'D$. Let AB
    be the given length.

    Construct chord $EF = AB$ and $PK \perp EF$.

    With P as center and $r = PK$ draw inner circle.

    Construct the common external tangent to this inner circle
    and circle P'.

    This external tangent, MN, is the required line.

SOLUTIONS OF LOCI PROBLEMS

[Chapter VI, pp. 52–54]

1. Let AB be the fixed hypotenuse.
   Construct the rt. $\triangle ACB$ and the median from C to AB.
   It can then be shown that $OC = \frac{1}{2} AB = OA = OB$. [See Prob. 15, Chap. VIII.]
   ∴ the rt. angle vertex C will always be at a distance OA from O.
   ∴ the locus is the circle having AB as its diameter, except for the points A and B since at these points we would not have a triangle.

2. See Example 1, Chapter VI.

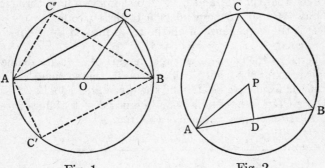

Fig. 1.   Fig. 2.

3. Given the fixed points A and B such that $AB = 8$ in.
   Draw the equilateral $\triangle ABC$; then $\angle BCA = 60°$.
   Circumscribe a circle about $\triangle ABC$; call its center P.
   Since $\angle BCA = 60°$, any angle whose vertex lies on the major arc AB and whose sides pass through A and B equals $60°$.
   Draw $PD \perp AB$ and connect A and P.
   $\triangle APD$ is a $90°$, $60°$, $30°$ $\triangle$ with $AD = 4$.
   ∴ $PD = \frac{4}{3}\sqrt{3}$ and $PA = r = \frac{8}{3}\sqrt{3}$. [See Prob. 11, Chap. VIII.]

4. Let the given circles have centers at C and C' and be tangent at D.

Draw the common internal tangent *MDN*.

On *MN* choose any point *P* and draw tangents *PA* and *PB*. Since tangents from the same point to a circle are equal, *PA = PD = PB*.

∴ the locus is the line *MN*, the common internal tangent.

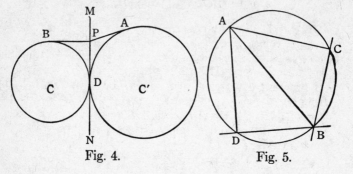

Fig. 4.   Fig. 5.

5. Given the points *A* and *B*. Fig. 5 shows two lines through *B*. Draw *AC* and *AD* perpendicular to these two lines.

AB is the hypotenuse of all the rt. ⩜ formed by the perpendiculars.

Therefore the locus is a circle having *AB* as its diameter, except for the point *A*. [See Prob. 1, this section.]

6. Let the fixed base be *AB* and the given area equal to △*ABC*. Draw *CD* ⊥ *AB*. The locus is composed of two lines parallel to *AB* and at a distance of *CD* from *AB*.

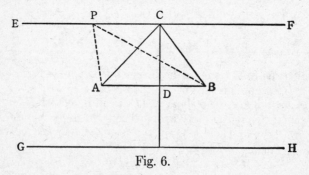

Fig. 6.

Proof: Given area $= \frac{1}{2}(\overline{CD} \times \overline{AB})$.

Draw *ECF* ∥ *AB* and let *P* be any point on *EF*.

Connect *P* with *A* and *B*.

Area of $\triangle APB = \frac{1}{2}$(altitude)(base)

$\qquad = \frac{1}{2}(\overline{CD})(\overline{AB}) =$ given area.

Similarly, for any point on $GH \parallel AB$.

7. Given the base AB and the vertex angle DCE.
   Extend EC to M and divide $\angle DCM$ into any two parts by NC.
   Construct $\triangle BAF$ with $\angle BAF = \angle MCN$, $\angle ABF = \angle NCD$.

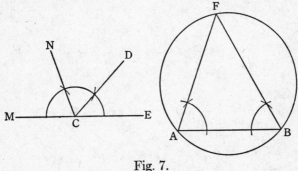

Fig. 7.

Then $\angle BFA = \angle DEC$ since $\angle ECM = 180°$.

Circumscribe a circle about $\triangle ABF$.

The locus is the arc AFB except for the end points.

Any angle with vertex on arc AFB and sides passing through A and B will equal $\angle AFB$ since it also will be measured by minor arc AB.

8. Given the circle C and chord AB of a given length.
   Draw $CD \perp AB$, then $AD = \frac{1}{2} AB$.
   Since P divides AB in the ratio $1 : 3$, $AP = \frac{1}{4} AB$.
   $\therefore PD = \frac{1}{2} AB - \frac{1}{4} AB = \frac{1}{4} AB$ and $\overline{CP}^2 = \overline{CD}^2 + \frac{1}{16} \overline{AB}^2$.
   Draw $A'B' = AB$ and $CD' \perp A'B'$.
   Then $CD' = CD$; $P'D' = \frac{1}{4} A'B' = \frac{1}{4} AB$;
   and $\overline{CP'}^2 = \overline{CD}^2 + \frac{1}{16} \overline{AB}^2$.
   $\therefore \quad CP = CP'$.
   The locus is a circle having C as center and $r = CP$.

9. Let the given square be $ACDB$.
   The locus is composed of four straight lines and four quadrant arcs, the four st. lines EF, GH, JK, and MN lying 2 ft. away from the nearest sides of the square and comprehended between the extensions of the sides, and the quadrants having radii of 2 ft. and centers at the corners of the square.

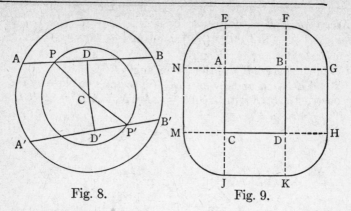

Fig. 8.   Fig. 9.

Area enclosed by the locus
  = square $ABCD$ + 4 equal rectangles $BGHD$, ... + 4 equal
    quadrants BFG, ...
  = $3^2 + 4(2 \times 3) + 4[\frac{1}{4}\pi(2)^2]$
  = $9 + 24 + 4\pi = 33 + 4\pi = 45.5664$ sq. ft.

10. From the point A draw any line to BC, for example AE.
    Let M divide AE into the ratio of $c : d$.
    Draw the lines AB and AC.
    Through M draw $DF \parallel BC$.
    Since a line parallel to the base of a triangle divides the sides
      into proportional parts, the required locus is the line DF.

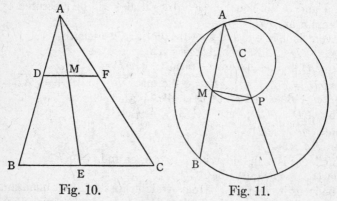

Fig. 10.   Fig. 11.

11. Let P be the center of the given circle and pick any point A.
    Draw the diameter AP and any chord AB.
    Let M be the midpoint of AB.

Since PM is the $\perp$ bis. of AB, $\angle AMP$ is a rt. $\angle$.

∴ the locus is a circle having AP as its diameter, except for the point A. [See Prob. 1, this section.]

12. Let the given segment be included between arc ACB and chord AB.

Since $CP = CB$, $\angle CPB = \angle CBP$ and $\angle ACB = 2\angle CPB$.

∴ $\angle CPB = \frac{1}{2}\angle ACB$ and the locus of P is the major arc of a circle having AB as its chord and having minor arc $= \angle ACB$.

To draw this locus proceed as in Prob. 7, this section.

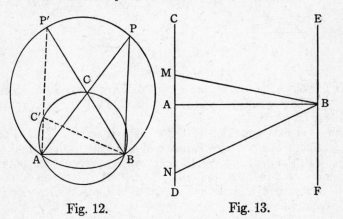

Fig. 12.   Fig. 13.

13. Let A and B be the given points.

The locus consists of the perpendiculars at A and B to the line joining A with B.

Proof: Draw AB, $CD \perp AB$ at A, and $EF \perp AB$ at B.

Consider any two points M and N on CD.

$\overline{MB}^2 - \overline{MA}^2 = \overline{AB}^2$ and $\overline{NB}^2 - \overline{AN}^2 = \overline{AB}^2$.

Since AB is a constant each of these differences equals a constant.

14. Given the base $AB = 4$ inches, the rectangle $CDEF$, and the acute $\angle EGD$.

By Prob. 7, this section, construct arc AJB which is the locus of all angles equal to $\angle EGD$.

Let P be the center of the inscribed circle of $\triangle ABJ$.

Then $\angle APB = 180° - (\frac{1}{2}\angle JAB + \frac{1}{2}\angle ABJ)$

$\qquad\qquad = 180° - \frac{1}{2}(180° - \angle AJB) = 90° + \frac{1}{2}\angle AJB$.

∴ $\angle APB$ is a constant.

By Prob. 7, this section, construct the locus of P.

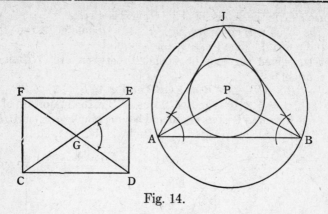

Fig. 14.

The locus is the minor arc of a circle having AB as its chord and having a major arc $= 2(90° + \frac{1}{2} \angle AJB)$.

15. See Example 3, Chapter II.

16. Since in every position of CD a right triangle is formed in which CD is the hypotenuse and since the median from O to P, the midpoint of CD, is always equal to $\frac{1}{2}$ the hypotenuse or 8 in. (see Prob. 15, Chap. VIII), the locus is the quadrant of a circle having O as its center and a radius equal to 8 in.

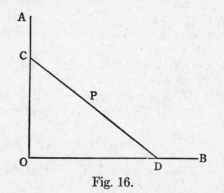

Fig. 16.

17. The locus is the $\perp$ bis. of the line joining the centers of the given circles.
    Proof: Given two equal circles whose centers are P and P'. Draw the line PP' and $CD \perp$ bis. of PP'.

Choose any point A on CD; draw AP intersecting circle P
at M and AP' intersecting circle P' at N.

Since $PM = P'N$ and $AP = AP'$, $AM = AN$.

Draw a circle with A as center and AM as radius.

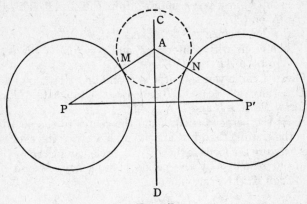

Fig. 17.

The circle will be tangent to circle P as a perpendicular to PM
at M also will be perpendicular to AM at M since PMA
is a straight line. Similarly, it is also tangent to circle P'.

18. Case I. If the given lines, AB and CD, intersect at E, the
locus consists of the bisectors of the angles at E except for
the point E (see Prob. 1, this section), since the bisector of
an angle is the locus of all points equally distant from the
sides.

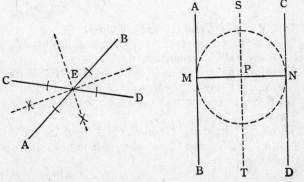

Fig. 18.

Case II. If AB and CD do not intersect, the locus is a line parallel to AB and CD and lying halfway between them.

Proof: Draw $ST \parallel AB \parallel CD$ and halfway between AB and CD.

From P, any point on ST, drop $PM \perp AB$ and extend to N on CD.

$PN \perp CD$ since $AB \parallel CD$ and $PM = PN$.

∴ a circle with center at P and $r = PM = PN$ is tangent to both AB and CD.

19. Given a circle whose center is P and an external point A.

Draw any two secants AB and AD; also tangents AM and AN. Draw $PC \perp AB$ and $PC' \perp AD$.

Since the perpendiculars from the center to the chords bisect the chords, C and C' are the midpoints of the chords.

Therefore the locus is the arc of a circle having AP as diameter and bounded by the points of tangency, M and N. [See Prob. 1, this section.]

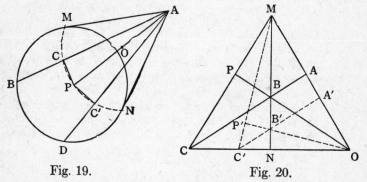

Fig. 19.   Fig. 20.

20. In $\triangle MCO$, MN and CA are altitudes.

Since altitudes are concurrent OP must also be an altitude.

Similarly, OP' is an altitude in $\triangle MC'O$.

Therefore the locus is a semicircle having MO for its diameter, except for the points M and O. [See Prob. 1, this section.]

21. Let C be the center of the given circle and let P be the given point.

Through P draw any chord ED and the diameter AB.

Let A', D', B', and E' be the midpoints of their respective segments.

Since $A'P = \frac{1}{2} AP$ and $PB' = \frac{1}{2} PB$, then $A'P + PB' = \frac{1}{2} AB = AC = r$.

$A'B' = A'C + CB' = A'C + AA'$; $\therefore CB' = AA' = A'P$.

Let F be the midpoint of $A'B'$.

Then $A'P + PF = FC + CB'$ and $PF = FC$.

$\therefore FE' = \frac{1}{2}CE = \frac{1}{2}r$. Similarly, $FD' = \frac{1}{2}r$.

Similarly with all chords through P.

Therefore the locus is a circle having a radius equal to $E'F$ or one-half radius of original circle and having its center situated midway between the dividing points A' and B' on the diameter of the original circle drawn through P,

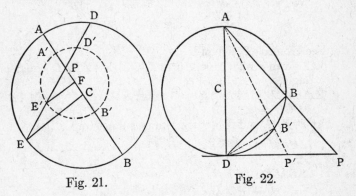

Fig. 21.   Fig. 22.

22. Let C be the center of the given circle; then the locus of P is the tangent to the circle at D, the extremity of the diameter ACD.

   Proof: $DB \perp AP$ since $\angle ABD$ is inscribed in semicircle ABD.

   ADP is a rt. $\triangle$ since DP is tangent to circle.

   $\therefore \overline{AD}^2 = \overline{AP} \times \overline{AB}$.

   Similarly, $\overline{AD}^2 = \overline{AP'} \times \overline{AB'}$.

   $\therefore \overline{AP} \times \overline{AB} = \overline{AP'} \times \overline{AB'} = $ constant.

23. Let EF be the given fixed base and let the square $ABCD$ be the given constant.

   Draw $GH = AB$ and at G draw $GJ \perp GH$ and $GJ = EF$.

   Draw $\angle JHK = \angle KJH$; $\therefore KH = KJ$.

   Also $\overline{KH}^2 - \overline{KG}^2 = \overline{GH}^2$ or $\overline{KJ}^2 - \overline{KG}^2 = \overline{GH}^2$.

   Measure off on EF, $EM = KG$ and $MF = KJ$.

   The perpendicular to EF at M is the required locus.

   $\overline{NF}^2 = \overline{MF}^2 + \overline{NM}^2$ and $\overline{NE}^2 = \overline{EM}^2 + \overline{NM}^2$.

   $\therefore \overline{NF}^2 - \overline{NE}^2 = \overline{MF}^2 - \overline{EM}^2 = \overline{KJ}^2 - \overline{KG}^2 = \overline{GH}^2 = \overline{AB}^2$

   $= $ constant.

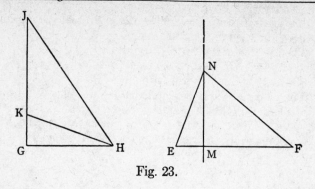

Fig. 23.

24. See Example 2, Chapter II.
25. Let given circle have center C and let $\angle BAD$ equal given angle.

Extend DA to M; at C construct $\angle ECF = \angle MAB$ and $\angle GCH = \angle MAB$.

At E, F, G, and H construct tangents meeting at J and K.

∴ $\angle GKH = \angle EJF = \angle BAD$, $\overset{\frown}{EF} = \overset{\frown}{GH}$, and chord EF = chord GH.

∴ $\triangle EJF \cong \triangle GKH$.

$\overline{JC}^2 = \overline{EJ}^2 + \overline{EC}^2$ and $\overline{CK}^2 = \overline{GC}^2 + \overline{GK}^2$.

∴ $\overline{JC}^2 = \overline{CK}^2$ or $JC = CK$.

Therefore the locus is a circle having CK as radius and center at C.

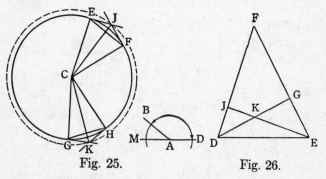

Fig. 25.   Fig. 26.

26. Let DE be the given base and $\angle C$, the vertex angle.
Fig. 26 shows one position with $\angle DFE = \angle C$.
JE and DG are altitudes meeting at K.

$\angle JKG = 180° - \angle DFE$ and $\therefore \angle DKE = 180° - \angle DFE$.

$\therefore \angle DKE$ is known and the problem is like Prob. 7, this section; the locus is the arc constructed upon DE and containing angles equal to DKE.

27. Let $PA = PN$; then $\angle PAN = \angle PNA$.

$\angle MPN = \angle PAN + \angle PNA = 2\angle PAN$.

$\therefore \angle PAN = \frac{1}{2} \angle MPN$.

Then since $\angle MPN$ is known $\angle PAN$ is known and the problem is like Prob. 7, this section, with MN as the given base and $\angle PAN$ as the vertex angle.

The locus is the arc constructed on MN as a chord and containing angles equal to angle PAN.

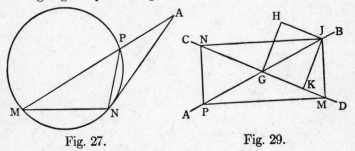

Fig. 27.   Fig. 29.

28. See Example 2, Chapter VI.

29. Given two intersecting lines AB and CD, and EF, a given length.

Draw $GH = EF$ and $GH \perp GD$.

Draw $HJ \perp GH$ and $JK \perp GD$.

$\therefore JK = HG = EF$. Mark off $GM = GJ$.

JM is part of the required locus since $\triangle GJM$ is an isosceles $\triangle$ and by Prob. 25, Chap. VIII, the sum of the distances of any point on JM to GJ and GM is equal to JK or EF.

Mark off GN and GP equal to GJ or GM; then NP is another part of the locus.

Similarly, NJ and PM are parts of the locus.

The whole locus is the parallelogram $NPMJ$.

30. See Example 3, Chapter VI.

31. Draw $BG \perp CD$ and $AR \perp EF$.

Take M any point on BS; draw $MN \perp CD$, $MP \perp EF$, and $BK \perp MN$.

Since $BGNK$ is a rectangle, $NK = BG$.

Since $BK \parallel CD$, $\angle KBM = \angle OAB = \angle OBA = \angle PBM$.

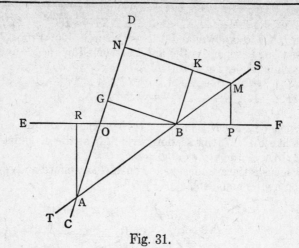

Fig. 31.

$\therefore$ rt. $\triangle KBM \cong$ rt. $\triangle MBP$ and $KM = MP$.

$NM - MP = NM - KM = NK = BG$.

Similarly with every point on BS.

Similarly, we can prove that every point on AT has distances from EF and CD whose difference equals AR, but $AR = BG$ since in rt. $\triangle ARO$ and OGB, $OA = OB$ and $\angle ROA = \angle GOB$.

32. Let the given circle have center at C; let AB be the given fixed line.

Draw $CD \parallel AB$ and extend so that $DE = AB$.

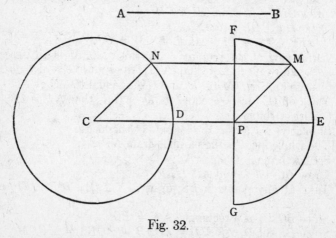

Fig. 32.

Mark off $CP = AB$.

The locus is the semicircle having P as its center, PE as its radius, and $FPG \perp CE$ as its diameter.

Proof: Consider any point M on the circumference.

Draw PM, $CN \parallel PM$, and join M to N.

Since $CP = AB$ and $DE = AB$, $CP = DE$ and $CD = PE$.

$\therefore PM = CN$.

Since $PM \parallel CN$, $PMNC$ is a parallelogram.

$\therefore MN \parallel CP \parallel AB$ and $MN = CP = AB$.

SOLUTIONS OF PROBLEMS ON POLYGONS

[Chapter VII, pp. 57–61]

1. Given the trapezoid $ABCD$ with $DC = 15$ in., $AB = 9$ in., and the altitude $MN = 4$ in.

   Extend the sides AD and BC to form $\triangle AEB$ and EDC.

   The altitudes are EN and EM.

   Since $AB \parallel DC$, $\triangle AEB \sim \triangle EDC$.

   $\therefore EM : EN = AB : DC$ or $EM : EM + 4 = 9 : 15$.

   $\therefore 15\,EM = 9\,EM + 36$ or $6\,EM = 36$ and $EM = 6$.

   $\therefore EN = EM + 4 = 6 + 4 = 10$.

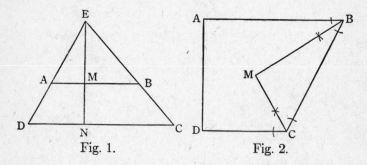

Fig. 1.   Fig. 2.

2. Given quad. $ABCD$ with $\angle BAD = \angle ADC = 90°$.

   Since sum of $\angle$ of quad. $= 360°$, $\angle ABC + \angle DCB = 180°$.

   $\therefore \frac{1}{2} \angle ABC + \frac{1}{2} \angle DCB = 90°$ or $\angle MBC + \angle MCB = 90°$.

   $\therefore \angle BMC = 90°$ since sum of $\angle$ in a $\triangle$ equals $180°$.

3. See Example 1, Chapter VII.

4. Since the angles form an arithmetic progression, their sum is given by

   $$\frac{n}{2} [2a + (n-1)d] = \frac{n}{2} [240 + (n-1)5] = \frac{n}{2} (235 + 5n).$$

   The sum of the angles of a polygon is also equal to $180(n-2)$.

   $\therefore 180(n-2) = \frac{n}{2} (235 + 5n);$

   $360n - 720 = 235n + 5n^2;$

   $n^2 - 25n + 144 = 0;$ $(n-16)(n-9) = 0.$

   $\therefore n = 16$ and 9.

152

5. Since $EB = BF$ and $\angle EBF = 90°$, $\angle BEF = \angle BFE = 45°$.
Similarly, $\angle AEH = 45°$.
$\therefore$ $\angle HEF = 180° - (\angle AEH + \angle BEF) = 180° - 90° = 90°$.
Similarly, $\angle EFG$, FGH, and GHE are each $90°$.
Since $BE = AE$, $BF = AH$, and $\angle ABC = \angle BAD$, $\triangle BEF \cong$
$\triangle EAH$.
$\therefore$ $EF = EH$. Similarly, $EH = HG = GF$.
$\therefore$ $EFGH$ is a square.
In rt. $\triangle EBF$: $\overline{EF}^2 = \overline{EB}^2 + \overline{BF}^2 = 2\,\overline{EB}^2$. $\therefore$ $EF = EB\sqrt{2}$.
Area of $EFGH = (\overline{EB}\sqrt{2})^2 = 2\,\overline{EB}^2$.
Area of $ABCD = \overline{AB}^2 = (2\,\overline{EB})^2 = 4\,\overline{EB}^2$.
$\therefore$ Area of $EFGH = \frac{1}{2}$ area of $ABCD$.

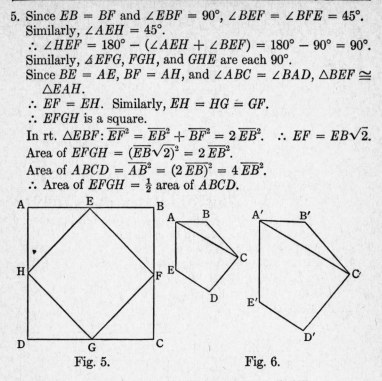

Fig. 5.   Fig. 6.

6. Since the polygons are similar, $\triangle ABC \sim \triangle A'B'C'$.
$\therefore$ $AB : A'B' = AC : A'C'$. But $\overline{AB}^2 : \overline{A'B'}^2 = 18 : 32$.
$\therefore$ $\overline{AC}^2 : \overline{A'C'}^2 = 18 : 32$ or $36 : \overline{A'C'}^2 = 18 : 32$.
Then $\overline{A'C'}^2 = 64$ or $A'C' = 8$.

7. Given the rectangle $ABCD$ and AM, BM, DN, and CN, the
bisectors of the angles.
Since $\angle FAD = \angle FDA = 45°$, $\angle FAD + \angle FDA = 90°$.
$\therefore$ $\angle AFD = 90°$ and $\angle NFM = 90°$.
Similarly, $\angle NEM = 90°$.
Since in $\triangle NDC$, $\angle NDC$ and NCD are each $45°$, $\angle DNC = 90°$.
Similarly, $\angle AMB = 90°$.
$\therefore$ $NEMF$ is a parallelogram.
$\triangle AFD \cong \triangle BEC$; $\therefore$ $DF = EC$.
Since $\angle NDC = \angle NCD$, $ND = NC$.
$\therefore$ $ND - DF = NC - EC$ and $NE = NF$.
Also $NE = EM = NF = FM$.

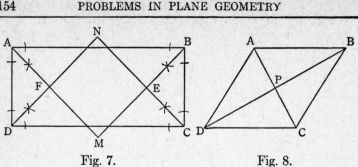

Fig. 7.   Fig. 8.

8. Given the rhombus $ABCD$ and the diagonals intersecting at P.
Since $AD = AB$ and $CD = CB$, AP is $\perp$ bis. of DB.

$\therefore$ area of $\triangle ADB = \frac{1}{2}\,\overline{DB} \times \overline{AP}$ and area of $\triangle CDB = \frac{1}{2}\,\overline{DB} \times \overline{PC}$.

$\therefore \ \triangle ADB + \triangle CDB = \frac{1}{2}\,\overline{DB}(\overline{AP} + \overline{PC}) = \frac{1}{2}\,\overline{DB} \times \overline{AC}$
$= $ area of rhombus.

9. Since $AE \parallel DB$, $\angle FAE = \angle ADB$.
Since $AB = AD$, $\angle ADB = \angle ABD$ and $\angle FAE = \angle ABD$.
Now $\angle ABD = \angle EAB = \angle FEA$.

$\therefore \ \angle FAE = \angle FEA$ and $FE = FA$.

$\therefore \ \triangle FAE$ is isosceles.

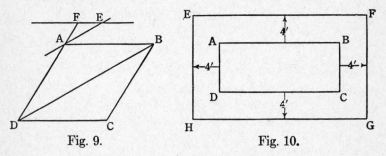

Fig. 9.   Fig. 10.

10. Let $ABCD$ be the rectangle and let $EFGH$ be the outer border
of the flower bed; let $AB = x$ ft. and $BC = y$ ft.
Area of lawn $= xy = 126$. $EF = x + 8$ and $FG = y + 8$.
Area of $EFGH = (x + 8)(y + 8)$.

$$
\begin{aligned}
\therefore \ (x + 8)(y + 8) - xy &= 264; & xy &= 126; \\
xy + 8y + 8x + 64 - xy &= 264; & x(25 - x) &= 126; \\
8(y + x) &= 200; & 25x - x^2 &= 126; \\
y + x &= 25; & x^2 - 25x + 126 &= 0; \\
y &= 25 - x; & (x - 18)(x - 7) &= 0.
\end{aligned}
$$

$\therefore x = 18$ or 7 and $y = 7$ or 18.

$\therefore$ the lawn is 18 ft. by 7 ft.

11. Given the quadrilateral $ABCD$ such that the opposite angles are supplementary.

Let O be the center of the circle passing through A, B, and C. This circle passes either above D, through D, or under D. Suppose it passes above D through E and F.

$\angle AEC + \angle ABC = \frac{1}{2}(\text{arc } ABC + \text{arc } AEC) = \frac{1}{2}(360°) = 180°$.

$\therefore \angle AEC = \angle ADC$ since both are supplementary to $\angle ABC$. But this is absurd since $\angle AEC$ is external angle of $\triangle ADE$, and

$\qquad \therefore \angle AEC > \angle ADC$.

Similarly, the circle cannot pass under D.

$\therefore$ the circle passes through D.

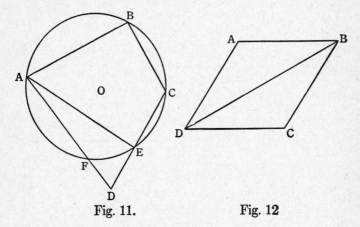

Fig. 11.   Fig. 12

12. Given rhombus $ABCD$ and diagonal BD.

Since $AB = AD$, $\angle ADB = \angle ABD$.

Since $AB \parallel DC$, $\angle BDC = \angle ABD$.

$\therefore \angle ADB = \angle BDC$.

Similarly for the other angles.

13. Let $ABCD$ be the given quadrilateral with E, F, G, and J as midpoints of the respective sides.

Then $FG \parallel AC$ and $FG = \frac{1}{2} AC$.

Similarly, $EJ \parallel AC$ and $EJ = \frac{1}{2} AC$.

$\therefore FG = EJ$ and $FG \parallel EJ$.

$\therefore FGJE$ is a parallelogram.

$FG = \frac{1}{2} AC$, $JG = \frac{1}{2} DB$, $EJ = \frac{1}{2} AC$, and $EF = \frac{1}{2} DB$.

$\therefore FG + JG + EJ + EF = AC + DB$.

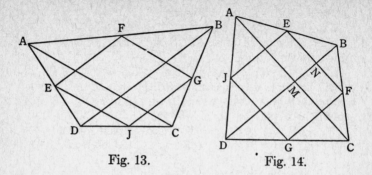

Fig. 13. Fig. 14.

14. Let $ABCD$ be the given quadrilateral and E, F, G, and J, the midpoints of the respective sides.

Since $EF \parallel AC$, $\triangle BEF \sim \triangle BAC$, $EF = \frac{1}{2} AC$, and $BN = \frac{1}{2} BM$.

$\therefore \triangle BEF : \triangle ABC = 1 : 4$ or $\triangle BEF = \frac{1}{4} \triangle ABC$.

Similarly, $\triangle AJE = \frac{1}{4} \triangle ADB$; $\triangle JDG = \frac{1}{4} \triangle ADC$, and $\triangle GCF = \frac{1}{4} \triangle CDB$.

$\therefore \triangle BEF + \triangle AJE + \triangle JDG + \triangle GCF$

$= \frac{1}{4}(\triangle ABC + \triangle ADB + \triangle ADC + \triangle CDB)$

$= \frac{1}{4}(2 \text{ quad. } ABCD) = \frac{1}{2} \text{ quad. } ABCD.$

Quad. $JEFG = \text{quad. } ABCD - (\triangle BEF + \triangle AJE + \triangle JDC + \triangle GCF)$

$= \text{quad. } ABCD - \frac{1}{2} \text{ quad. } ABCD$

$= \frac{1}{2} \text{ quad. } ABCD.$

15. Given the regular pentagon $ABCDE$ with diagonals AC and BD intersecting at P.

Since $ABCDE$ is a regular polygon a circle can be circum-

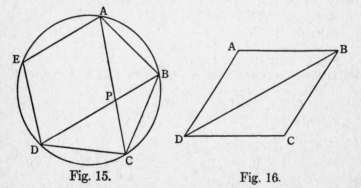

Fig. 15. Fig. 16.

scribed and since the sides of the pentagon are equal, **the** arcs AB, BC, CD, DE, and EA are equal.

$\angle APB = \frac{1}{2} AB + \frac{1}{2} CD$; $\angle ABD = \frac{1}{2} AE + \frac{1}{2} ED$.

$\therefore\ \angle APB = \angle ABD$ and $AP = AB$.

Similarly, $PD = DC$.

16. Given the parallelogram $ABCD$ with $\angle ABD = \angle DBC$.
Since $AB \parallel DC$, $\angle BDC = \angle ABD$.
$\therefore\ \angle BDC = \angle DBC$ and $DC = BC$.
But $BC = AD$; $\therefore\ DC = BC = AD = AB$.

17. Given the hexagon $ABCDEF$ inscribed in circle O.
$\angle A = \frac{1}{2}$ arc $BCDEF$; $\angle C = \frac{1}{2}$ arc $DEFAB$; and
$\angle E = \frac{1}{2}$ arc $FABCD$.

$$\therefore\ \angle A + \angle C + \angle E = \tfrac{1}{2}(\text{arc } BCDEF + \text{arc } DEFAB$$
$$+ \text{arc } FABCD)$$
$$= \tfrac{1}{2}(720°) = 360°.$$

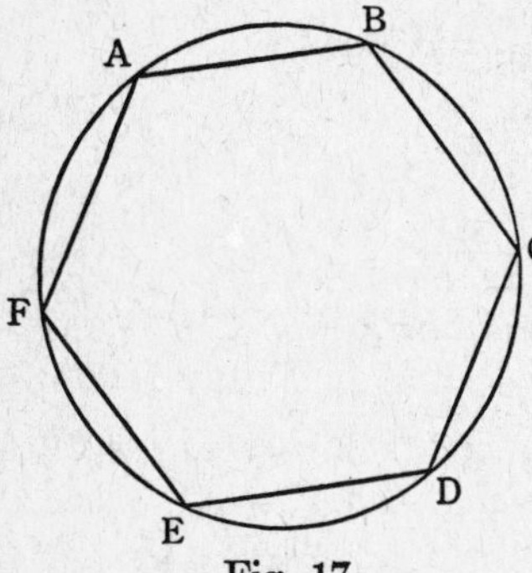

Fig. 17. 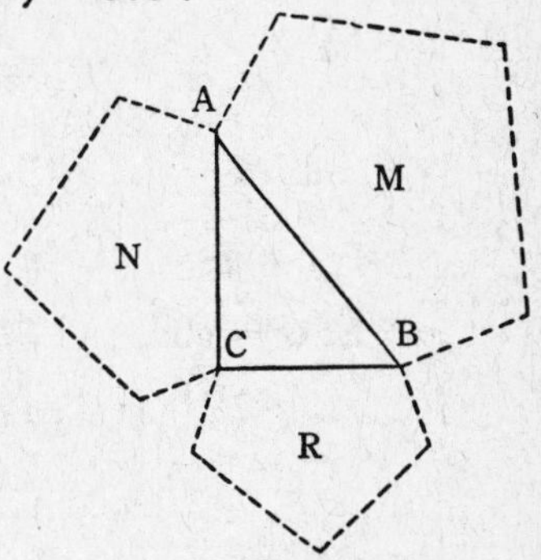   Fig. 18.

18. Given the right $\triangle ACB$.
Call the polygons on AB, AC, and BC, respectively, M, N, and R.

$$\therefore\ \frac{N}{M} = \frac{\overline{AC}^2}{\overline{AB}^2}; \frac{R}{M} = \frac{\overline{BC}^2}{\overline{AB}^2}; \frac{N + R}{M} = \frac{\overline{AC}^2 + \overline{BC}^2}{\overline{AB}^2} = \frac{\overline{AB}^2}{\overline{AB}^2} = 1.$$

$\therefore\ N + R = M$.

19. See Example 2, Chapter VII.

20. Given $\square ABCD$ with $AB = 8$, $BC = 6$, and $AC = 12$.
Draw $AM \perp CD$ extended.
Then in rt. $\triangle ADM$: $36 = \overline{AM}^2 + \overline{MD}^2$.
In rt. $\triangle AMC$:
$$144 = \overline{AM}^2 + (\overline{MD} + 8)^2 = \overline{AM}^2 + \overline{MD}^2 + 16\,MD + 64.$$
$$108 = 16\,MD + 64 \text{ or } MD = \tfrac{44}{16} = \tfrac{11}{4}.$$

$\therefore AM = \sqrt{36 - \frac{121}{16}} = \frac{1}{4}\sqrt{455} = \frac{1}{4}(21.33073).$

$\therefore$ area of $\square ABCD = 8(AM) = 2(21.33073) = 42.6615$ sq. in.

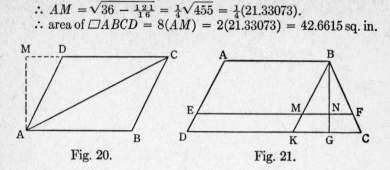

Fig. 20.   Fig. 21.

21. Given trapezoid $ABCD$ with $DC = 10$, $BG \perp DC$ and $BG = 4$, and $EF \parallel DC$ and 1 ft. above DC.

Area of $ABCD = 32 = \frac{1}{2}(10 + AB)4 = 20 + 2AB$, or $AB = 6$.

Draw $BK \parallel AD$; then $DK = 6$ and $KC = 4$.

Since $MF \parallel KC$, $\triangle BMF \sim \triangle BKC$. $\therefore MF : KC = BN : BG$. $BG = 4$ and $NG = 1$. $\therefore BN = 3$.

$\therefore MF : 4 = 3 : 4$ or $MF = 3$.

Since $EM = 6$, then $EM + MF = 9$.

22. Given trapezoid $ABCD$ with $AB = 15$, $DC = 9$, and $CB = DA = 5$.

Draw CM and DN perpendicular to AB.

Since $CB = AD$ and $CM = DN$, rt. $\triangle CMB \cong$ rt. $\triangle AND$.

$\therefore MB = AN = 3$, since $AB = 15$ and $NM = 9$.

$\therefore$ in rt. $\triangle CMB$: $\overline{CM}^2 = 25 - 9 = 16$; $\therefore CM = 4$.

Since $\angle BAC = \angle DCA$ and $\angle DBA = \angle CDB$, $\triangle AEB \sim \triangle DEC$ and $AE : EC = 15 : 9$.

Draw $RS \parallel AB$ and through E.

Then $AE : EC = MV : CB = 15 : 9$ or $9MV = 15CV$ or $CV = \frac{9}{15}MV$.

$\therefore \frac{3}{5}MV + MV = 4$ or $MV = \frac{5}{2}$.

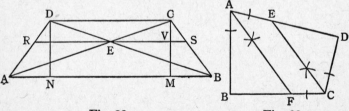

Fig. 22.   Fig. 23.

MV is the altitude of $\triangle AEB$.

∴ area of $\triangle AEB = \frac{1}{2}(15)(\frac{5}{2}) = \frac{75}{4} = 18.75$ sq. ft.

23. Given $ABCD$ with $\angle B = \angle D = 90°$; EC and AF, the bisectors of $\angle BCD$ and DAB. To prove that $EC \parallel AF$.

Since $\angle B + \angle D = 180°$, $\angle BCD + \angle BAD = 180°$.

∴ $\frac{1}{2}\angle BCD + \frac{1}{2}\angle BAD = 90°$ or $\angle BCE + \angle BAF = 90°$.

$\angle BFA + \angle BAF = 90°$ since $\angle B = 90°$.

∴ $\angle BCE = \angle BFA$ and ∴ $EC \parallel AF$.

24. Let $ABCD$ be the given trapezoid and E and F the midpoints

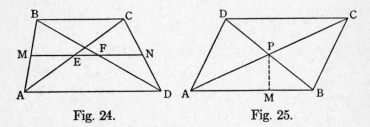

Fig. 24.　　　　　Fig. 25.

of AC and BD; let M be the midpoint of AB.

In $\triangle ABC$, $ME \parallel BC \parallel AD$.

If ME is extended, it must pass through F since in $\triangle ABD$, $MF \parallel AD$ and bisects AB.

∴ $EF = MF - ME = \frac{1}{2}AD - \frac{1}{2}BC$.

25. Let $ABCD$ be the given parallelogram and let $AC = 28$, $DB = 18$, and $AB = 20$.

Area of $\triangle APB = \sqrt{s(s-a)(s-b)(s-c)}$. [See Prob. 79, Chap. VIII.]

Draw $PM \perp AB$; then area of $\triangle APB = 10\,PM$.

∴ $10\,PM = \sqrt{s(s-a)(s-b)(s-c)}$.

$$
\begin{array}{l|l}
a = 20 & s - a = \frac{3}{2} \\
b = 14 & s - b = \frac{15}{2} \\
c = 9 & s - c = \frac{25}{2} \\
\hline
2s = 43 & s = \frac{43}{2} \\
s = \frac{43}{2} &
\end{array}
\quad
\begin{array}{l}
\sqrt{s(s-a)(s-b)(s-c)} \\
= \sqrt{\frac{43}{2}(\frac{3}{2})(\frac{15}{2})(\frac{25}{2})} \\
= \frac{1}{4}(5)(3)\sqrt{215} \\
= \frac{15}{4}\sqrt{215}.
\end{array}
$$

∴ $10\,PM = \frac{15}{4}\sqrt{215}$ and $PM = \frac{3}{8}\sqrt{215} = 5.50$ in.

26. Area of trapezoid $ABCD = \frac{1}{2}(9 + 15)7 = 84$.

Area of $EFGJ = \frac{1}{2}(84) = 42$. [See Prob. 14, this section.]

27. Let regular hexagon be $ABCDEF$ and let $\triangle ACE$ be formed by connecting alternate vertices.

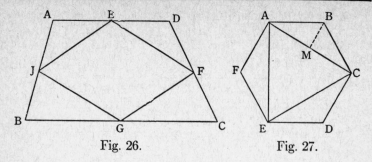

Fig. 26.   Fig. 27.

$$\angle ABC = \frac{180(n-2)°}{n} = \frac{180(4)°}{6} = 120°.$$

Draw $BM \perp AC$; then $\triangle ABM$ is a 90°, 60°, 30° $\triangle$.

$\therefore BM = 2$ and $AM = 2\sqrt{3}$; $\therefore AC = 4\sqrt{3}$. [See Prob. **11**, Chap. VIII.]

Since $\triangle ABC \cong \triangle DEC \cong \triangle AFE$, $AC = CE = AE$.

$\therefore$ area of $\triangle ACE = \frac{48}{4}\sqrt{3} = 12\sqrt{3} = 20.785$ sq. ft.

[See Prob. **12**, Chap. VIII.]

28. Let $AEBFCGDJ$ be the inscribed octagon; $ABCD$, inscribed square; $MRST$, circumscribed square; r = radius of circle having P as center.

In rt. $\triangle APB$: $AB = r\sqrt{2}$.

$\therefore$ area of $ABCD = 2\,r^2$ and $KP = AK = \frac{1}{2}\,r\sqrt{2}$.

$EK = EP - KP = r - \frac{1}{2}\,r\sqrt{2}$.

Area of $\triangle AEB = \overline{AK} \times \overline{EK} = \frac{1}{2}\,r\sqrt{2}(r - \frac{1}{2}\,r\sqrt{2})$

$\qquad = \frac{1}{2}\,r^2(\sqrt{2} - 1).$

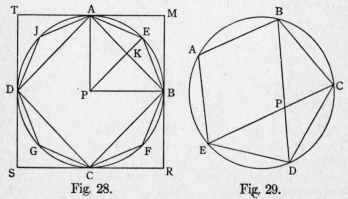

Fig. 28.   Fig. 29.

∴ area of AEB + area of BFC + area of DGC + area of $AJD = 2\,r^2(\sqrt{2} - 1)$.

Area of octagon $= 2\,r^2 + 2\,r^2(\sqrt{2} - 1) = 2\,r^2\sqrt{2}$.

Since $\triangle AMB$ is a 90°, 45°, 45° $\triangle$ and $AB = r\sqrt{2}$, then $MB = r$.

∴ $MR = 2\,r$.

∴ area of rectangle having sides AB and MR
$\quad = (r\sqrt{2})(2\,r) = 2\,r^2\sqrt{2} = $ area of octagon.

29. Since $ABCDE$ is a regular polygon, a circle can be circumscribed about it.

In $\triangle BDC$ and PDC, $\angle PDC$ is common and $\angle DBC = \angle ECD$.

∴ $\triangle DBC \sim \triangle DPC$.

∴ $BD : CD = BC : PC$ or $BD : BC = BC : PC$.

$\angle BCP = \angle BPC$ since they are measured by equal arcs.

∴ $BC = BP$ and similarly $PC = PD$.

∴ $BD : BP = BP : PD$.

30. Let A and B be regular polygons of the same number of sides, with sides, respectively, 5 ft. and 12 ft.

Let s be the side of polygon C, whose area $= A + B$.

Then $A : C = 25 : s^2$ and $B : C = 144 : s^2$.

∴ $(A + B) : C = 169 : s^2$.

But since $A + B = C$ we have $169 = s^2$ or $s = 13$.

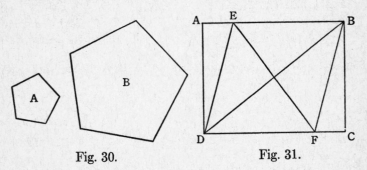

Fig. 30.   Fig. 31.

31. Let $ABCD$ be the given paper with $AB = 24$ and $BC = 18$; let EF be the crease when the paper is folded so that point B falls on point D.

By the process of folding $EB = ED$ and $BF = DF$.

If $AE = x$, then $EB = 24 - x = ED$.

In rt. $\triangle AED$: $x^2 + 18^2 = (24 - x)^2$ and $x = AE = 5\frac{1}{4}$.

∴ $EB = ED = 24 - 5\frac{1}{4} = 18\frac{3}{4}$.

Similarly, if $FC = y$, then $DF = BF = 24 - y$ and in rt. $\triangle BCF$: $18^2 + y^2 = (24 - y)^2$ or $y = 5\frac{1}{4} = FC$ and $BF = 18\frac{3}{4} = DF$.

$\therefore$ $EBFD$ is a rhombus.

In rt. $\triangle BCD$: $18^2 + 24^2 = \overline{BD}^2$ or $BD = 30$.

Area of rhombus $= \overline{DF} \times \overline{BC} = (18\frac{3}{4})(18)$.

Area of rhombus $= \frac{1}{2} \overline{BD} \times \overline{EF} = 15 \, EF$. [See Prob. 8, this section.]

$\therefore$ $15 \, EF = (18\frac{3}{4})(18)$ or $EF = 22\frac{1}{2}$ in.

32. In fig. $ANBP$, $AN = PB$ and $AN \parallel PB$.

$\therefore$ $ANBP$ is a $\square$ and $NB \parallel AP$.

In $\triangle MND$: $AC \parallel ND$ and bisects MN.

$\therefore$ AC bisects MD and $MC = CD$.

Similarly, in $\triangle PCO$, $OD = DC$.

$\therefore$ $MC = CD = DO$.

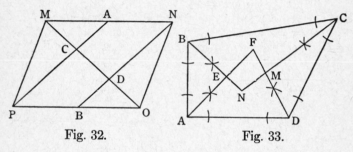

Fig. 32.   Fig. 33.

33. Let $EFMN$ be the quadrilateral formed by the bisectors of the angles of $ABCD$.

$\angle ABC + \angle BCD + \angle CDA + \angle DAB = 360°$.

$\therefore$ $\frac{1}{2} \angle ABC + \frac{1}{2} \angle BCD + \frac{1}{2} \angle CDA + \frac{1}{2} \angle DAB = 180°$.

$\therefore$ $\angle ABE + \angle FAB + \angle NCD + \angle FDC = 180°$.

But $\angle ABE + \angle FAB + \angle NCD + \angle FDC + \angle BEA + \angle CMD = 360°$.

$\therefore$ $\angle BEA + \angle CMD = 180°$.

Then since $\angle NEF = \angle BEA$ and $\angle NMF = \angle CMD$, we have $\angle NEF + \angle NMF = 180°$.

Similarly, $\angle EFM$ is supplementary to $\angle ENM$.

34. In $\triangle APD$ and DCQ: $AP = AB = DC$, $AD = BC = CQ$, and $\angle PAD = \angle DCQ$ since $\angle PAD = 60° + \angle DAB$ and $\angle DCQ = 60° + \angle DCB$.

$\therefore$ $\triangle PAD \cong \triangle DCQ$ and $PD = DQ$.

In $\triangle PBQ$: $\angle PBQ = 360° - 120° - \angle ABC$
$$= 240° - (180° - \angle DAB)$$
$$= 60° + \angle DAB$$
$$= \angle PAD.$$
$PB = PA$ and $BQ = AD.$
$\therefore \triangle PAD \cong \triangle PBQ$ and $PQ = PD = DQ.$

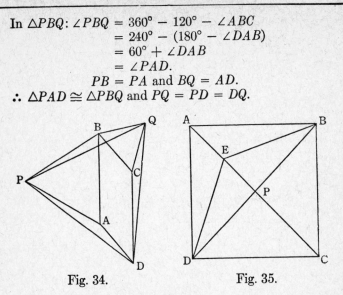

Fig. 34.   Fig. 35.

35. Let $AB = s$, then area of $ABCD = s^2$ and area of $\triangle ABD = \frac{1}{2} s^2$. In rt. $\triangle ABD$: $BD = s\sqrt{2}$ and $EP = \frac{1}{4} AC = \frac{1}{4} s\sqrt{2}$.

$\therefore$ area of $\triangle DEB = (\frac{1}{2} s\sqrt{2})(\frac{1}{4} s\sqrt{2}) = \frac{1}{4} s^2$.

$\therefore$ area of $ABED = \triangle ABD - \triangle DEB = \frac{1}{2} s^2 - \frac{1}{4} s^2 = \frac{1}{4} s^2$.

The square on $AE = \overline{AE}^2 = \overline{EP}^2 = \frac{1}{8} s^2$.

$\therefore$ area of $ABED$ is twice the area of square on AE.

36. Let $ABCD$ and $A'B'C'D'E'F'$ be any two polygons circumscribed about circle having R as its center; let $r =$ ra-

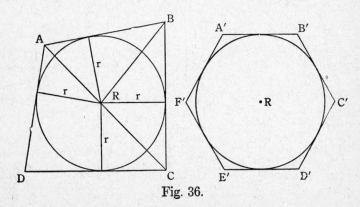

Fig. 36.

dius of circle; p, perimeter of $ABCD$; and P, perimeter of $A'B'C'D'E'F'$.

Divide $ABCD$ into △ by lines from the center R.

$$\text{Area of } ABCD = \triangle ARB + \triangle BRC + \triangle DRC + \triangle ARD$$
$$= \tfrac{1}{2}\, r(AB) + \tfrac{1}{2}\, r(BC) + \tfrac{1}{2}\, r(CD) + \tfrac{1}{2}\, r(AD)$$
$$= \tfrac{1}{2}\, r(AB + BC + CD + AD) = \tfrac{1}{2}\, rp.$$

Similarly, area of $A'B'C'D'E'F' = \tfrac{1}{2}\, rP$.

∴ area of $ABCD$: area of $A'B'C'D'E'F' = p : P$.

37. Let $ABCD$ be the given rectangle.

Draw $AN \perp BD$; from P, draw $PE \perp BD$ and $PM \perp AC$; draw $PR \perp AN$.

Fig. $PENR$ is a rectangle and ∴ $PE = RN$.

$PR \parallel BD$ since both are perpendicular to AN.

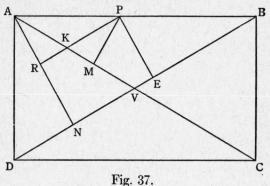

Fig. 37.

∴ $\angle APR = \angle ABD$.

$\angle ABD = \angle BAC$ since $BV = AV$.

$\angle APR = \angle BAC$ and $PK = AK$.

$\angle PKM = \angle AKR$; ∴ $\triangle PKM \cong \triangle AKR$ and $AR = PM$.

∴ $AR + RN = AN = PM + PE$.

Similarly, we can prove that, no matter where P is on the perimeter, $PM + PE$ will always equal AN and therefore equals a constant.

38. Let $AEBFCGDJ$ be the given regular octagon and circumscribe a circle about it; let P be the center of the circle.

Inscribe the square $ABCD$ and let $r = AP$.

$\triangle AKP$ is a 90°, 45°, 45° △; ∴ $AK = KP = \tfrac{1}{2}\, r\sqrt{2}$.

$EK = EP - KP = r - \tfrac{1}{2}\, r\sqrt{2}$.

Since perimeter of octagon is 40, $AE = 5$.

∴ in rt. $\triangle AEK$: $25 = \tfrac{1}{2}\, r^2 + (r - \tfrac{1}{2}\, r\sqrt{2})^2$

or
$$r^2 = \frac{25}{2-\sqrt{2}}.$$

Draw $PM \perp AE$; $\therefore$ in rt. $\triangle APM$: $r^2 = PM^2 + \frac{25}{4}$ and
$PM = \frac{5}{2}(\sqrt{3 + 2\sqrt{2}})$.

Area of octagon $= \frac{1}{2}(40)(PM) = 20\ PM = 50(\sqrt{3 + 2\sqrt{2}})$
$\qquad\qquad\qquad = 120.706$ sq. ft.

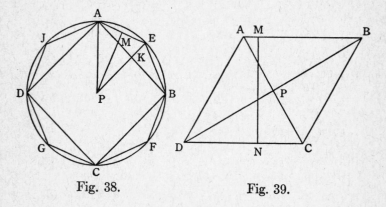

Fig. 38.　　　　　　Fig. 39.

39. Given the rhombus $ABCD$ with $AC = 30$ in. and $BD = 50$ in.
Since the diagonals of a rhombus bisect each other at rt. $\measuredangle$,
$\quad\triangle APB$ is a rt. $\triangle$ and $15^2 + 25^2 = \overline{AB}^2$ or $AB = 29.155 = DC.$
Area of rhombus $= \frac{1}{2}\ \overline{BD} \times \overline{AC} = \frac{1}{2}(30)(50) = 750.$
Let MN be the perpendicular between bases; then area of
rhombus equals $\overline{DC} \times \overline{MN} = 750$ or $MN = \dfrac{750}{29.155} = 25.725.$

40. Let $ABCD$ be the given trapezoid with $AB = 8$ and $DC = 18$.
Let P be the center of inscribed circle.
Since trapezoid is isosceles, $\angle DAB = \angle ABC$.
PA and PB bisect the angles at A and B; $\therefore \angle PAB = \angle ABP$.
Thus $AP = PB$ and $PE = PE$ so that $\triangle APE \cong \triangle PEB$.
$\therefore AE = EB = 4$ and $AJ = 4 = BF$.
Let $x = AD = BC$, then $JD = x - 4 = FC = DG = GC$ and
$\quad x - 4 + x - 4 = 18$ or $x = 13 = AD = BC.$
Draw AM and $BN \perp DC$.
Since $\triangle ADM \cong \triangle BNC$, $DM = NC$.
Since $MN = 8$, $DM + NC = 10$ or $DM = 5$.
In rt. $\triangle ADM$: $13^2 = 5^2 + AM^2$ or $AM = 12.$

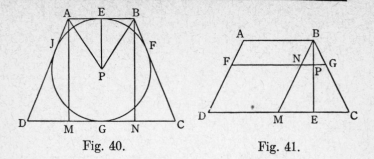

Fig. 40. Fig. 41.

41. Let $ABCD$ be the given trapezoid with $AB = 1$, $DC = 2$,
   $BE \perp DC$, and $BE = 1$. Let FG divide trapezoid in ratio
   $7 : 20$ and let $7a$ equal the area of $ABGF$.
   Then $20\,a$ = area of $FGCD$ and
   $$27\,a = \text{area of } ABCD = \tfrac{1}{2}(1 + 2)(1) = \tfrac{3}{2}.$$
   $\therefore a = \tfrac{1}{18}$ and area of $ABGF = \tfrac{7}{18}$.
   Draw $BNM \parallel AD$; then $ABGF = \square ABNF + \triangle BNG$
   $$= 1(BP) + \tfrac{1}{2}\,\overline{NG} \times \overline{BP}.$$
   $\triangle BNG \sim \triangle BMC$; $\therefore NG : MC = BP : BE$ or
   $$NG : 1 = BP : 1 \text{ and } NG = BP.$$
   $\therefore$ area of $ABGF = BP + \tfrac{1}{2}\,\overline{BP}^2 = \tfrac{7}{18}$.
   $9\,\overline{BP}^2 + 18\,BP - 7 = 0$ or $(3\,\overline{BP} + 7)(3\,\overline{BP} - 1) = 0$ and
   $BP = \tfrac{1}{3}$.

42. In $\triangle MBN$ and AMC, $\angle NBM = \angle MCA$ and $\angle N = \angle A$.
   $\therefore \triangle MBN \sim \triangle AMC$ and $NB : AM = MN : AC$ or $\overline{NB} \times \overline{AC}$
   $= \overline{AM} \times \overline{MN}$.
   Since $\overline{AM} \times \overline{MN}$ is a constant, then $\overline{NB} \times \overline{AC}$ is a constant.

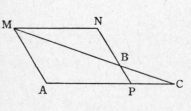

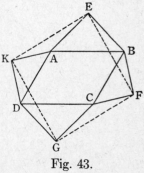

Fig. 42. Fig. 43.

43. Let $ABCD$ be the given parallelogram and let $\triangle ABE$, BCF, DCG, and DKA be the given external isosceles rt. $\triangle$.

In rt. $\triangle AKD$ and BCF: $BC = AD$, $\angle KAD = 45° = \angle CBF$.

$\therefore \triangle AKD \cong \triangle BCF$ and $AK = BF$.

$AE = BE$; $\angle KAE = 360° - 90° - \angle DAB = 270° - \angle DAB$.

$\angle EBF = 90° + \angle ABC = 90° + 180° - \angle DAB$
$\qquad = 270° - \angle DAB$.

$\therefore \angle KAE = \angle EBF$, $\triangle EBF \cong \triangle KAE$, and $KE = EF$.

$\angle AEB = 90° = \angle AEF + \angle FEB = \angle AEF + \angle KEA$
$\qquad = \angle KEF = 90°$.

Similarly, we can prove $EF = FG = KG$ and $\angle GFE = 90° = \angle FGK = \angle GKE$.

44. Let G be midpoint of BC, then EB and DG trisect AC. [See Prob. 32, this section.]

$\therefore FC = 2 AF$.

Since $\triangle AEF$ and EFC have the same altitudes,
$\quad \triangle AEF : \triangle EFC = AF : FC = AF : 2 AF = 1 : 2$.

In $\triangle AFE$ and BCF: $\angle AFE = \angle BFC$ and $\angle FAE = \angle FCB$.

$\therefore \triangle AFE \sim \triangle BCF$.

$\therefore \triangle AEF : \triangle BCF = \overline{AF}^2 : \overline{FC}^2 = \overline{AF}^2 : (2\,\overline{AF})^2 = 1 : 4$.

In $\triangle ABE$, AF bisects $\angle EAB$.

$\therefore EF : FB = AE : AB = 1 : 2$, and $2\,EF = FB$ or $EB = 3\,EF$.

Since $\triangle AEF$ and AEB have the same altitude,
$\quad \triangle AEF : \triangle AEB = EF : EB = EF : 3\,EF = 1 : 3$.

45. See Example 3, Chapter VII.

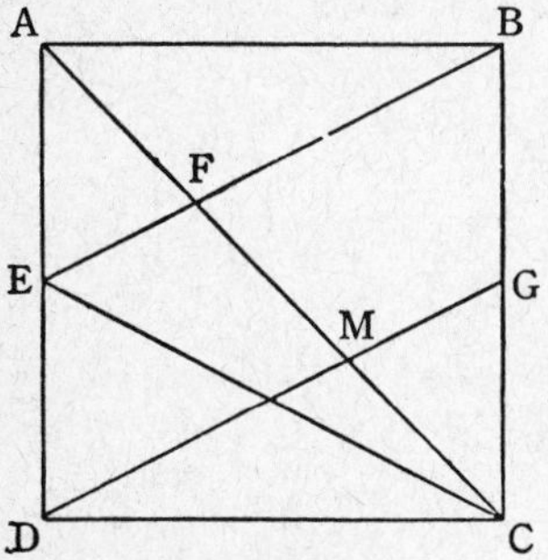

Fig. 44. 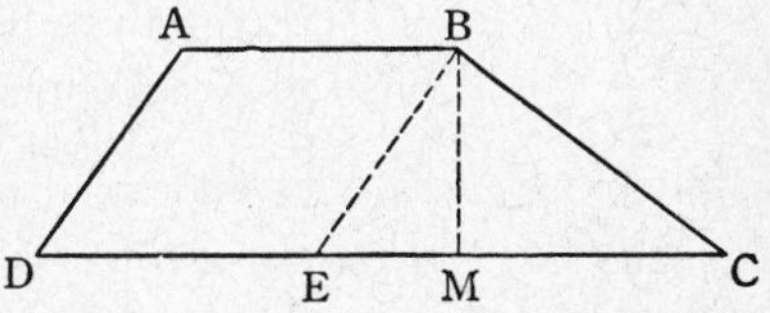   Fig. 46.

46. Let $ABCD$ be the given trapezoid with $AB = 17$, $DC = 42$, $AD = 15$, and $BC = 20$.

Draw $BE \parallel AD$; then $DE = 17$, $EC = 25$, and $BE = 15$.

Then since $25^2 = 15^2 + 20^2$, $\triangle EBC$ is a rt. $\triangle$.

∴ area of $\triangle EBC = \frac{1}{2}(20)(15) = 150$.

If we take EC as base and BM as altitude,

   area of $\triangle EBC = \frac{1}{2}(25)(BM) = 150$; ∴ $BM = 12$.

Area of trapezoid $= \frac{1}{2}(17 + 42)12 = 354$ sq. ft.

47. Let $ABCD$ be the given quadrilateral.

Draw AE so that $\angle DAE = \angle CAB$; then $\angle DAC = \angle BAE$.

$\angle DCA = \angle ABD$ since they are measured by the same arc.

∴ $\triangle ABE \sim \triangle ACD$.

Then $AB : AC = BE : CD$ or $\overline{AB} \times \overline{CD} = \overline{AC} \times \overline{BE}$.

In $\triangle ABC$ and ADE, $\angle DAE = \angle CAB$ and $\angle ADE = \angle ACB$.

∴ $\triangle ABC \sim \triangle ADE$.

Then $BC : DE = AC : AD$ or $\overline{BC} \times \overline{AD} = \overline{DE} \times \overline{AC}$.

∴ $\overline{AB} \times \overline{CD} + \overline{BC} \times \overline{AD} = \overline{AC} \times \overline{BE} + \overline{DE} \times \overline{AC}$

$$= \overline{AC}(\overline{BE} + \overline{DE}) = \overline{AC} \times \overline{BD}.$$

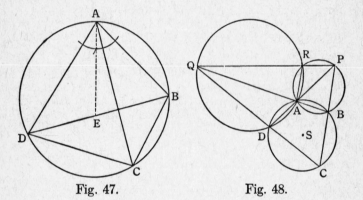

Fig. 47.   Fig. 48.

48. Let $ABCD$ be the given quadrilateral inscribed in a circle with center at S. Let outside circles meet again at R.

Since $ARPB$ is inscribed quadrilateral, $\angle ARP$ is supplement of $\angle PBA$.

Since $\angle ABC$ is supplement of $\angle PBA$, $\angle ARP = \angle ABC$.

Similarly, $\angle QDA = \angle ABC = \angle ARP$.

$\angle QDA$ is supplement of $\angle QRA$.

∴ $\angle ARP$ is supplement of $\angle QRA$ and QR and RP form a straight line.

49. In $\triangle ADN$ and BCM: $BC = AD$, $\angle BCM = \angle DAN$, and $\angle ADN = \angle MBC$.

∴ $\triangle ADN \cong \triangle BCM$ and $AN = CM$.

∴ $BN = DM$ and $BN \parallel DM$ so that $NBMD$ is a $\square$.

∴ $RS \parallel PQ$, $\angle ADN = \angle NDM = \angle AND$, and $AD = AN = BC$.
Since $\angle BAQ = \frac{1}{3} \angle BAD$ and $\angle BCR = \frac{1}{3} \angle DCB$,
  $\angle NAQ = \angle BCR$.
∴ $\angle RBC = \angle RBN = \angle QNA$ and $\triangle ANQ \cong \triangle BRC$ and
  $NQ = BR$.
$NQ \parallel BR$ and therefore $NQRB$ is a $\square$.
∴ $QR \parallel NB$.
Similarly, we can prove $PS \parallel DM$ and ∴ $PS \parallel QR$ and $PQRS$
  is a $\square$.

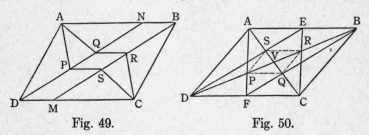

Fig. 49.   Fig. 50.

50. AC is trisected by DE and BF. [See Prob. 32, this section.]
  ∴ $AS = SQ = QC$.
  Similarly, $BR = RP = PD$; $AV = VC$.
  ∴ $AV - AS = VC - QC$ or $SV = VQ$.
  Similarly, $VR = VP$ and ∴ $PQRS$ is a $\square$.
  Since $SV : AS = 1 : 2$ and $VR : RB = 1 : 2$, then $SR \parallel AB$.
  ∴ $\triangle VSR \sim \triangle VAB$.
  Since $VS = \frac{1}{2} AS$, $VA = 3 VS$ or $VS : VA = 1 : 3 = SR : AB$.
  But since $\triangle SVR \sim \triangle AVB$, $\triangle SVR : \triangle AVB = \overline{SR}^2 : \overline{AB}^2 = 1 : 9$.
  Similarly, we can prove that $\triangle VRQ = \frac{1}{9} \triangle VBC$,
    $\triangle VPQ = \frac{1}{9} \triangle VDC$, and $\triangle VSP = \frac{1}{9} \triangle VAD$.
  ∴ $\square PQRS = \frac{1}{9} \square ABCD$.

SOLUTIONS OF PROBLEMS ON TRIANGLES

[Chapter VIII, pp. 66–72]

1. Given $\triangle ABC$ and the median BD.
   Draw $AE \perp BD$ and $CF \perp BD$; to prove that $AE = CF$.
   Since D is the midpoint of AC, $AD = DC$.
   $\angle ADE = \angle FDC$.
   $\therefore$ rt. $\triangle ADE \cong$ rt. $\triangle FDC$ and $AE = FC$.

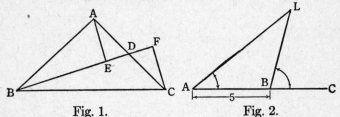

Fig. 1.   Fig. 2.

2. $\angle LBC = 73° = \angle LAB + \angle BLA = 36° 30' + \angle BLA.$
   $\therefore \angle BLA = 36° 30' = \angle LAB.$
   $\therefore LB = AB = 5.$
3. $BD = BC - DC = 37.5 - DC.$
   Since AD is the bisector of $\angle BAC$, $AB : AC = BD : DC.$
   Then $27 : 18 = (37.5 - DC) : DC$ or $DC = 15.$
   $\therefore BD = 37.5 - 15 = 22.5.$

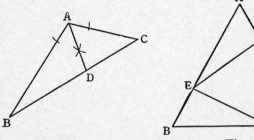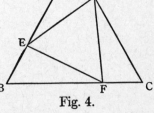

Fig. 3.   Fig. 4.

4. Since $\triangle ABC$ is equilateral, $\angle EAD = \angle EBF.$
   Since $AB = BC$ and $EB = FC$, then $AB - EB = BC - FC$
   or $AE = BF$ and $AD = BE.$

$\therefore \triangle AED \cong \triangle BEF$ and $ED = EF$.

Similarly, we can prove that $EF = DF$.

$\therefore ED = EF = DF$ and $\triangle DEF$ is equilateral.

5. Let $\triangle ABC$ represent the field whose area is 156,250 sq. ft.; let $A'B'C'$ be the triangular plan with $A'B' = 1$ ft., $B'C' = \frac{17}{12}$ ft., and $A'C' = \frac{25}{12}$ ft.

Area of $\triangle A'B'C' = \sqrt{s(s-a)(s-b)(s-c)} = K$. [See Prob. 79, this section.]

$$a = 1 \qquad s - a = \frac{15}{12} \qquad K = \sqrt{\left(\frac{27}{12}\right)\left(\frac{15}{12}\right)\left(\frac{10}{12}\right)\left(\frac{2}{12}\right)}$$

$$b = \frac{17}{12} \qquad s - b = \frac{10}{12} \qquad = \frac{(9)(5)(2)}{(12)(12)}$$

$$c = \frac{25}{12} \qquad s - c = \frac{2}{12} \qquad = \frac{5}{8}.$$

$$2s = \frac{54}{12} \qquad s = \frac{27}{12}$$

$$s = \frac{27}{12}$$

Since $\triangle ABC \sim \triangle A'B'C'$, $156{,}250 : K = \overline{AB}^2 : \overline{A'B'}^2 = \overline{AB}^2 : 1$.

Thus $\overline{AB}^2(K) = 156{,}250$ or $\overline{AB}^2 = 156{,}250(\frac{8}{5}) = 250{,}000$.

$\therefore AB = 500$ ft.

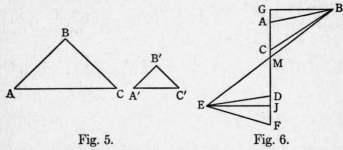

Fig. 5.   Fig. 6.

6. Let the given $\triangle$ be ABC and DEF with $AC = DF$.

Draw BG and $EJ \perp AF$.

Since areas of $\triangle$ are equal and $AC = DF$, then $BG = EJ$.

In rt. $\triangle BGM$ and MEJ: $BG = EJ$ and $\angle BMG = \angle EMJ$.

$\therefore \triangle BGM \cong \triangle MEJ$ and $BM = ME$.

7. See Example 1, Chapter VIII.

8. Since E and G are midpoints, respectively, of AD and AB, $GE \parallel BD$ and $GE = \frac{1}{2} BD$.

Similarly, $FH \parallel BD$ and $FH = \frac{1}{2} BD$.

$\therefore EG = FH$.

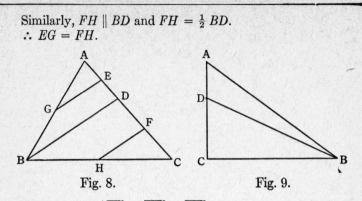

Fig. 8.   Fig. 9.

9. In rt. $\triangle BDC: \overline{BD}^2 = \overline{DC}^2 + \overline{BC}^2$.

   In rt. $\triangle ACB: \overline{AC}^2 = \overline{AB}^2 - \overline{BC}^2$.

   $\therefore \overline{BD}^2 + \overline{AC}^2 = \overline{DC}^2 + \overline{BC}^2 + \overline{AB}^2 - \overline{BC}^2 = \overline{DC}^2 + \overline{AB}^2$.

10. Since $AB > AC$, $\angle ACB > \angle ABC$.

    In $\triangle PBC$ and BCQ, $BC = BC$, $BP = CQ$, and $\angle QCB > \angle PBC$.

    $\therefore BQ > PC$.

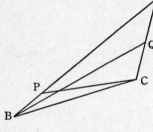

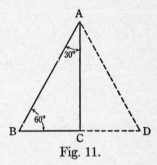

Fig. 10.   Fig. 11.

11. Given $\triangle ABC$ with $AB = h$, $\angle B = 60°$, $\angle C = 90°$, and $\angle BAC = 30°$.

    Extend BC to D so that $CD = BC$ and draw AD.

    In $\triangle ABC$ and ACD: $AC = AC$, $BC = CD$, and $\angle ACB = 90° = \angle ACD$.

    $\therefore \triangle ABC \cong \triangle ACD$ and $\angle D = \angle B = 60°$.

    Then $\angle DAC = \angle BAC = 30°$ and $\angle BAD = 60°$.

    Thus $\triangle ABD$ is equiangular and equilateral.

    Then $BD = AB$ and since $BC = \frac{1}{2} BD$, $BC = \frac{1}{2} AB = \frac{1}{2} h$.

    In rt. $\triangle ABC: \overline{AB}^2 = \overline{BC}^2 + \overline{AC}^2$ or $h^2 = \frac{1}{4} h^2 + \overline{AC}^2$.

    $\therefore AC = \frac{1}{2} h \sqrt{3}$.

12. Given the equilateral $\triangle ABC$.

Draw $AM \perp BC$; then $\triangle ABM$ is a 90°, 60°, 30° $\triangle$.

$\therefore BM = \frac{1}{2} AB$ and $AM = BM\sqrt{3} = \frac{1}{2} AB\sqrt{3}$.   [See
Prob. 11, this section.]

$\therefore$ area of $\triangle ABC = \frac{1}{2}\overline{BC} \times \overline{AM} = \frac{1}{2}\overline{AB}(\frac{1}{2}\overline{AB}\sqrt{3})$

$$= \frac{1}{4}\overline{AB}^2\sqrt{3} = \frac{s^2}{4}\sqrt{3}.$$

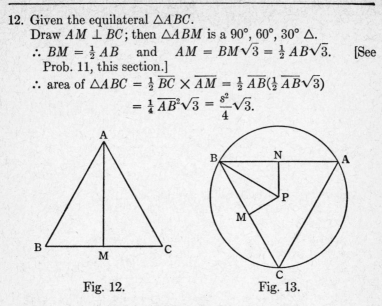

Fig. 12.   Fig. 13.

13. Given equilateral $\triangle ABC$ inscribed in circle with center at P.

Draw PM and $PN \perp BC$ and AB, respectively.

Since $BC = AB$, $PM = PN$ and $BP = BP$.

$\therefore$ rt. $\triangle PBM \cong$ rt. $\triangle PBN$ and $\angle PBM = \triangle PBN = 30°$.

$\therefore$ rt. $\triangle PBM$ is a 90°, 60°, 30° $\triangle$.

Then $PB = 1$, $BM = \frac{1}{2}\sqrt{3}$, and $BC = \sqrt{3}$. [See Prob. 11,
this section.]

$\therefore$ area of $\triangle ABC = \frac{3}{4}\sqrt{3}$. [See Prob. 12, this section.]

$\therefore$ area of isosceles $\triangle = (\frac{3}{2})\frac{3}{4}\sqrt{3} = \frac{9}{8}\sqrt{3}$.

Since base of isosceles $\triangle = 2$, $\frac{9}{8}\sqrt{3} = \frac{1}{2}(2)(h)$.

$\therefore$ altitude $= h = \frac{9}{8}\sqrt{3}$.

14. Given the rt. $\triangle ABC$ with $\angle ACB = 90°$ and $AB = 2 BC$.

Extend BC to D so that $CD = BC$; then $BD = AB$.

In rt. $\triangle ACB$ and ACD:

$AC = AC$, $BC = CD$, and $\angle ACB = \angle ACD$.

$\therefore \triangle ACB \cong \triangle ACD$ and $AD = AB = BD$.

$\therefore \triangle ABD$ is equiangular and $\angle B = 60°$.

Then since $\angle ACB = 90°$, $\angle BAC = 30°$.

15. Given the rt. $\triangle ACB$ with $\angle ACB = 90°$ and CD, the median
to AB.

Draw $DM \perp AC$; then $DM \parallel BC$.

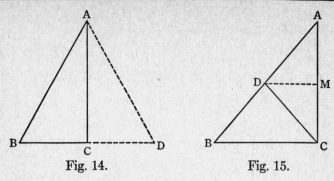

Fig. 14.   Fig. 15.

Since DM bisects AB, it bisects AC.

∴ $AM = MC$, $DM = DM$, and $\angle DMA = \angle DMC$.

∴ $\triangle ADM \cong \triangle DMC$ and $DC = AD$.

Since $AD = \frac{1}{2}$ hypotenuse, then $DC = \frac{1}{2}$ hypotenuse.

16. Given the rt. $\triangle ACB$ with $\angle ACB = 90°$ and $\angle A = 2\angle B$.

$\angle A + \angle B = 90° = 2\angle B + \angle B = 3\angle B$ or $\angle B = 30°$ and $\angle A = 60°$.

∴ $AB = 2AC$. [See Prob. 11, this section.]

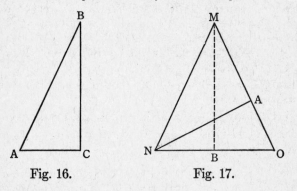

Fig. 16.   Fig. 17.

17. Draw MB, the bisector of $\angle NMO$.

$\triangle MNB \cong \triangle MBO$ (s.a.s. = s.a.s.).

∴ $\angle MBN = \angle MBO = 90°$.

In $\triangle NAO$ and BMO: $\angle MON = \angle MON$, $\angle MBO = \angle NAO$.

∴ $\angle ONA = \angle BMO = \frac{1}{2} \angle NMO$.

18. Given the equilateral $\triangle ABC$ with BP and PC, the respective bisectors of $\angle ABC$ and ACB; given also $PM \parallel AB$ and $PN \parallel AC$.

Since $PM \parallel AB$, $\angle BPM = \angle ABP = \angle PBM$; $PM = BM$.

$\angle PMN = \angle PBM + \angle BPM = 30° + 30° = 60°.$
Similarly, $\angle PNM = 60°$; then $\angle MPN = 60°$ and
$$PM = MN = BM.$$
Similarly, in $\triangle NPC$: $\angle NPC = \angle NCP$ and $NC = PN.$
Then, since $PN = MN$, we have $BM = MN = NC.$

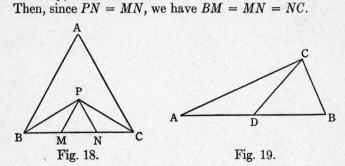

Fig. 18.   Fig. 19.

19. $\angle ACB = \angle CAB + \angle ABC.$
Since $\angle ACB + \angle CAB + \angle ABC = 180°$, then
$\angle ACB + \angle ACB = 180°$ or $\angle ACB = 90°.$
$\therefore AB$ is the hypotenuse of a rt. $\triangle$ and $AB = 2\,CD.$
[See Prob. 15, this section.]

20. Given $\triangle ACB$ with $\overline{AC}^2 + \overline{BC}^2 = \overline{AB}^2.$
Draw $\triangle A'B'C'$ with $B'C' = BC$, $A'C' \perp B'C'$, and $A'C' = AC.$
$\therefore \overline{A'C'}^2 + \overline{B'C'}^2 = \overline{A'B'}^2 = \overline{AC}^2 + \overline{BC}^2 = \overline{AB}^2.$
$\therefore A'B' = AB.$
Then $\triangle ABC \cong \triangle A'B'C'$ and $\angle C = \angle C' = 90°.$

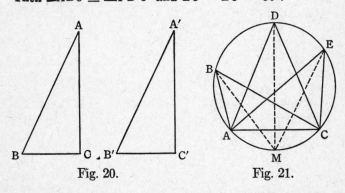

Fig. 20.   Fig. 21.

21. Let AC be the given base, and $\angle ABC$, ADC, and AEC, equal
    vertical angles.
    A circle can be circumscribed about A, B, D, E, and C.

[See Prob. 7, Chap. VI.]

Draw BM, the bisector of $\angle ABC$; then $\angle ABM = \frac{1}{2}$ arc AM.

Draw DM; then $\angle ADM = \frac{1}{2}$ arc $AM = \angle ABM = \frac{1}{2} \angle ABC$ $= \frac{1}{2} \angle ADC$.

$\therefore$ DM bisects $\angle ADC$.

Similarly for EM, etc.

22. Given $\triangle ABC$ and DEF with $AB = DE$, $\angle B = \angle E$, and equal areas.

Draw $AM \perp BC$ and $DN \perp EF$.

In rt. $\triangle ABM$ and DEN: $AB = DE$ and $\angle B = \angle E$.

$\therefore$ $\triangle ABM \cong \triangle DEN$ and $AM = DN$.

Area of $\triangle ABC =$ area of $\triangle DEF$.

$\therefore$ $\frac{1}{2} \overline{BC} \times \overline{AM} = \frac{1}{2} \overline{EF} \times \overline{DN}$ and $BC = EF$.

$\therefore$ $\triangle ABC \cong \triangle DEF$ (s.a.s. = s.a.s.).

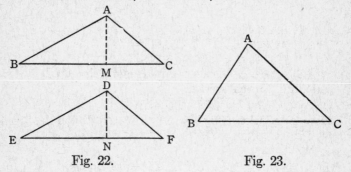

Fig. 22.   Fig. 23.

23. Given any $\triangle ABC$.

$AB < AC + BC$ and $AB = AB$.

$\therefore$ $AB + AB < AC + BC + AB$ or $2 AB < AC + BC + AB$.

Then $AB < \frac{1}{2}(AC + BC + AB)$.

Similarly for BC and AC.

24. See Example 2, Chapter VIII.

25. Given $\triangle ABC$ with BM as altitude to AC, and $AC = BC$.

From any point D on AB draw $ED \perp AC$ and $DF \perp BC$.

Connect C with D.

Area of $\triangle ABC = \frac{1}{2} \overline{AC} \times \overline{BM}$.

Area of $\triangle ABC = \triangle ACD + \triangle DCB$

$\qquad = \frac{1}{2} \overline{AC} \times \overline{ED} + \frac{1}{2} \overline{BC} \times \overline{DF}$

$\qquad = \frac{1}{2} \overline{AC} \times \overline{ED} + \frac{1}{2} \overline{AC} \times \overline{DF}$

$\qquad = \frac{1}{2} \overline{AC}(\overline{ED} + \overline{DF})$.

$\therefore$ $\frac{1}{2} \overline{AC} \times \overline{BM} = \frac{1}{2} \overline{AC}(\overline{ED} + \overline{DF})$ and $BM = ED + DF$.

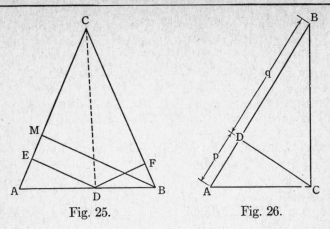

Fig. 25.   Fig. 26.

26. Given the rt. $\triangle ACB$ with $\angle C = 90°$, $CD \perp AB$, $AD = p$, and $DB = q$.

Area of $\triangle ACB = \frac{1}{2}\overline{AB} \times \overline{DC}$.

Since $AB = p + q$ and $AD : DC = DC : BD$ or $\overline{DC}^2 = \overline{AD} \times \overline{DB} = pq$, we have area of $\triangle ACB = \frac{1}{2}(p + q)\sqrt{pq}$.

27. Let ABC be the given triangle with CD and BF as medians to AB and AC; given also $CD = DE$ and $BF = FM$.

Connect E with A and A with M.

In $\triangle EDA$ and DBC:

    $DA = DB$, $ED = DC$, and $\angle EDA = \angle BDC$.

$\therefore \triangle EDA \cong \triangle BDC$ and $\angle EAD = \angle DBC$.

$\therefore EA \parallel BC$.

Similarly, we can prove $\triangle AFM \cong \triangle BFC$ and $AM \parallel BC$.

$\therefore$ AM and EA form a straight line since through one point only one line can be drawn parallel to another line.

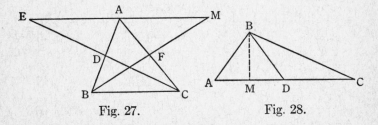

Fig. 27.   Fig. 28.

28. Given $\triangle ABC$ with $AC = 12$, median $BD = 5$, and area $= 24$.
Draw $BM \perp AC$.

Then $24 = \frac{1}{2}\overline{AC} \times \overline{BM} = \frac{1}{2}(12\,BM) = 6\,BM$ or $BM = 4.$

Then in rt. $\triangle BMD$: $BD = 5$ and $BM = 4$; $\therefore$ $MD = 3$ and $AM = 3.$

Since $\overline{AB}^2 = \overline{BM}^2 + \overline{AM}^2 = 16 + 9$, we have $AB = 5.$

Further, $\overline{BC}^2 = \overline{BM}^2 + \overline{MC}^2 = 16 + 81 = 97$ and $BC = \sqrt{97}.$

29. Draw fig. 29 from the data and draw $DM \perp AE.$

In rt. $\triangle ADM$ and ACB: $\angle DMA = \angle ACB$ and $\angle MAD = \angle BAC.$

$\therefore$ $\triangle ADM \sim \triangle ACB$ and $MD : BC = DA : AB.$

Now $BC = 15$ and $DA = 5$; further, $\overline{AB}^2 = 15^2 + 8^2 = 289$ or $AB = 17.$

Then $MD : 15 = 5 : 17$ or $MD = \frac{75}{17}.$

Area of $\triangle ABC = \frac{1}{2}(8)(15) = 60 = \frac{1}{2}\overline{EA} \times \overline{MD} = \frac{1}{2}EA\left(\frac{75}{17}\right).$

$\therefore$ $EA = \frac{136}{5} = 27.2$ in.

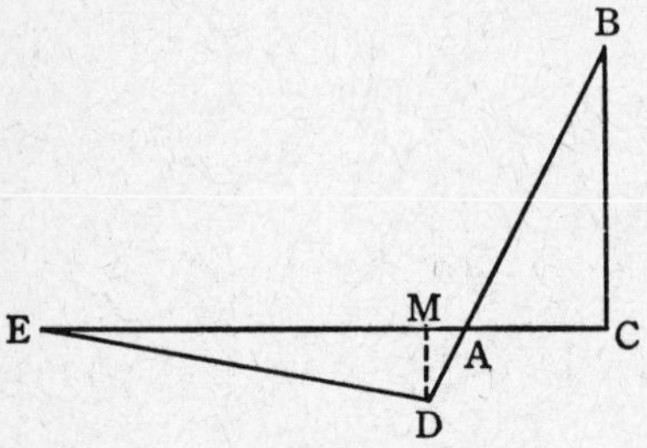

Fig. 29. 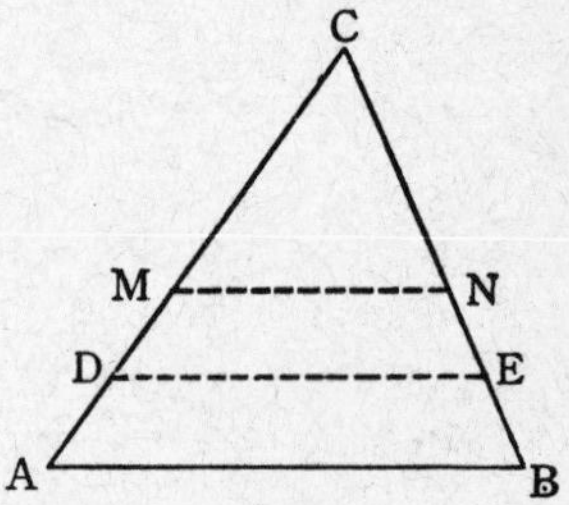   Fig. 30.

30. Given $\triangle ABC$ with $AB = 12.$

Let DE mark the crease and let MNC be the projection beyond the base.

Since $MN \parallel AB$, $\triangle MNC : \triangle ABC = 36 : 100.$

$\therefore$ $\overline{MN}^2 : 144 = 36 : 100$ and $MN = 7.2.$

Since in the process of folding DE coincides with DE and MN coincides with AB, the perpendicular distance between MN and DE equals the perpendicular distance between DE and $AB.$

$\therefore$ DE is the median of trapezoid $MNBA.$

Then $DE = \frac{1}{2}(7.2 + 12)$ or $DE = 9.6.$

31. Since $DE \parallel AC$, $\angle EDB = \angle BCA = \angle ABC$; $\therefore$ $ED = EB.$

Since $DF \parallel AB$, $\angle FDC = \angle ABC = \angle BCA$; $\therefore$ $FD = FC.$

$\therefore$ $AF + FD + ED + AE = AF + FC + EB + AE$
$$= AB + AC = 10.$$

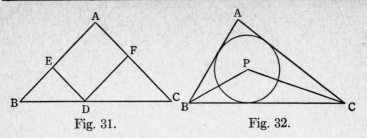

Fig. 31.   Fig. 32.

32. Given $\triangle ABC$ and the inscribed circle with center at **P**.
Since P lies on the bisectors of the angles,
$\angle PBC = \frac{1}{2} \angle ABC$ and $\angle PCB = \frac{1}{2} \angle ACB$.
$$\angle BPC = 180° - (\angle PBC + \angle PCB)$$
$$= 180° - (\tfrac{1}{2} \angle ABC + \tfrac{1}{2} \angle ACB)$$
$$= 180° - \tfrac{1}{2}(180° - \angle BAC)$$
$$= 90° + \tfrac{1}{2} \angle BAC.$$

33. Given $\triangle ABC$ and P, any point in the triangle.
$PC + AP > AC; PC + PB > BC;$ and $PB + PA > \mathbf{AB}$.
$\therefore 2PC + 2AP + 2PB > AC + BC + AB$
or $PC + AP + PB > \frac{1}{2}(AC + BC + AB)$.
The sum of two lines from a point to the ends of a line is
greater than the sum of two other lines similarly drawn but
included by the first two lines.
$\therefore AC + AB > PC + PB; AB + BC > AP + PC;$ and
$BC + AC > AP + PB$.
$\therefore 2AC + 2AB + 2BC > 2PC + 2PB + 2AP$
or $AC + AB + BC > PC + PB + AP$.

34. See Example 3, Chapter VIII.

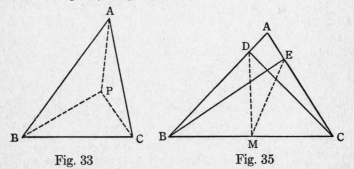

Fig. 33   Fig. 35

35. Given $\triangle ABC$ with $CD \perp AB$, $BE \perp AC$, and M, the midpoint of BC.

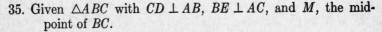

In rt. $\triangle BDC$: DM is a median;

$\therefore DM = \frac{1}{2} BC$. (See Prob. 15, this section.)

In rt. $\triangle BEC$: EM is a median; $\therefore EM = \frac{1}{2} BC$.

$\therefore EM = DM$.

36. Given rt. $\triangle ACB$ with $\angle C = 90°$, $CD \perp AB$, $AB = 25$, and $CD = 12$.

$\therefore AD : DC = DC : DB$ or $AD : 12 = 12 : 25 - AD$.

$\therefore AD = 16$ or 9.

$AB : AC = AC : AD$ or $25 : AC = AC : (16$ or $9)$.

$\therefore AC = 20$ or 15.

$AB : BC = BC : BD$ or $25 : BC = BC : (9$ or $16)$.

$\therefore BC = 15$ or 20.

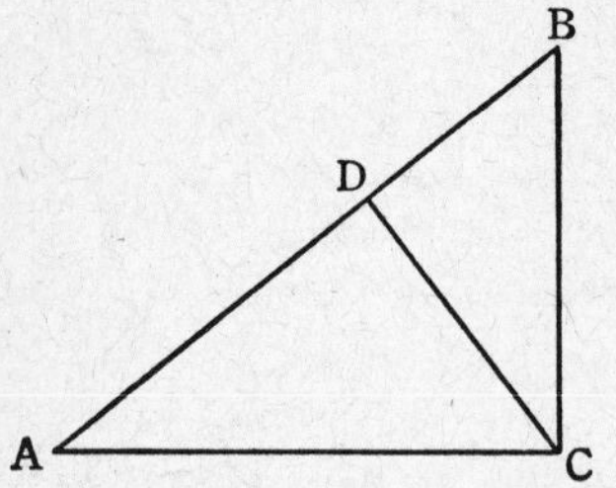

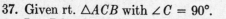

Fig. 36. 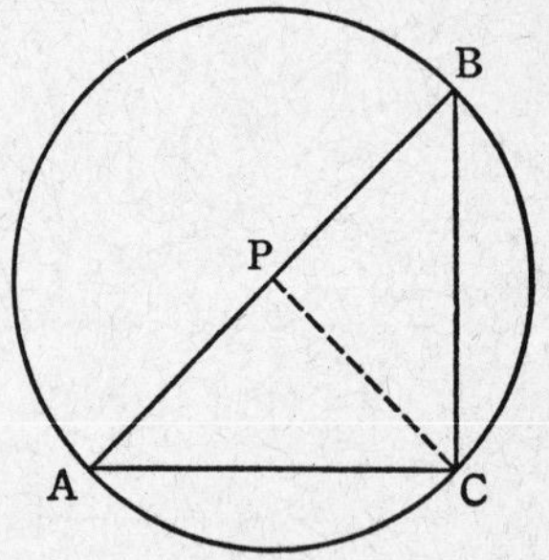   Fig. 37.

37. Given rt. $\triangle ACB$ with $\angle C = 90°$.

Let P be the midpoint of AB; then since $CP = PA = PB$, P is the center of circle passing through A, C, and B. [See Prob. 15, this section.]

$\therefore PC = 25 = PA$ and $AB = 50$.

Let d = common arithmetic difference and $AC = x$.

Then $AC + 2d = x + 2d = AB = 50$ and $BC = AC + d = x + d$.

$\therefore 50^2 = x^2 + (x + d)^2$.

$d = \frac{1}{2}(50 - x)$.

Then $x + d = x + 25 - \frac{1}{2}x = \frac{1}{2}(x + 50)$ and

$50^2 = x^2 + \frac{1}{4}(x + 50)^2 = x^2 + \frac{1}{4}(x^2 + 100x + 50^2)$;

$4(50)^2 = 4x^2 + x^2 + 100x + 50^2$;

$5x^2 + 100x - 3(50)^2 = 0$;

$x^2 + 20x - 30(50) = 0$;

$(x - 30)(x + 50) = 0$;

$x = 30$ and $d = \frac{1}{2}(50 - 30) = 10$.

$\therefore AC = 30$, $BC = 40$, and $AB = 50$.

38. Given isosceles $\triangle ABC$ and D, any point on BC.

Draw $FD \parallel AC$ and $DE \parallel AB$; then $DEAF$ is the $\square$.

In Prob. 31, this section, it was shown that $DE + DF + FA + AE = AB + AC$.

Since $AB + AC$ is a constant, the perimeter of $DEAF$ is a constant.

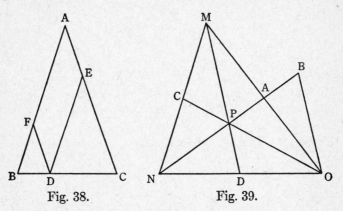

Fig. 38.   Fig. 39.

39. Since the medians of a triangle meet at a point which is $\frac{2}{3}$ the distance from the vertex to the midpoint of the opposite side, $MP = \frac{2}{3} MD$, $NP = \frac{2}{3} NA$, and $OP = \frac{2}{3} OC$.

$\therefore PA = \frac{1}{3} NA = AB$ and $PA + AB = \frac{2}{3} NA$.

In $\triangle MPA$ and OAB: $MA = AO$, $PA = AB$, and $\angle MAP = \angle OAB$.

$\therefore \triangle MPA \cong \triangle OAB$ and $OB = MP = \frac{2}{3} MD$.

40. $\angle A = 180° - (\angle ANO + \angle NOA)$

$= 180° - (\frac{1}{2} \angle MNO + \angle MON + \angle MOA)$

$= 180° - (\frac{1}{2} \angle MNO + \angle MON + \frac{1}{2}[180° - \angle MON])$

$= 180° - (\frac{1}{2} \angle MNO + \frac{1}{2}[180° + \angle MON])$

$= 180° - \frac{1}{2}(\angle MNO + \angle MON + 180°)$

$= 180° - \frac{1}{2}(180° - \angle M + 180°)$

$= 180° - 180° + \frac{1}{2} \angle M$

$= \frac{1}{2} \angle M$.

41. Given $\triangle ABC$, with $CD \perp AB$ and P, the center of the circumscribed circle.

Connect B with M.

In $\triangle ADC$ and CBM: $\angle A = \angle CMB$ and $\angle ADC = \angle CBM$.

$\therefore \triangle ADC \sim \triangle CBM$ and $AC : CM = CD : CB$.

$\therefore \overline{AC} \times \overline{CB} = \overline{CM} \times \overline{CD}$.

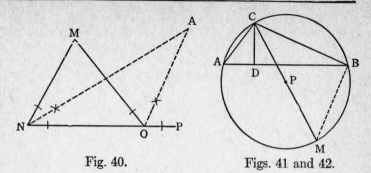

Fig. 40.   Figs. 41 and 42.

42. Given $\triangle ABC$ and P, the center of the circumscribed circle.
Draw $CD \perp AB$.
Area of $\triangle ABC = \frac{1}{2} \overline{AB} \times \overline{CD}$.
From Prob. 41, this section, $\overline{AC} \times \overline{CB} = \overline{CD} \times \overline{CM}$.
$$\therefore CD = \frac{\overline{AC} \times \overline{CB}}{\overline{CM}}.$$

Then area of $\triangle ABC = \frac{1}{2}\left(\overline{AB} \times \dfrac{\overline{AC} \times \overline{CB}}{\overline{CM}}\right)$

$$= \frac{\overline{AB} \times \overline{AC} \times \overline{CB}}{2\,\overline{CM}}.$$

43. Connect A with D, then $AD \perp BC$.
In rt. $\triangle BED$ and ADB: $\angle DEB = \angle ADB$ and $\angle B = \angle B$.
$\therefore \triangle BED \sim \triangle ADB$ and $BD : BE = AB : BD$.
Since $BD = \frac{1}{2} BC = \frac{1}{2} AB$, $\frac{1}{2} AB : BE = AB : \frac{1}{2} AB$ or
$\overline{BE} \times \overline{AB} = \frac{1}{4}\overline{AB}^2$.
$\therefore BE = \frac{1}{4} AB$.

44. See Example 4, Chapter VIII.

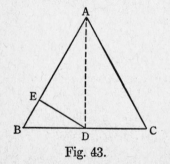

Fig. 43.

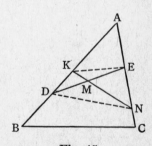

Fig. 45.

45. Given $\triangle ABC$ with DE bisected at M.

Draw KN, any other line through M and terminating inside AB and AC.

If M were the midpoint of KN, then $KM = MN$ and since $DM = ME$, $KEND$ would be a parallelogram.

$\therefore EN \parallel KD$ but this is absurd since EN and KD meet at A.

$\therefore M$ cannot be the midpoint of KN.

46. Given $\triangle ABC$ and circumscribed circle having P as its center.

Let M be midpoint of arc BC; then $\angle BAM = \angle MAC$.

$\therefore AM$ is the bisector of $\angle BAC$.

Let DE be the $\perp$ bis. of BC.

Since the perpendicular bisector of a chord bisects the arcs of the chord, DE passes through M.

$\therefore DE$ and AM intersect at M.

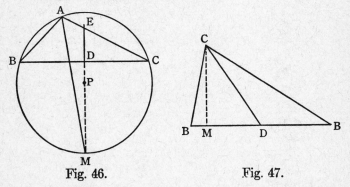

Fig. 46.   Fig. 47.

47. Given $\triangle ABC$ with $AB = 16$, $AC = 9$, $CD = 11$, and $AD = BD = 8$.

Draw $CM \perp AB$; then $AM = 8 - DM$.

In rt. $\triangle CDM$: $11^2 = \overline{CM}^2 + \overline{DM}^2$.

In rt. $\triangle CMA$: $81 = \overline{CM}^2 + (8 - \overline{DM})^2$.

$\therefore DM = \frac{13}{2}$ and $CM = \frac{1}{2}\sqrt{315}$.

In rt. $\triangle CMB$: $\overline{BC}^2 = \overline{CM}^2 + (8 + \overline{DM})^2$

$$= \frac{315}{4} + (8 + \frac{13}{2})^2 = \frac{1156}{4}.$$

$\therefore BC = 17$.

48. Given the rt. $\triangle ACB$ with $\angle C = 90°$, $AB = 5$, $AC = 4$, $BC = 3$, and $AD = 2$.

Draw $CM \perp AB$.

Area of $\triangle ABC = \frac{1}{2} \overline{AC} \times \overline{BC} = \frac{1}{2} \overline{AB} \times \overline{CM} = \frac{1}{2}(4)(3)$

$$= \frac{1}{2}(5)CM.$$

$\therefore CM = \frac{12}{5}$.

In rt. $\triangle CMB$: $9 = \overline{BM}^2 + (\frac{12}{5})^2$ or $BM = \frac{9}{5}$.

Since $BD = 3$, $MD = 3 - BM = 3 - \frac{9}{5} = \frac{6}{5}$.

In rt. $\triangle CMD$: $\overline{DC}^2 = \overline{CM}^2 + \overline{MD}^2 = \frac{144}{25} + \frac{36}{25} = \frac{180}{25}$.

$\therefore DC = \frac{6}{5}\sqrt{5}$.

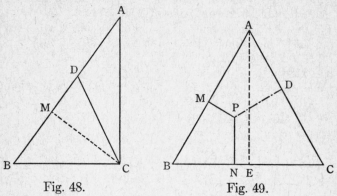

Fig. 48.   Fig. 49.

49. Given equilateral $\triangle ABC$ with perimeter $= 30$, $PM = 2$, and $PN = 3$.

Draw $AE \perp BC$ and $PD \perp AC$.

Then $PM + PN + PD = AE$. [See Prob. 34, this section.]

Since $\triangle ABE$ is a $90°$, $60°$, $30°$ $\triangle$ and $AB = 10$, then $BE = 5$ and $AE = 5\sqrt{3}$. [See Prob. 11, this section.]

$\therefore 2 + 3 + PD = 5\sqrt{3}$ or $PD = 5(\sqrt{3} - 1) = 3.66$ ft.

50. Given $\triangle ABC$ with $AB = 7$, $AC = 15$, and $BC = 20$; then $\angle ACB$ is the smallest angle.

Let CM bisect $\angle ACB$; then $AM : MB = 15 : 20$.

Since $MB = AB - AM = 7 - AM$, $AM : (7 - AM) = 15 : 20$ or $AM = 3$.

Draw $CD \perp BA$ extended.

In rt. $\triangle BCD$: $400 = \overline{CD}^2 + (7 + \overline{AD})^2$.

In rt. $\triangle CAD$: $225 = \overline{CD}^2 + \overline{AD}^2$.

Then $AD = 9$ and $CD = 12$.

In rt. $\triangle CMD$: $\overline{CM}^2 = \overline{MD}^2 + \overline{DC}^2 = (3 + \overline{AD})^2 + 144$.

$\therefore CM = 12\sqrt{2}$.

51. Given $\triangle ABC$ with CD the median to BA.

Represent BC by a, AC by b, AB by c, and CD by x.

Draw $CE \perp BD$ and represent CE by h and ED by m.

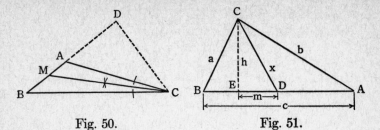

Fig. 50.   Fig. 51.

Then $BE = BD - m = \frac{1}{2}c - m$.

In rt. $\triangle CBE$: $(\frac{1}{2}c - m)^2 + h^2 = a^2$.

In rt. $\triangle CEA$: $(m + \frac{1}{2}c)^2 + h^2 = b^2$.

Solve these simultaneous equations for m and h^2:

$$m = \frac{b^2 - a^2}{2c} \text{ and } h^2 = a^2 - \frac{1}{4}\left(\frac{c^2 - b^2 + a^2}{c}\right)^2.$$

In rt. $\triangle CED$: $x^2 = h^2 + m^2$

$$= a^2 - \frac{1}{4}\left(\frac{c^2 - b^2 + a^2}{c}\right)^2 + \left(\frac{b^2 - a^2}{2c}\right)^2$$

$$= \tfrac{1}{4}(2a^2 - c^2 + 2b^2).$$

$\therefore x = \frac{1}{2}\sqrt{2a^2 - c^2 + 2b^2}$.

52. Given $\triangle ABC$ with $AB = 5$, $AC = 10$, and AD, the median to BC, equal to $6\frac{1}{2}$.

By Prob. 51, this section,

$$AD = \tfrac{1}{2}\sqrt{2\,\overline{AB}^2 - \overline{BC}^2 + 2\,\overline{AC}^2}.$$

$$6\tfrac{1}{2} = \tfrac{1}{2}\sqrt{50 - \overline{BC}^2 + 200} = \tfrac{1}{2}\sqrt{250 - \overline{BC}^2}.$$

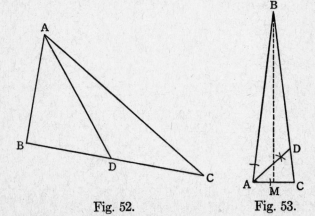

Fig. 52.   Fig. 53.

$\therefore \overline{BC}^2 = 81$ and $BC = 9$ in.

Area of $\triangle ABC = \sqrt{s(s-a)(s-b)(s-c)}$
$$= \sqrt{12(7)(2)(3)} = 6\sqrt{14} = 22.45 \text{ sq. in.}$$
[See Prob. 79, this section.]

53. Given $\triangle ABC$ with $AB = BC = 40$ and $AC = 10$.

Draw AD bisecting $\angle BAC$; then $BD : DC = AB : AC$, or
$BD : (40 - BD) = 40 : 10$ so that $BD = 32$ and $DC = 8$.

Draw $BM \perp AC$; then $40^2 = \overline{BM}^2 + 25$ and $BM = 15\sqrt{7}$.

Area of $\triangle ABC = K = \frac{1}{2}(\overline{AC} \times \overline{BM}) = 5(15\sqrt{7}) = 75\sqrt{7}$.

$\triangle ADC$ and ABC have the same altitude, the $\perp$ from A to BC.

$\therefore \triangle ABC : \triangle ADC = BC : DC$ or $75\sqrt{7} : \triangle ADC = 40 : 8$.

$\therefore$ area of $\triangle ADC = 15\sqrt{7}$.

Area of $\triangle ABD = K - \triangle ADC = 75\sqrt{7} - 15\sqrt{7} = 60\sqrt{7}$.

54. Connect M with C.

The perpendicular from C to AB is the altitude of $\triangle CMB$ and CAB.

$\therefore \triangle CMB : \triangle CAB = BM : BA = 1 : 2$.

$\therefore \triangle CMB = \frac{1}{2} \angle CAB$.

Since $MD \parallel PC$, the $\perp$ from P to $MD = \perp$ from C to MD;
then $\triangle PMD$ and MCD have equal altitudes and the same
base, MD.

$\therefore$ area of $\triangle PMD =$ area of $\triangle MCD$.

$\triangle PBD = \triangle BMD + \triangle MPD = \triangle BMD + \triangle MCD = \triangle CMB$
$= \frac{1}{2} \triangle CAB$.

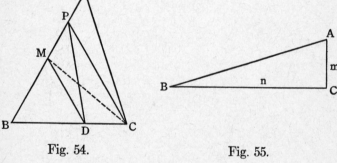

Fig. 54.   Fig. 55.

55. Given rt. $\triangle ACB$ with $\angle C = 90°$, $p = 56$, and $K = 84$.

Let $AC = m$ and $BC = n$; then $AB = 56 - m - n$.

$$\therefore \begin{cases} (56 - m - n)^2 = m^2 + n^2. \\ \tfrac{1}{2}\,mn = 84. \end{cases}$$

$$112(m + n) = 112(31) \text{ or } m + n = 31.$$

$$n^2 - 31\,n + 168 = 0 \text{ or } (n - 24)(n - 7) = 0.$$

$\therefore n = 24$ or 7.

Then $m = 31 - n = 7$ or 24 and $AB = 56 - 31 = 25$.

$\therefore$ the sides are 7, 24, and 25.

56. Given isosceles $\triangle ABC$ with $AB = AC = 50$, $BC = 60$, and $FDEJ$ the inscribed square.

Draw $AM \perp BC$; then M is the midpoint of BC and $BM = 30$.

In $\triangle AMB$: $50^2 = \overline{AM}^2 + 30^2$ or $AM = 40$.

In $\triangle JEC$ and FDB: $\angle B = \angle C$ and $FD = JE$.

$\therefore \triangle JEC \cong \triangle FDB$ and $EC = BD$.

Let $EC = y$, then $DE = 60 - 2\,y = JE$.

$JE \parallel AM$; $\therefore \triangle JEC \sim \triangle AMC$.

Then $40 : (60 - 2\,y) = 30 : y$, or $y = 18$ and $JE = 24$.

Area of square $= \overline{JE}^2 = (24)^2 = 576$ sq. ft.

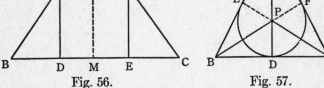

Fig. 56. Fig. 57.

57. Given $\triangle ABC$ with $AB = AC = 17$, $AD = 15$, and $AD \perp BC$.

In rt. $\triangle ABD$: $17^2 = 15^2 + \overline{BD}^2$ and $BD = 8$.

Center of inscribed circle lies on bisectors of the angles.

$\therefore$ since AD bisects $\angle BAC$, the center, P, lies on AD.

Since BC is tangent to circle P, the radius from P is $\perp BC$.

$\therefore PD$ is a radius since $PD \perp BC$.

Area of $\triangle ABC = \tfrac{1}{2}(\overline{BC} \times \overline{AD}) = \tfrac{1}{2}(16)(15) = 120$.

Area of $\triangle ABC = \triangle PBC + \triangle APB + \triangle APC$

$$= \tfrac{1}{2}(16)PD + \tfrac{1}{2}(17)EP + \tfrac{1}{2}(17)PF$$
$$= 8\,PD + \tfrac{1}{2}(17)PD + \tfrac{1}{2}(17)PD$$
$$= \tfrac{1}{2}\,PD(16 + 17 + 17) = 25\,PD.$$

$\therefore 25\,PD = 120$ and $PD = 4.8$ in.

58. Given $\triangle ABC$ with AD, the bisector of $\angle BAC$, $AD = 8$, $AB = 7$, and $BD = 3$.

Area of $\triangle ABD = \sqrt{s(s-a)(s-b)(s-c)}$
$$= \sqrt{9(2)(1)(6)} = 6\sqrt{3}.$$

[See Prob. 79, this section.]

Draw $AM \perp BD$; then

area of $\triangle ABD = \frac{1}{2}(\overline{BD} \times \overline{AM}) = \frac{3}{2}\,AM = 6\sqrt{3}.$

$\therefore\ AM = 4\sqrt{3}.$

In rt. $\triangle AMD$: $64 = \overline{AM}^2 + \overline{MD}^2$ or $MD = 4$.

Since AD bisects $\angle BAC$, $BD : BC = AB : AC$ or $7\,DC = 3\,AC$.

In rt. $\triangle AMC$: $\overline{AC}^2 = \overline{AM}^2 + \overline{MC}^2 = \overline{AM}^2 + (\overline{MD} + \overline{DC})^2$
$$= \overline{AM}^2 + (\overline{MD} + \tfrac{3}{7}\,\overline{AC})^2$$
$$= 48 + \tfrac{1}{49}(28^2 + 168\,AC + 9\,\overline{AC}^2).$$

$\therefore\ 49\,\overline{AC}^2 = (48)(49) + 28^2 + 168\,AC + 9\,\overline{AC}^2;$

$5\,\overline{AC}^2 - 21\,AC - 392 = 0$ or $(5\,AC - 56)(AC + 7) = 0.$

$\therefore\ AC = 11.2.$

$BC = BD + DC = 3 + \tfrac{3}{7}\,AC = 3 + \tfrac{3}{7}(11.2) = 7.8.$

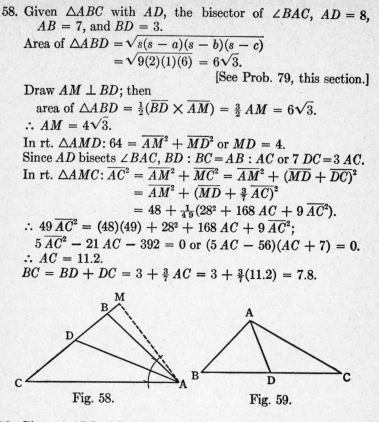

Fig. 58.   Fig. 59.

59. Given $\triangle ABC$ with $AB = 4$, $AC = 6$, and $BC = 8$.

Let AD be the median to BC.

By Prob. 51, this section,
$$AD = \tfrac{1}{2}2\,\overline{AB}^2 - \overline{BC}^2 + 2\,\overline{AC}^2$$
$$= \tfrac{1}{2}\sqrt{32 - 64 + 72} = \tfrac{1}{2}\sqrt{40} = \sqrt{10}.$$

60. Given the rt. $\triangle ACB$ with $\angle C = 90°$, AP and PB bisecting, respectively, $\angle BAC$ and CBA, and $PM \perp BC$.

Since $\triangle ACB$ is a rt. $\triangle$, $\overline{AB}^2 = 12^2 + 5^2$ and $AB = 13$.

Draw PN and PR respectively $\perp AC$ and AB.

Since the bisectors of $\angle$ of a $\triangle$ meet at a point equally distant from the sides, $PM = PN = PR$ and $PNCM$ is a square.

$\therefore\ PM = NC$ and $AN = AC - NC = 12 - PM$.

$\triangle APN \cong \triangle APR$ since $AP = AP$ and $PN = PR$.

$\therefore AN = AR = 12 - PM$.

$BR = AB - AR = 13 - (12 - PM) = 13 - 12 + PM$
   $= 1 + PM$.

$\triangle BPR \cong \triangle BPM$ since $BP = BP$ and $PR = PM$.

$\therefore BR = BM = 1 + PM$.

Since $BM = BC - MC = 5 - PM$, then $1 + PM = 5 - PM$.

$\therefore PM = 2$.

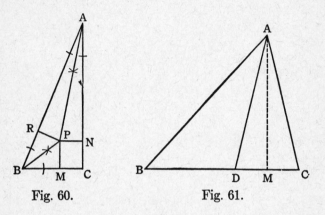

Fig. 60.   Fig. 61.

61. Given $\triangle ABC$ with AD bisecting $\angle BAC$, $BD = 4$, $DC = 3$,
    and $AD = 6$.

    Since AD bisects $\angle BAC$, $BD : DC = AB : AC = 4 : 3$.

    $\therefore$ let $AB = 4y$ and $AC = 3y$.

    Draw $AM \perp BD$ and let $BM = z$; then $MD = z - 4$.

    Since $\overline{AM}^2 = \overline{AB}^2 - \overline{BM}^2$ and $\overline{AM}^2 = \overline{AD}^2 - \overline{MD}^2$, we have
       $\overline{AB}^2 - \overline{BM}^2 = \overline{AD}^2 - \overline{MD}^2$

    or $16y^2 - z^2 = 36 - (z - 4)^2 = 36 - z^2 + 8z - 16$

    or $16y^2 - 8z - 20 = 0$.   (1)

    In rt. $\triangle AMC$: $\overline{AM}^2 = \overline{AC}^2 - \overline{MC}^2$

    or $16y^2 - z^2 = 9y^2 - (DC - MD)^2 = 9y^2 - (4 - z + 3)^2$

    or $7y^2 - 14z + 49 = 0$.   (2)

    We then solve the simultaneous equations (1) and (2) and get
       $z = 5.5$ and $y = 2$.

    Then $AB = 8$ and $AC = 6$.

62. Given $\triangle ABC$ with AD the median to BC.

    Extend AD to E so that $DE = AD$.

    Since $BD = DC$ and $AD = DE$, $ACEB$ is a $\square$.

    $\therefore BE = AC$.

Since $AE < AB + BE$, $AE < AB + AC$, or
  $2\,AD < AB + AC$ since $AE = 2\,AD$.
$\therefore AD < \frac{1}{2}(AB + AC)$.

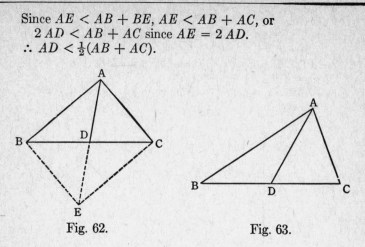

Fig. 62.   Fig. 63.

63. Given $\triangle ABC$ with AD the median to BC.
  $AD + BD > AB$ and $AD + DC > AC$.
  $\therefore 2\,AD + BD + DC > AB + AC$ or $2\,AD + BC > AB + AC$.
  $\therefore 2\,AD > AB + AC - BC$ or $AD > \frac{1}{2}(AB + AC) - \frac{1}{2}BC$.
64. Given $\triangle ABC$ with medians CM, BN, and AP.
  $AP < \frac{1}{2}(AB + AC)$. [See Prob. 62, this section.]
  $CM < \frac{1}{2}(BC + AC)$ and $BN < \frac{1}{2}(AB + BC)$.
  $\therefore AP + CM + BN < \frac{1}{2}(AB + AC) + \frac{1}{2}(BC + AC) + \frac{1}{2}(AB + BC)$
  or $AP + CM + BN < AB + AC + BC$.

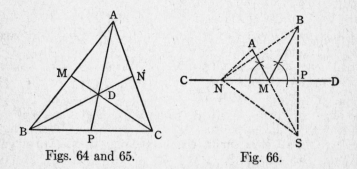

Figs. 64 and 65.   Fig. 66.

65. Given $\triangle ABC$ with medians CM, BN, and AP.
  Let medians be concurrent at D.
  $DC + DP > PC$, $DP + DB > BP$, $DB + DM > BM$,
   $DM + DA > AM$, $DA + DN > AN$, $DN + DC > NC$.

$\therefore 2\,DC + 2\,DP + 2\,DB + 2\,DM + 2\,DA + 2\,DN$
$> PC + BP + BM + AM + AN + NC$
$= BC + AB + AC.$

$\therefore 2(DC+DM)+2(DP+AD)+2(DB+DN)>BC+AB+AC$
or $2\,CM + 2\,AP + 2\,BN > BC + AB + AC,$
and $CM + AP + BN > \frac{1}{2}(BC + AB + AC).$

66. Given two points A and B external to line CD.
    M is so placed that $\angle BMD = \angle AMC.$
    Let lines from A and B meet at another point N.
    Extend AM to S so that $BM = MS.$
    Connect B with S and N with S.
    $\angle AMC = \angle SMD = \angle DMB.$
    $\therefore$ in $\triangle BMP$ and MPS: $MS = BM, MP = MP,$ and
    $\angle SMP = \angle PMB.$
    $\therefore \triangle BMP \cong \triangle MPS.$
    Then $BP = PS$ and $\angle MPB = \angle MPS = 90°.$
    $\therefore MP$ is $\perp$ bis. of BS and $NS = BN.$
    $\therefore AM + BM < AN + BN$ since $AM + MS < AN + NS.$

67. Given $\triangle ABC$ with $AD \perp BC$ and AE bisecting $\angle BAC.$
    $\angle DAE = 90° - \angle AED = \angle ADE - \angle AED$
    $\quad\quad\quad = \angle B + \angle BAD - \angle C - \angle CAE$
    $\quad\quad\quad = \angle B + \angle BAE - \angle DAE - \angle C - \angle BAE$
    $\quad\quad\quad = \angle B - \angle DAE - \angle C.$
    $\therefore 2\angle DAE = \angle B - \angle C.$
    $\therefore \angle DAE = \frac{1}{2}(\angle B - \angle C).$

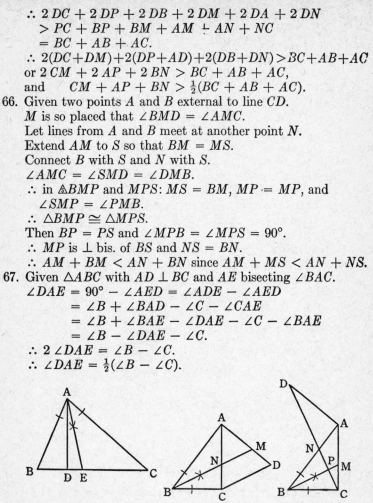

Fig. 67.   Fig. 68a   Fig. 68b.

68. Given rt. $\triangle ACB$ with $\angle C = 90°,$ $AD = AC$ and $AD \perp AB,$
    and $BM,$ the bisector of $\angle ABC.$
    In rt. $\triangle AMB$: $\angle AMB = 90° - \angle ABM = 90° - \frac{1}{2}\angle ABC.$
    In rt. $\triangle NBC$: $\angle BNC = 90° - \angle CBN = 90° - \frac{1}{2}\angle ABC.$
    $\therefore \angle BNC = \angle AMB.$
    Since $\angle BNC = \angle ANM,$ $\angle ANM = \angle AMN$ and $AN = AM.$

Since $AC = AD$, then $AN : AC = AM : AD$.

$\therefore NM \parallel CD$ and $BM \parallel CD$.

In fig. 68(b): $\angle D = 90° - \angle AND = 90° - \angle BNC$.

Since $AD = AC$, $\angle D = \angle ACD = 90° - \angle BCN$.

$\therefore 90° - \angle BCN = 90° - \angle BNC$ and $\angle BCN = \angle BNC$.

$\therefore BN = BC$.

In $\triangle BPN$ and BPC: $BN = BC$, $BP = BP$, and $\angle NBP = \angle PBC$.

$\therefore \triangle BPN \cong \triangle BPC$ and $\angle BPN = \angle BPC = 90°$.

$\therefore BM \perp CD$.

69. Given rt. $\triangle ABC$ with $\angle A = 90°$, and $BCDE$, a square erected on BC.

Since the diagonals of a square intersect at rt. $\angle$s, $\angle BOC$ is a rt. $\angle$. Further, $\angle BAC$ is a rt. $\angle$.

$\therefore$ a circle having BC as its diameter will pass through O and A. [See Prob. 11, Chap. VI.]

$\triangle BDC \cong \triangle BEC$ (s.a.s. = s.a.s.).

$\therefore BD = EC$.

Since diagonals of a $\square$ bisect each other, $BO = OC$.

$\therefore$ arc $BO =$ arc OC and $\angle BAO = \angle OAC$.

$\therefore AO$ is the bisector of $\angle BAC$.

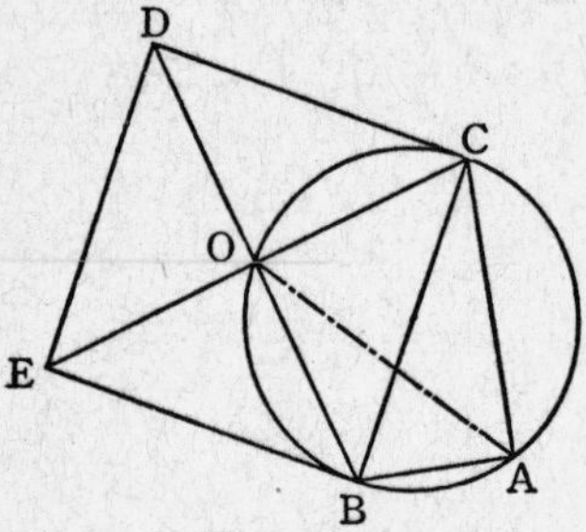

Fig. 69. 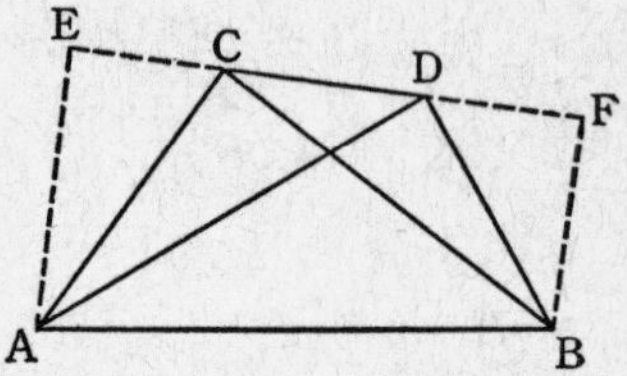   Fig. 70.

70. In rt. $\triangle AEC$: $\overline{CE}^2 = \overline{CA}^2 - \overline{EA}^2$.

In rt. $\triangle BFC$: $\overline{CF}^2 = \overline{BC}^2 - \overline{BF}^2$.

$\therefore \overline{CE}^2 + \overline{CF}^2 = \overline{CA}^2 - \overline{EA}^2 + \overline{BC}^2 - \overline{BF}^2$

$\qquad = \overline{AB}^2 - (\overline{EA}^2 + \overline{BF}^2)$.

In rt. $\triangle DEA$: $\overline{DE}^2 = \overline{AD}^2 - \overline{AE}^2$.

In rt. $\triangle DFB$: $\overline{DF}^2 = \overline{BD}^2 - \overline{BF}^2$.

$\therefore \overline{DE}^2 + \overline{DF}^2 = \overline{AD}^2 - \overline{AE}^2 + \overline{BD}^2 - \overline{BF}^2$

$\qquad = \overline{AB}^2 - (\overline{AE}^2 + \overline{BF}^2)$.

$\therefore \overline{CE}^2 + \overline{CF}^2 = \overline{DE}^2 + \overline{DF}^2$.

71. Since C and D are respectively the nearest points to A and B, then AC and $BD \perp CD$.

Extend BD to D' making $DD' = BD$. Connect A with D'.

Then the point M, where AD' meets CD, is the point where the shortest road from A to B touches CD.

[Since MD is the $\perp$ bis. of BD', $\angle BMD = \angle DMD'$, but $\angle DMD' = \angle AMC$ and $\therefore \angle AMC = \angle BMD$; then by Prob. 66, this section, AMB is the shortest line under the required conditions.]

In $\triangle ACM$ and MDD', $\angle ACM = \angle MDD'$ and
$\angle AMC = \angle D'MD$.

$\therefore \triangle ACM \sim \triangle MDD'$ and $CM : MD = AC : DD' = 1 : 4$.

$\therefore 4\,CM = MD$.

Since $CM + MD = 12$, $CM + 4\,CM = 5\,CM = 12$ and $CM = \frac{12}{5}$.

$\overline{AM}^2 = 1^2 + (\frac{12}{5})^2 = \frac{169}{25}$ and $AM = \frac{13}{5}$.

$\overline{BM}^2 = 4^2 + \overline{MD}^2 = 16 + (4\,\overline{CM})^2 = 16 + 16(\frac{12}{5})^2 = 16(\frac{169}{25})$.

$\therefore BM = \frac{52}{5}$.

Then $AM + BM = \frac{1}{5}(52 + 13) = 13$.

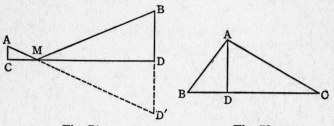

Fig. 71.   Fig. 72.

72. Given $\triangle ABC$ with $AB = 10$, $AC = 17$, and $BC = 21$.
Draw $AD \perp BC$.

Area of $\triangle ABC = K = \sqrt{s(s-a)(s-b)(s-c)}$
$$= \sqrt{24(14)(7)(3)} = (7)(3)(4) = 84.$$
[See Prob. 79, this section.]

$K = \frac{1}{2}(\overline{BC} \times \overline{AD}) = \frac{1}{2}(21\,AD) = 84.$

$\therefore AD = 8$ in.

Let m represent diameter of circumscribed circle, then $\overline{AB} \times \overline{AC} = \overline{AD} \times m$. [See Prob. 41, this section.]

$\therefore (10)(17) = 8\,m$ and $m = 21.25$ in.

73. Since medians intersect at a point $\frac{2}{3}$ the distance from their vertices to the opposite sides, $BF = \frac{2}{3}\,BE$ or $BF : FE = 2 : 1$.

Since $\triangle AFB$ and AFE have the same altitude (the $\perp$ from A to BE), $\triangle AFB : \triangle AFE = BF : FE = 2 : 1$.

$\therefore \triangle AFB = 2 \triangle AFE$.

Let K represent the area of $\triangle AFE$; then $\triangle AFB = 2\,K$ and $\triangle ABE = 3\,K$.

Since $\triangle ABE$ and ABC have the same altitude,

$\triangle ABC : \triangle ABE = AC : AE = 2 : 1$.

$\therefore \triangle ABC = 2 \triangle ABE = 6\,K$.

Area of $CEFD$ = area of $\triangle AFB$. [See Prob. 44, this section.]

$\therefore CEFD = 2\,K$ and $CEFD : \triangle ABC = 2\,K : 6\,K = 1 : 3$.

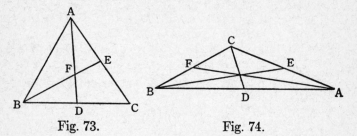

Fig. 73.   Fig. 74.

74. Given $\triangle ABC$ with medians CD, BE, and AF.

Let $BC = a = 5$, $AC = b = 7$, and $AB = c = 11$.

$\therefore$ by Prob. 51, this section,

$$CD = \tfrac{1}{2}\sqrt{2\,a^2 + 2\,b^2 - c^2} = \tfrac{1}{2}\sqrt{50 + 98 - 121} = \tfrac{1}{2}\sqrt{27} = \tfrac{3}{2}\sqrt{3};$$

$$AF = \tfrac{1}{2}\sqrt{2\,c^2 + 2\,b^2 - a^2} = \tfrac{1}{2}\sqrt{242 + 98 - 25} = \tfrac{1}{2}\sqrt{315} = \tfrac{3}{2}\sqrt{35};$$

$$BE = \tfrac{1}{2}\sqrt{2\,a^2 + 2\,c^2 - b^2} = \tfrac{1}{2}\sqrt{50 + 242 - 49} = \tfrac{1}{2}\sqrt{243} = \tfrac{9}{2}\sqrt{3};$$

$\therefore CD = \tfrac{3}{2}\sqrt{3}$ is the shortest median.

That CD is the shortest median can also be shown analytically and this is left as an exercise for the reader.

75. See Example 5, Chapter VIII.

76. Connect E with D.

Since $AE : AC = 1 : 3$ and $AD : AB = 1 : 3$, then

$AE : AC = AD : AB$.

$\therefore ED \parallel CB$ and $ED : CB = AE : AC = 1 : 3$.

In $\triangle EFD$ and FCB:

$\angle DEF = \angle FBC$ since $ED \parallel CB$.

$\angle EDF = \angle FCB$ since $ED \parallel CB$.

$\therefore \triangle EFD \sim \triangle FCB$ and $FD : FC = ED : CB = 1 : 3$.

Since $\triangle BFD$ and BCF have equal altitudes,

$\triangle BFD : \triangle BFC = DF : FC = 1 : 3$.

$\therefore \triangle BFC = 3 \triangle BFD$.

Let area of $\triangle BFD = K$; then $\triangle BFC = 3\,K$ and $\triangle BCD = 4\,K$.

$\triangle BCD$ and BCA have the same altitude;

$\quad \therefore \triangle BCD : \triangle BCA = BD : BA = 2 : 3$.

$\therefore 2 \triangle BCA = 3 \triangle BCD = 12\,K$ and $\triangle BCA = 6\,K$.

Since $\triangle BFC = 3\,K$, $\triangle BFC = \frac{1}{2} \triangle BCA$.

Since $\triangle BEA$ and BCA have the same altitude,

$\quad \triangle BAE : \triangle BCA = AE : AC = 1 : 3$.

$\therefore 3 \triangle BAE = \triangle BCA = 6\,K$ or $\triangle BAE = 2\,K$.

Quad. $ADFE = \triangle ABE - \triangle BDF = 2\,K - K = K = \triangle BDF$.

Similarly, we can prove that quad. $ADFE = \triangle CEF$.

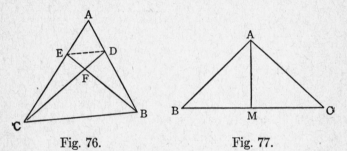

Fig. 76. Fig. 77.

77. Given $\triangle ABC$ with $\angle B$ acute, $AM \perp BC$, and BM, the projection of AB on BC.

$$\overline{AC}^2 = \overline{AM}^2 + \overline{MC}^2 = \overline{AB}^2 - \overline{BM}^2 + \overline{MC}^2$$
$$= \overline{AB}^2 - \overline{BM}^2 + (\overline{BC} - \overline{BM})^2$$
$$= \overline{AB}^2 - \overline{BM}^2 + \overline{BC}^2 - 2\,\overline{BC} \times \overline{BM} + \overline{BM}^2$$
$$= \overline{AB}^2 + \overline{BC}^2 - 2\,\overline{BC} \times \overline{BM}.$$

78. Given rt. $\triangle BAC$ with $\angle CAB = 90°$, CM and BN respectively bisecting BA and CA, and $DE \parallel BC$.

Connect M with N.

Since M and N are midpoints of BA and AC, $MN \parallel BC$.

Since $ED \parallel BC$, we have $MN \parallel ED$.

In $\triangle CAE$: $MN \parallel AE$ and bisects AC.

$\therefore MN$ bisects CE or $CM = ME$.

Similarly, $BN = ND$ or $CE = 2\,CM$ and $BD = 2\,BN$.

$$\overline{CM}^2 = \overline{AC}^2 + \overline{AM}^2 = \overline{AC}^2 + (\tfrac{1}{2}\,\overline{AB})^2.$$
$$\therefore \overline{CE}^2 = 4\,\overline{CM}^2 = 4\,\overline{AC}^2 + \overline{AB}^2.$$
$$\overline{BN}^2 = \overline{BA}^2 + \overline{AN}^2 = \overline{BA}^2 + (\tfrac{1}{2}\,\overline{CA})^2 \text{ or}$$
$$\overline{BD}^2 = 4\,\overline{BN}^2 = 4\,\overline{BA}^2 + \overline{CA}^2.$$

$$\therefore\ \overline{CE}^2 + \overline{BD}^2 = 4\,\overline{AC}^2 + \overline{AB}^2 + 4\,\overline{BA}^2 + \overline{CA}^2$$
$$= 5\,\overline{AC}^2 + 5\,\overline{AB}^2 = 5(\overline{AC}^2 + \overline{AB}^2)$$
$$= 5\,\overline{BC}^2.$$

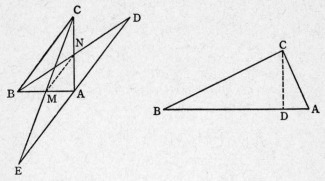

Fig. 78.   Fig. 79.

79. Given $\triangle ABC$ with $CD \perp BA$.
Let $BC = a$, $AC = b$, and $BA = c$.
By Prob. 77, this section,
$$b^2 = a^2 + c^2 - 2\,c(BD)$$

or $BD = \dfrac{c^2 + a^2 - b^2}{2\,c}$.

In rt. $\triangle CDB$:
$$\overline{CD}^2 = a^2 - \overline{BD}^2 = a^2 - \frac{(c^2 + a^2 - b^2)^2}{4\,c^2}$$
$$= \frac{(a + c + b)(a + c - b)(b + c - a)(b - c + a)}{4\,c^2}$$
$$= \frac{1}{4\,c^2}\,[(a + c + b)(a + c + b - 2\,b)(a + c + b - 2\,a)$$
$$(a + c + b - 2\,c)].$$

Since $s = \tfrac{1}{2}(a + b + c)$, then $2\,s = a + b + c$.
$$\therefore\ \overline{CD}^2 = \frac{1}{4\,c^2}\,[2\,s(2\,s - 2\,b)(2\,s - 2\,a)(2\,s - 2\,c)]$$
$$= \frac{1}{4\,c^2}\,[16\,s(s - b)(s - a)(s - c)]$$
$$\frac{1}{c^2}\,[4\,s(s - b)(s - a)(s - c)].$$

$$\therefore CD = \frac{2}{c} \sqrt{s(s-b)(s-a)(s-c)}.$$

Area of $\triangle ABC = \frac{1}{2} c \times CD$

$$= \sqrt{s(s-b)(s-a)(s-c)}.$$

80. Given $\overline{AB} \times \overline{AM} = \overline{AN}^2$.

Since $AP = AN$, then $\overline{AB} \times \overline{AM} = \overline{AP}^2$ or
$AB : AP = AP : AM$.

Then further, since $\angle A = \angle A$, $\triangle APM \sim \triangle APB$.

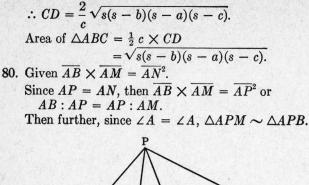

Fig. 80.

$\therefore \angle AMP = \angle APB$ and $\angle APM = \angle B$.

$\angle AMP = \angle MPB + \angle B$

$$= \angle MPN + \angle NPB + \angle APM.$$

Since $AP = AN$, $\angle APM + \angle MPN = \angle MNP$.

$\angle AMP = \angle MNP + \angle MPN$.

$\therefore \angle MPN + \angle NPB + \angle APM = \angle MNP + \angle MPN$ and
$\angle NPB + \angle APM = \angle MNP = \angle APM + \angle MPN$.

$\therefore \angle NPB = \angle MPN$ and PN bisects $\angle MPB$.